Becoming a Family

OTHER TITLES IN THE SERIES

BEING PREGNANT, GIVING BIRTH
Mary Nolan

WORK AND HOME
Teresa Wilson

BREASTFEEDING YOUR BABY
Jane Moody, Jane Britten and Karen Hogg

Becoming a Family

Anna McGrail

A
NATIONAL CHILDBIRTH TRUST GUIDE

Published by HMSO in collaboration with
National Childbirth Trust Publishing Ltd.

NCT
EDITIONS

Picture Acknowledgements
The publishers would like to thank the following for their permission to reproduce photographs: Zefa/Michael Keller: Cover; David Muscroft: pxiv; Johnson's Baby: p34; Michael Bassett: pp94, 126; Format Photography/Brenda Prince: p152; The Image Bank/Anne Rippy: p178; Joanne O'Brien: p196.

Illustrations: Jo Dennis.

Design by Tim McPhee.

Production in association with Book Production Consultants plc, 25–27 High Street, Chesterton, Cambridge CB4 1ND, UK.

Printed by Hillman Printers (Frome) Ltd, Frome, Somerset.

Published by HMSO in collaboration with National Childbirth Trust Publishing Ltd, 25-27 High Street, Chesterton, Cambridge CB4 1ND, UK.

© 1996 NCT Publishing Ltd,

A CIP catalogue record for this book is available from the British Library.

ISBN 0 11 701934 8

Published by HMSO and available from:

HMSO PUBLICATIONS CENTRE
(Mail, fax and telephone orders only)
PO Box 276, London SW8 5DT
Telephone orders 0171 873 9090
General enquiries 0171 873 0011
(queuing system in operation for both numbers)
Fax orders 0171 873 8200

HMSO BOOKSHOPS

49 High Holborn, London WC1V 6HB
(counter service only)
0171 873 0011 Fax 0171 831 1326

68-69 Bull Street, Birmingham B4 6AD
0121 236 9696 Fax 0121 236 9699

33 Wine Street, Bristol BS1 2BQ
0117 926 4306 Fax 0117 929 4515

9-21 Princess Street, Manchester M60 8AS
0161 834 7201 Fax 0161 833 0634

16 Arthur Street, Belfast BT1 4GD
01232 238451 Fax 01232 235401

71 Lothian Road, Edinburgh EH3 9AZ
0131 228 4181 Fax 0131 229 2734

The HMSO Oriel Bookshop
The Friary, Cardiff CF1 4AA
01222 395548 Fax 01222 384347

HMSO's Accredited Agents
(see Yellow Pages)
and through good booksellers

Contents

About the author

ANNA WAS BORN in Liverpool but now lives in Brighton. She and her partner Peter have two children, Benjamin and Christiane. Anna was a full-time mother for four years, which is when she first became involved in the NCT. She was postnatal support co-ordinator for her local Brighton branch before going on to edit the branch newsletter and then to contribute to *New Generation,* the journal of the NCT.

Anna now works as an editor of health and social services books and journals, and also writes: she won the Ian St James Fiction Award in 1994 and her first novel, *Blood Sisters,* was published in 1995.

Publisher's note

ALL COMMENTS and personal accounts were given to us in confidence, so out of respect for our contributors' privacy we have changed all the names.

We have endeavoured where possible to reproduce quotations verbatim, but where editing has been applied, the integrity of the quotation has been maintained.

Dedication

For Benjamin and Christiane.

Introduction

THE WORDS of the parents in this book have been drawn from the conversations and interviews I have had with parents over the past six years, eight months and twenty-five days. I can pinpoint this time so accurately as this was the date our son was born. No sooner had he arrived, than I was plunged from the relatively ordered world of singles and partners to the chaos of babies and families.

Being a parent is one of the most difficult and demanding jobs we will ever be asked to undertake. It is also one of the most rewarding. But steering a path between the difficulties to reach the rewards is sometimes harder than we would ever have dreamed possible.

Becoming a family is something most of us undertake as a couple, relying on the strength and support our partner can give. For some, choice and circumstances mean that we take the step alone, or carry most of the responsibility alone.

Nevertheless, whether you are with a partner or a lone parent, the way our society is structured, and the way the world works, means that a great deal of the shock of babies is borne by the mother. Very often the proud father can return to work, accept the congratulations, and get on with business as usual. It is the new mother who needs to negotiate her way around this new world . . . usually without a map.

That is how it felt to me. In fact, it felt worse. I felt like I was bobbing around on a sea without a lifeboat, and all reference points were gone. And that is why I have spent so much of the past six years, eight months and twenty-five days talking to other parents, finding out if it felt like this for them, too, finding out just what I was meant to do, and how I was meant to do it.

I live in Brighton, but not all the parents whose voices you will hear in this book do: in my role as an editor on the local NCT newsletter, and then for the NCT national journal *New Generation*, I have met and talked to new families from all over Britain. When I was asked to write this book, I contacted a lot more parents, many of whom have made written contributions to this final manuscript. I have them all to thank. I have them all to thank twice over, because when you are a new family, time is at its most precious.

I'd also like to thank Sue Orchard and Heather Welford who gave their time and expertise and made valuable contributions to the final typescript.

The aim of this book is to let the voices of these mothers and fathers act like beacons for all those currently adrift on the sea of parenthood: whether you are bobbing happily along on the waves and wondering where to go next, or whether you are caught up in darker currents and confusions. Now my daughter is four and safely off to school this September, I feel I have negotiated another major milestone in the path of parenthood, but still, hearing other people tell of what it's like from their point of view continues to be one of the most valuable ways for me of defining where I want to go, even if it is just a matter of deciding – well, I don't want to do *that*.

For all those brave and generous enough to talk to me so openly and generously, thank you. Your names have been changed but you know who you are.

For all those still coming to terms with being a family, this book is for you.

Anna McGrail,
September 1995.

CHAPTER <u>***one***</u> *You and your newborn*

THE MOMENT of birth may be exactly that: a moment, a joyous, unforgettable moment, or an unpleasant experience we'd rather forget. Becoming a parent, however, can take a bit of getting used to. Even if your pregnancy was planned, the baby's room is decorated and the cupboards are well stocked, don't be surprised if life as a parent isn't what you thought it would be. There is a word for it: 'babyshock'.

JOURNEY INTO THE UNKNOWN

The first twenty-four hours

WE CANNOT know what parenthood will be like until it happens. Yet many couples find that the first few months are much harder than they expected. After the elation and excitement of the birth, they are tired, stressed and bewildered. Although you are delighted that your baby is here, even those first twenty-four hours can be more difficult than you envisaged.

Katharine found both her baby and the hospital experience overwhelming: *'It was dreadful. Max wouldn't settle and I had a catheter in which was uncomfortable, and the room was hot and stifling and the corridor outside was noisy. I was awake most of the night and so shattered the next day I couldn't take in all the information that people kept popping in to tell me. The room was like Victoria Station. People were in and out and I didn't know who half of them were: midwives, paediatrician, someone bringing a bunch of flowers from my mum and then other people looking for a vase to put them in . . .'*

COUPLES OFTEN find that with the demands of a new baby it can take a while to calm down, and discover just what it is that you *do* feel.

Lynn found the first few days of motherhood a real eye-opener: *'Looking back, I was very naive. I hadn't a clue what new babies were like: the only babies I'd had much to do with before were older, about nine or ten months old, so I was used to seeing them sitting up and playing, smiling…eating biscuits, for Heaven's sake. Just to have Adam so completely helpless, so dependent on me, was terrifying.'*

Olivia kept being surprised by her daughter: *'I don't think I had ever pictured her, physically. I don't think you do. You picture them more as toddlers and what they're going to look like when they're people. For instance, I did think that all babies looked the same and I was amazed in hospital how they didn't. For a start, mine was the most beautiful on the ward, of course! And Robert kept saying, "You know, even objectively, I'm sure she's the most beautiful. There's no doubt. And I'm not just saying this because I'm her father." And I couldn't convince him that everyone on the ward thought the same about their own baby. So that was nice, really, that she was so lovely.'*

CAESAREANS

PARENTS WHOSE baby was delivered by caesarean often find that they have particular problems adjusting to the fact of the baby's arrival. After all, at the last minute, the decisions were taken out of their hands.

Eileen had a long labour and eventually needed an emergency caesarean: *'After what seemed like hours they finally wheeled me in to the operating theatre and the anaesthetist said, "You'll feel a pressure round your neck now . . ." and that's the last thing I can remember before coming round. And when I did come round, neither the baby nor Mick was there, so I thought, "Oh, I haven't had the baby yet, then," so when Mick did walk in, I said, "What are you doing here?" Mick said they'd taken the baby up to the Unit as he wasn't breathing properly, and I said he should be with the baby, so he went, and then the nurse came in when I was awake a bit more and said, "What are you going to call him then?" and I got terrified because I thought it meant that we were going to have to baptise the baby straight away because he was so ill with his breathing and going to die. So I wailed, "Oh, call him Michael after his father." She looked at me very oddly because I think they just wanted to know what to write on his cot tag up in the Unit.'*

Sometimes a caesarean can lessen the feeling of continuity, as it did for Sushma: *'They brought him in about five o'clock for a feed. He was all washed then and wrapped in a white blanket, very clean, and so calm – big, dark eyes looking round. I felt like I was being introduced to a stranger, though, who had just dropped in. I was very glad to meet him and all of that, but I didn't get the feeling that this was the little being I had laboured for so many hours to produce. I felt no connection between this baby in a blanket and the pregnancy I'd had. This baby was here, and I wasn't pregnant any more, but they didn't seem to coincide, somehow.'*

WHEN YOU'RE preparing for the birth, it may be a good idea to read up about caesareans. That way, if things do turn out not quite the way you planned during your labour, you will be better informed to make choices about the sort of caesarean birth you want.

TWINS OR MORE

ONE IN EVERY 90 births in this country is of twins, triplets or more. If this is your situation, you may find many of the problems of adjusting to life as a family doubled (or tripled). In particular, the physical demands can be exhausting, as Dawn and her husband found out: *'Sometimes we do despair. The sheer volume of work – washing, drying, bottles, nappies – and the effort involved in lifting three of them into the bath, out of the bath, into the highchair, out of the highchair, into the cot, out of the cot . . . And the noise! Just when you've got the last one off, the other two wake up and start shouting.'*

STATISTICS SHOW that unfortunately twins, triplets and other higher order births experience medical problems more frequently in the early months of life, and spend more time in special care.

Colin, whose twins did need special care, used to envy parents who only had one: *'I just seemed to lurch from worry to worry and they had so much more time. So it was useful to be reminded occasionally just how special the twins were. Although I envied parents who only had one, I would never have swapped the twins for just one, or had them one at a time.'*

MOST OF US, when we envisage ourselves with a child, envisage exactly that: a one-to-one relationship. Right from the start, therefore, if you've given birth to twins, you have to adjust the dream to the reality in a fairly major way.

Jess felt she was giving neither of her children the attention they deserved: *'Other parents might have time to show their babies a book, or take them for walks, but I hardly had time to smile at them. If one was being quiet, I'd rejoice, because it meant that I could change the other one's nappy in peace. Most of the time, though, in those first few months, I felt as if I was listening to a constant grizzle, because – except when it came to feeding – whatever I was giving one, it meant I wasn't giving it to the other.'*

PARENTING IN the way or to the standard you'd imagined may not be possible with twins or more, and individual attention may be at a premium, but twins have each other for companionship and, as they

grow older, a guaranteed play partner, in ways that singletons can never know.

Widening the circle can be more difficult, however: the efforts involved in getting out and socialising are multiplied more than seems fair when you have more than one. With her triplets, Dawn found it especially complicated: *'Sometimes it can seem like too much trouble to put on three pairs of shoes and three coats just so you can wheel them all to the corner shop. But I know from experience that if I don't go, and if I allow Peter to bring things back from work with him at the end of the day, like milk or a loaf of bread, then I might have no reason to go out, and if I don't have a reason, I won't go, and if I don't go, I'll just stay in and get more and more miserable. So it's worth the effort.'*

HOWEVER, most parents of twins (or triplets) will confirm the old cliché: that even if the demands and problems are doubled (or tripled) so are the joys and delights.

NEWBORN NICETIES

Some of the physical features of newborns that may cause surprise or anxiety include:

- Birth marks (if it's going to be a mark that's permanent, someone should come to talk to you about it)
- Heads that are moulded (from labour) so that they look squashed; the bones will return to normal within days
- Spots (usually entirely harmless, however disappointing)
- Hair (either too much or too little, depending on what the parents had thought the baby would have, but any amount is normal)
- The sex organs – those on some little boys can appear out of proportion (he will grow into them), those on some little girls may be red and swollen as a reaction to the hormones in her mother's body. Swollen breasts and even occasionally small amounts of milk are caused by the mothers' hormones. Breast size will reduce and milk disappear over the first few days
- A squint (which often disappears as the baby learns to focus her eyes).

LOOKS

HOW MANY of us new parents were prepared for the black umbilical stump? For the blotchy skin which newborns are prone to? For the way our newborn's hands and feet can turn blue after a long nap, a sign that the circulation is not yet efficient or mature? In fact, in many respects the picturebook baby you were expecting may bear no resemblance to the child you've actually got, as Lynn discovered: *'It was only when I changed Adam's nappy for the first time that I got a good look at the umbilical cord . . . which was definitely something I hadn't been prepared for. There was this black thing, with a clip on it. What was I supposed to do? The nurse had said "Oh, sprinkle on some of this powder when you clean him", so I stood there with this talcum powder tin trying to guess if I should move the stump to one side, or lift it up, or just sprinkle all around it. I hadn't a clue. I was petrified of hurting him. I was convinced that whatever I did, it would be wrong: the clamp would come off, it would bleed, I'd knock it off and do him dreadful damage. Then Adam did a wee all over me and I stopped worrying about the cord and started worrying about that instead.'*

THERE ARE MANY kinds of marks on your baby's body that may worry you, although most need no worrying about whatsoever. There are two kinds of birthmarks: vascular, which are to do with the blood vessels, and pigmented, which are to do with skin colouration. Philippa's daughter, Sophie, was born with a birthmark: *'Sophie was born with a red mark on her forehead and at first we never gave it a second thought. The midwives said it was probably a pressure mark from the birth and we were quite happy with that explanation – and relieved. At the six-*

week check, the doctor was more specific: *"It's a strawberry birthmark – my daughter had one. Don't worry – it'll go away on its own."* We were due to go back when Sophie was six months old, but we went back long before then as the mark began to get darker and to swell and we were worried it was some sort of tumour. We saw a skin specialist in London when she was three months old. She started on steroids and almost immediately the mark stopped growing. We were lucky, they think there won't be a permanent mark, but those first months of her life were dreadful. There was all that uncertainty, all that fear for the future, and all that guilt. Even though this wasn't a life-threatening condition, and it didn't mean she had any permanent disability, that mark takes away the enjoyment and all the joy of her arrival even now. I look back at photographs of her when she was newly born and I think: *"I should be thinking what a beautiful baby she was"*, but I'm not. I'm thinking: *"Look at that red mark. Little did we know."* '

DURING THE first 24 hours after the birth, a paediatrician will visit you to check over your baby. The paediatrician will check things like:

- Your baby's hips – to make sure they are fitting nicely in their socket and have not been slightly dislocated by the birth
- The fontanelles: your baby will have two main fontanelles – soft spots on her head where the skull bones haven't yet grown over and fused together.

BIRTHMARKS

- **A brown mark** – these are present in about ten per cent of babies: sometimes dark brown, sometimes a pale, milky coffee colour. Harmless. May not fade but no treatment necessary.
- **Mole** – a very few babies are born with a mole; raised, flat, dark or light, of any shape. They are only a cause for concern if they suddenly get larger, itch or bleed. If this happens, see your GP.
- **Mongolian blue spot** – a large, blue-grey or brown mark which occurs reasonably frequently in dark-skinned babies, usually on their back or bottom. Harmless. Soon fades.
- **Port wine stain** – a flat, purple-red birthmark caused by blood vessels under the skin; usually harmless but can be distressing for parents, and permanent without treatment. Nowadays, laser treatment can remove these birthmarks safely and effectively in four or five treatments, which can usually be started almost immediately.
- **Stork bites** – small pink blotches, usually near the eyelid. Harmless. Will fade. No treatment required.
- **Strawberry birthmarks** – raised, red marks. Usually occur on the face or neck. They eventually stop growing – although they may initially get larger before they shrink again – and usually fade completely during childhood. May need treatment if it is near your baby's eyes, or in an awkward place where it could cause her discomfort. In these cases, the mark can be removed with laser therapy.
- **Tiny brown marks** – usually round... stop panicking – it's a freckle.

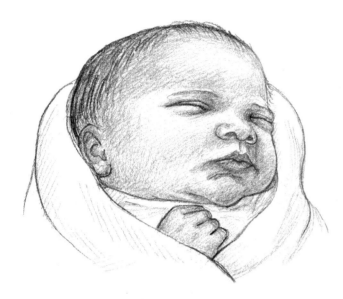

IT'S NORMAL for the fontanelles to appear slightly indented, and you may notice a pulse beating through the skin. You may worry that they are very fragile, but they are covered by toughened membranes. If they do become very sunken or raised, this is a useful warning sign that your baby is unwell, possibly dehydrated and needs medical attention.

All babies, while in the womb, are covered with a fine fuzz of hair called lanugo. Sometimes there will still be a little of this lanugo left when the baby is born – but it will soon rub off.

Some babies may be born with coarse hair, often across the shoulder blades or down the spine, which can alarm parents. Most of this will fall out – it just rubs off.

In fact, the hair your baby is born with on his head may well not last – if you look at new babies a couple of weeks old, you will notice that they have a little bald patch on the back of their heads where the hair has been rubbed away by the mattress. All the hair is gradually replaced, and the colour it will finally be cannot be judged from the colour he started out with – many babies change from fair to dark, and some vice-versa.

A blister on the baby's upper lip concerns some parents, but it is only a 'sucking blister', an indication of your baby's enthusiasm for feeding. The blister may disappear between feeds, it may not. Babies seem entirely oblivious to the blisters and they soon fade as feeding frequency decreases.

If there's anything that worries you, ask your midwife or health visitor. They will be visiting you regularly to check things like this. If your baby has a condition which needs further treatment, you will be given further information and often the names and contact numbers of support groups. If in doubt, ask.

Vitamin K

Vitamin K has been much in the news the last few years as health authorities and trusts have been rethinking their policies on this issue.

A few years ago, almost every newborn baby in this country was automatically given an injection of vitamin K just after birth with the aim of preventing haemorrhagic disease – a rare but dangerous condition in which the baby's blood fails to clot in the event of any bleeding. Vitamin K prevents this disease developing and thus the injection programme gained widespread acceptance. No one knows why babies are born with low levels of vitamin K compared to adults, but it may be a safety measure in the womb when cells are dividing very quickly.

Then a study was published which showed a possible link between vitamin K injections and childhood cancer. Although the link was never proven, many health authorities decided to err on the side of caution and replace the routine injection with an oral dose of vitamin K, which was not linked with any problems.

You will find that your baby will be offered a preventive dose of vitamin K shortly after she is born. It is up to you and your partner to decide, well beforehand, whether and how you want her to have this. The disease it prevents is rare, but possibly fatal, and it isn't possible to predict which babies will develop the disease. Babies who develop bleeding are usually found to have an underlying liver problem. If you want more information before making your decision, discuss it with your midwife.

First attempts

There are many new skills to learn, but all new parents experience this daunting realisation: just how much they have to learn. Rose, like many new mothers, had to start from the beginning: *'"Have you fed and changed him?" the nurse said to me at six o'clock in the morning, when I'd only had him at ten the night before. And I thought, "What? Me? No." So I went and looked for the stuff I'd need and I didn't know where it was, and everyone had just left me. Then this other nurse came round and I was in tears. She said, "Are you alright, love?" I said, "No, I don't know what I'm doing!" So she showed me. She was really nice. She had two little boys of her*

own and showed me which bits to wipe and which bits to use where...you know, all that stuff they give you in hospital, all those gauze things...you don't know which end to use what on. The gauze was for wiping his bottom, apparently and I'd been trying to wash his face with it.'

BEING IN hospital can make things very public, as Hilary found: 'It was awful, that first time. I felt like I was on show, like everyone was watching me. I'm sure they weren't, they were all too busy with their own nappies, but it was a very testing time. And I felt like Lucy was made out of china. I didn't want to fasten the nappy too tight, so it fell off, and then I did it too loose and it leaked. Mind you, you get used to it very quickly.'

Sometimes no knowledge can be a good thing, says Chloë: 'Nobody ever came along and told us what we had to do or should be doing, because once he was born, they just left us on our own for the rest of the day and then we came home that same evening, so nobody was there to guide us. So that evening we thought we'd better change him and it was . . . I found it very exciting. It was very frightening, too, that first time, because he had meconium and I was worried in case he was suffering, and I kept thinking, "Is this normal?" But the most important thing was the excitement. I felt very excited to have him home and very happy. I wanted it like that.'

John reckons it's often the simple tasks that worry you most, in the beginning: 'There were obvious things I didn't know. Like, I didn't know what the cream was for. I didn't realise it was a barrier cream. It's obvious now but I didn't realise then, so I put as little of it as possible on and he got very bad nappy rash. So I could have done with a bit more guidance in those early days.'

YOUR BABY'S TEMPERAMENT

ONE THING that will determine how tough or how easy you find the transition to parenthood is your baby's temperament. Some are easier than others. Some babies actually seem to like being babies, and thus help make their babyhood a more enjoyable experience for all concerned, too; other babies seem to actively dislike being a baby. There are sighs of relief all round when they sit up, or walk, or turn into a toddler, whichever great achievement they seem to have been pining for.

Wakeful

IF YOU HAVE a baby who seems to need very little sleep – lucky you! You have an intelligent, smart child with great potential who will obviously do very well in life. At least that's what everyone will tell

you. And, if it's any consolation, they're probably right. Some babies are born wanting more – more of everything: more colour, more shapes, more talk, more walks in the park, more discussions over whether he'd like his bath now or later, or after the news.

If the wakefulness just lasts during the day, it's going to mean hard work for you, but parents often find that this sort of baby, hungry for stimulation, is quite happy to be passed from friend to friend and all around the grandparents. Invite round old friends, distant relatives – anyone who'll dandle the baby on their knee while you get on with calm and relaxing tasks like cooking dinner for 35.

Never underestimate how exhausting a wakeful baby can be. No matter how much you love someone, and no matter how much you love being in their company, it is very wearing to be 100% responsible for all their entertainment, as well as their meals, hygiene and bodily functions.

This is where partners need to be very supportive of each other. Whoever comes home from a hard day at work needs to remember that the person who's spent all day with the baby is in far more need of a break. They should try not to show *too* much surprise if greeted at the door by a partner holding the baby at arm's length.

If your baby's wakefulness lasts late into the night as well – you have my sympathy. This is an exhausting phase. Everything you do will be coloured by your lack of sleep if you are dealing with sleepless nights. You will feel irritable, cross and desperate. But it is only a phase. For you *and* the baby. There are only two things which will cure your exhaustion:

- Time – all children sleep through the night eventually
- Sleep – can you have a nap when the baby does? Why not? Whatever needs doing, can't it be put off? Your rest and your health come first.

Sad

SOME BABIES spend a lot of time crying. There's no denying it. And there's no denying that for much of the time in those very early days, we won't be able to work out exactly why they are crying.

Rose never discovered what upset her son as a baby: *'One of the most useful things anyone ever said to me, in Sainsbury's, when Thomas had griz-zled for days non-stop was, "He's one of those that just doesn't like being a baby. He'll be different as a child." That really kept me going, because, as he grew, I began to see that it was true.'*

Cross

AFTER WAITING for so long to meet your baby, and being overjoyed at his arrival, it can come as something of a disappointment to find that your baby seems less than enthusiastic about the world. Some babies seem to find it very hard to come to terms with the stresses and strains of babyhood: hunger, tiredness, the need to meet strangers – think how cross all these things can make *you*, and you get some idea of how your baby might be feeling.

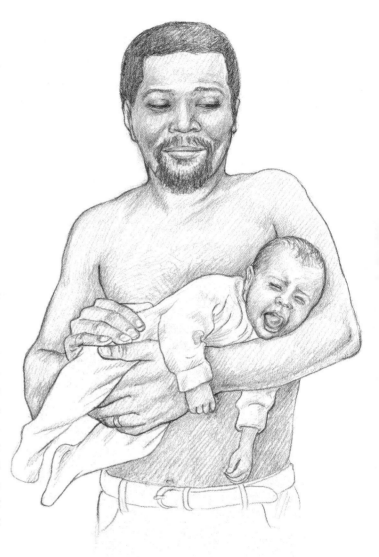

Louise's son would scream and scream for hours at a time: *'Nothing would calm him, nothing. No tears. Just this red face and so much anger.'*

CRYING IS at its worst in the first year of life, and at its very worst in the first three months. Unfortunately, this is just the time when you are most unsure of your skills as a new parent, and the crying can sound like an unfair judgement on your ability to care for your child.

Chloë comments: *'I used to think that I must be the world's worst mother. He was only three weeks old and already I'd somehow got it monumentally wrong. Other women from my antenatal group had babies who'd taken regular naps practically since birth and it seemed like it was just me. It made me feel lonelier than ever when we were awake in the dark.'*

IT DOES HELP if you don't compare your baby to other people's. How can there be any comparison between, say, a breastfed baby who weighed 6lb 7oz at birth, and a baby who is given a bottle every four

CRYING CHECKLIST

If it makes you feel better, you can prepare a list of possible reasons for your baby's crying:

● Hunger
● Wet nappy
● Temperature – too hot or too cold?
● Wind.

And it will probably make you feel better if you have a list of things to do:

● Feed the baby (and yourself if necessary)
● Change the nappy
● Add – or remove – a blanket
● Walk up and down.

You'll find yourself pacing up and down anyway...

It is always worth trying a feed if your baby is very unhappy, especially if your baby is breastfed: breast milk is so perfectly absorbed into the body and so quickly digested that your baby may need to be fed quite often. This is also true if your baby is very tiny; his stomach capacity may mean that he had all he could hold at the last feed but he now needs a bit more. If you can, it's worth spending some time just cuddling your baby and letting him feed whenever he wants to so that you build up your milk supply. This can also double as a time for you to replenish your reserves of energy: crying is tiring and miserable for the baby, but to listen to it can be just as tiring and unhappy for the parents.

hours and who weighed 12lb at birth? How can, in fact, there be any comparison between your own highly-gifted offspring and any other baby in the universe?

Clingy

FOR MANY babies who cry, the answer will simply be that he wants to be held, especially in these very early days. Some babies have a very strong, instinctive desire to be held and soothed. If you have one of these, then you have the sort of baby who's fine and happy while you are holding her, pacing the bedroom, or patting her soothingly on her back, but who starts wailing the instant you put her back in her cot. A surprisingly large proportion of these babies, with practice, develop a magic ability to know when you are moving towards the cot and start wailing in protest before you get there. A few – and this is a theory largely maintained by fathers deranged from pacing the bedroom floor once too often – after a quiet period in which they've lulled you into a false sense of security, know when you are just *thinking* that perhaps you might just move towards the cot again and instantly start howling, before you've so much as actually lifted a hopeful foot in that direction.

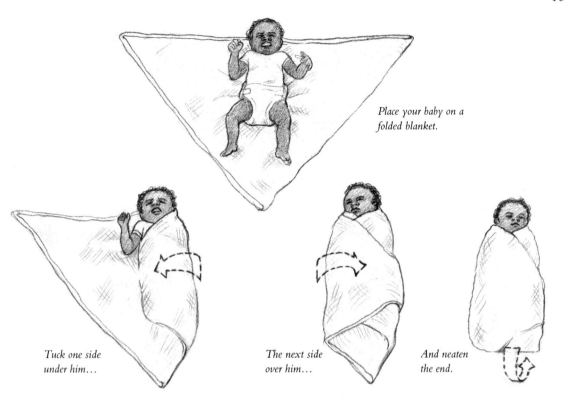

Place your baby on a folded blanket.

Tuck one side under him...

The next side over him...

And neaten the end.

You can try:

- Swaddling – see right and above, or ask your midwife or health visitor to show you how
- Doing shifts: taking it in turns to hold her.

Emerging patterns

BY ABOUT three months of age, the causes of your baby's crying will have become much clearer: you will also have got to know her patterns and can predict or anticipate what she needs. Olivia found this made motherhood easier and more rewarding: *'I can usually tell what's the matter with her, yes. It surprised Robert the first couple of times I did it. I was having a*

SWADDLING

Swaddling with a cotton sheet is a tried-and-tested method for calming and soothing newborns. Anyone who has watched a newborn can see the sense in it – those flailing arms and legs can't be very conducive to sleep. It stands to reason that a baby who has been used to being warmly cushioned in the warm waters of the womb may find the sudden change to fresh air and unlimited space rather frightening. Swaddling can give a sense of security, and enables you to rock your newborn or hold him close to you gently and firmly – which babies like. The only word of warning concerns overheating, which can happen quite quickly to some babies if they are overwrapped. So swaddle your baby to sleep, but don't overload him with blankets as well.

bath and he was walking up and down with her because she was crying and all he could say was: "What is it?" I said, "Has she got a dirty nappy?" And of course he was most peeved to find out that she had. Now I can say, "She's hungry", or "She's bored". But the best one to learn to understand was, "She's tired". If Robert's with her and she makes that cry, I can say, "She's tired, she just wants to go to sleep. Stop playing with her, stop trying to keep her amused". It had often happened, I realised, that we'd been waving toys in her face and all she wanted to do was to go to sleep.'

THE GROWTH OF LOVE

IF YOU'VE GOT a baby who's behaving in a way you find hard to cope with – whether because she sleeps all the time, is awake all the time, is cross or clingy, you may find it very hard to love your baby. And, if you feel that way, you probably feel guilty, too. Guilt is an unpleasant, gnawing feeling, so, if you feel guilty, you probably resent the baby for having made you feel that way. And you love her less.

Such vicious emotional cycles are sometimes easy to get into in the first few weeks of a baby's life and hard to break out of again. The best thing to do if you're beginning to feel like this is to tell someone about it: your midwife, your GP, your health visitor, a friend, your mum . . . Getting your feelings out into the open is often the first positive step we can take in admitting how we feel and then dealing with it, as Ingrid discovered for herself: *'I could have gone on pretending everything was alright. After all, the house was immaculate, Rosie was obviously well cared for, and I had this smile plastered on my face every time the doorbell rang and someone came visiting. I think I was worried that no one would believe me if I said I felt there was something wrong. But in the end all I had to do was mention to*

RELATING TO YOUR BABY

If you're finding it hard to relate to your baby:

- Give it time . . . some relationships are slower than others, that's all

- Remember that you cannot 'spoil' a new baby. If it's fear of indulging her that's holding you back, give in. Allow yourself to cuddle and kiss her as much as you want

- Share your worries with your partner, a friend or a relative. Talk it through as much as you can

- The birth of your baby may have stirred up unpleasant memories or worries about your own childhood. If this is the case, it is worth telling your GP that you'd like to talk to someone about this

- Trust your own instincts – if you feel there's something wrong with your baby or you, keep asking for professional help until you get it.

my GP that I wasn't feeling right and he said, "Oh, we'll send one of the community nurses round to have a chat with you." And she was round the next day. And said she'd come back in a couple of days. Just knowing that someone was going to come, who was interested in me, interested in how I was feeling, and wasn't just going to ask questions about the baby all the time, made all the difference. I knew I'd get time to talk about me, and that's what I needed.'

IT CAN TAKE time for love to grow between you and your baby, just as it takes time for love to grow between any two people. Once you realise that this is not unusual, you may be half-way to feeling better.

WHEN THINGS AREN'T AS YOU EXPECTED

Special care

IF YOUR BABY arrives early, or is poorly just after the delivery, you may find that much of the responsibility for day-to-day care is taken out of your hands, especially if she needs to be looked after in the Special Care Baby Unit (SCBU).

If your baby is in an incubator, it can be a very scary experience. Kay found it hard to relate to her premature baby at first: *'I gave birth under anaesthetic on the Monday afternoon at 2.34pm when he was at 32 weeks' gestation, and he was taken straight off to the SCBU. A few hours later, when I was coming round, the nurses gave me a Polaroid of him. I thought, "Oh, well, they're looking after him there much better than I ever could here." And I wanted to go back to sleep. My throat was very sore – they say that sometimes happens after a general anaesthetic – and all I could think about was having drinks of cool water to try to stop it burning. The rest of the time, I was very fuzzy. By Tuesday lunchtime, the catheter had been removed and, with the aid of the wonderful suppositories that they used for pain relief, I was able to shuffle down, very slow and careful, to see him. He looked very odd, all old and just-born at the same time, very cross and very wrinkled and slightly bluey-pink. After three days, they put some clothes on him. At one-week-old he moved into a cot with a lid. Then they started talking about when I could take him home and I started to panic. I still didn't feel like he was my baby, and we still didn't have a name for him.'*

Susanne wasn't sure throughout her pregnancy how well her baby would be: *'Perhaps because there had been bleeding in the pregnancy, I had kept my emotional distance from this baby. I wasn't going to believe the trouble was over till it was over. Even when she was born, I still found it hard to let myself get close to her. She was being looked after by so many different people and they all seemed to know much better than I did how she was doing from day to day.'*

Your baby may need to go into special care if she is:
- Premature - usually if she has arrived before 34 weeks
- Small - weighing under 4lb
- Having breathing difficulties or has other medical problems.

IT MAY BE impossible at first for medical staff to answer questions on quite what is the matter with your baby if he's been whisked off to the SCBU. All they may be able to say is that he's not breathing well, or had the umbilical cord around his neck, but they'll let you know – trust them. Whether your baby is admitted to the SCBU for treatment or simply for observation, you will be kept informed of progress and developments every step of the way.

It can be very comforting, if your baby is taken to the SCBU immediately after delivery, for your birth partner to go up to the Unit to see your baby settled and report back to you in detail. You will be able to visit as soon as your own physical care has been sorted out.

Kangaroo care for premature babies

THE REASON THAT premature babies are looked after in incubators is that early babies are often unable to maintain a steady body temperature. An incubator provides an environment where the temperature can be kept stable easily. Now, a new method of caring, called kangaroo care, is being tried out by some neonatal units.

Babies are placed in skin-to-skin contact with their mother, against their mother's chest, and covered with a blanket. The baby is thus close to her parent, and the mother, it has been found, is so in tune with her infant that her own skin temperature rises and falls to keep the baby's stable. Another advantage of this form of care is that breast-feeding is easier and it encourages more women to breastfeed successfully. So, if your baby needs special care, perhaps it is worth asking the staff if anyone with an interest in kangaroo care would be willing to let you have a go. While it isn't something that everyone will want to try, as some mothers feel much happier if their infant remains in the care of technology, for some mothers – and indeed fathers – it will be a golden opportunity to get closer to their baby sooner than they could otherwise have hoped for.

Special babies

SOMETIMES, either immediately at the birth, or in the first few days after the birth, some parents are faced with the devastating news that their child isn't the 100% healthy being they had hoped for. There may be an illness, a disability or a learning disorder, something that won't just disappear in a few days.

Bridget's daughter, Lois, had a cleft lip and palate: *'It sounds awful, but I didn't even know what this was. I'd never seen it before. John hadn't, either, so we thought it was something dreadful, and that she'd never be normal.'*

PART OF THE insidious nature of many genetically transmitted diseases, like cystic fibrosis (CF), is that one or both parents can be a carrier of the disease and not know it. It can pass undetected from generation to generation, and only when two carriers of the defective gene have a child does the disease come to light. Vicky's son, Anthony, was diagnosed at birth: *'I was lucky in a way because Anthony was born with a bowel blockage, which is one of the indications of CF, so he was diagnosed early. We knew what we were dealing with right from the start.'*

FOR OTHER parents, the illness or the diagnosis are more uncertain.

The doctors didn't diagnose Mary's daughter Katie at first: *'They went out and told Michael, who was waiting in the corridor, that we had a little girl and everything was fine, so of course, he couldn't wait, didn't even wait for me to come out of theatre, he went off and called his mum and my mum, and other people who had been waiting to hear the news, and it was only the next day that they came back to us and said things weren't so good after all. Well, we'd already suspected – nothing definite, but there was something . . . And*

*then when they came back and said she had Down's, well, we had her by
then, and we loved her, so the worst thing was Michael having to go and
phone everyone back again and tell them that things weren't quite so wonderful after all. But we knew her then, so it was different.'*

Stephen's reaction seems dramatic, but is quite typical: *'I didn't want to
touch her, I didn't want to pick her up. All I could think of was that there was
something wrong with her heart, and I felt like she was made of glass. She
wasn't mine. That's all I could think. She wasn't the baby I expected to have.'*

IF YOUR BABY has been born with a disability, then you may well feel
confused and resentful. More: you may feel angry, bitter, cheated.
You may not even know *how* you feel except that you don't feel right.
  During this sad time, there is no right or wrong way to feel. Allow
yourself time to come to terms with your feelings, and don't think
that this will happen overnight.

One of the main things you need, if you are struggling to come to terms with the child you have rather than the child you thought you were going to have, is information. The **Directory** at the end of this book gives details of many organisations who are there to offer you advice and support, and will help you through any difficulties, often by putting you in touch with other parents who have been through similar experiences. Other parents are often all too willing to help; they know what it is like. They know, better than anyone else, what you are going through. Make the most of them. But take it slowly . . .

Mary and Vicky express their inability to see beyond their own grief and shock: *'Yes, we needed a lot of information, but there was also so much going on, every day, that we couldn't take all the information in.'*

'I wasn't coping on any level – physically, spiritually, emotionally. And I couldn't read a Factsheet, the words didn't make sense.'

Remember: Everyone needs to take the time they need. You know your needs. Take your time.

Learning to adjust to the reality of your baby's condition also takes time, as Stephen and Bridget discovered: *'Sometimes I felt really protective towards her, other times, if someone had come in and asked me if I wanted her taken away, I'd have said yes. And I'd have never looked back. But they didn't come in. And then she was mine.'*

BABIES WITH DISABILITIES

There are some specific stages that most parents whose baby is born with a disability will go through:

Shock:
Nothing can prepare you for this news; expect simply to feel numb: If someone asks, you may find yourself saying, 'I don't know how I feel.'

Denial:
There are not many parents who won't ask the doctor: 'How can you be sure?'

Grief:
Many parents whose baby is born with a disability or a developmental problem find that they go through a time of sorrow and grief – just as if they were grieving for someone. And they are. Parents need time to mourn the loss of the perfect baby they dreamed of before they can whole-heartedly welcome the child they have.

Anger:
This is another natural reaction. The anger can be directed at anyone, including your partner and your friends, especially if your friend's own child is healthy. You may find yourself saying, 'Why us?'

Guilt:
Many parents feel guilty, even if they are told categorically it could not have been their fault. You may find yourself thinking back over the events in your pregnancy and saying, 'What did we do wrong?'

> ### SHARING
>
> When it comes to sharing what has happened, **remember:**
>
> - Most people will know very little about what has happened to your child. Be willing to explain as much as they need
> - Choose a time for talking when you can talk privately and without hurry
> - Have a positive attitude: it will help everyone be positive
> - It may help to have a checklist to cover important points.

'What was awful was never knowing what was best. Other people knew best all the time. They had experience of this, and we hadn't. We didn't know anything. All the time we were having to say: "Is this how you do it? Is this what you do?" I expected just to get on with it, and I couldn't.'

ONE PARTICULAR hurdle that parents whose child is born with a disability must face is telling others. How and when you tell people is your decision to make. Most parents, though, find that telling others as soon as possible is more helpful than not, and it is the best way to prevent misunderstandings.

Bereavement

IF YOUR BABY dies either just before birth (a stillbirth) or just after being born (a neonatal death) you will feel more anguish and pain than you ever thought was possible.

Some of you who are reading this book before your baby arrives will turn past these pages, not wanting to read them. 'It doesn't bear thinking about.' That would have been my reaction, too. But for some parents, they have to think about it, the hardest thing of all: a death in a place where there is no place for it, in a room where we give birth.

It is beyond the scope of this book to support families through the loss of their baby. Only talking and specialised support can do that, and for this reason we include the names and addresses of specific organisations that can help in the **Directory**.

What we can also do here is to let parents think in advance of how they might cope with the loss of their baby, and to let you know some positive ways in which you can help each other through such a difficult and distressing time.

George speaks for many other grieving fathers: *'People somehow expected me to be affected less than Anita. I was the one making the funeral* arrangements, going to see the Registrar, all of that. It was as if I just had to get all that done and then I could go back to work and forget about it.'

Anita expresses her own anguish: 'I was going to be a mother...and then I wasn't... and then I realised I was a mother, and always would be, even if I didn't have my baby with me any more.'

THERE ARE MANY local support groups run by and for parents who suffer a bereavement. They will allow you and your partner the opportunity to talk about how you both feel, express your feelings and grief and to share ways of coping.

TRANSITION

IF YOUR BABY has been born in a hospital, you may find that leaving what feels like absolute safety, where there are experts and paediatricians on call 24 hours a day, and returning home, is a daunting experience. Parents whose baby

---

REASONS

If you and your partner suffer a bereavement:

- Find out as much information as you want and need as to the causes. This will help you to understand and to come to terms with what has happened
- Do talk about the baby to each other. One of the saddest things about losing a baby near the time of birth is that no one else has had the chance to get to know this new little person. You know her better than anyone and can share your knowledge with each other
- Give yourself plenty of time to grieve. Do not expect to pick up the threads of life again as if nothing had happened
- Give your baby a name. This will help you to talk about her and see her as a person in her own right
- Ask for a photograph of your baby. This will help you to remember her
- Don't blame each other – you are both angry; you have a right to be angry, but you need to find other ways of expressing that anger
- Support each other – remember that your partner has also lost a child.

---

has been born at home often feel something similar when the last of the midwives finally leaves and they are on their own – at last, with their new arrival. Although there is a physical journey involved in the transition from hospital to home, for all parents there is an emotional journey to be made. When you left, there were two of you, now there are three.

The reality may not hit you until you are actually back at home, as it did Kay: 'I was in hospital for a week and all that time I kept thinking at the back of my mind that they'd never really let me leave with this baby because he wasn't really mine. Of course, I'm saying all this, I knew he was mine, I knew it rationally, but deep down . . . I just kept having this niggling doubt *that I'd have to hand him back before I got in the lift to go home. It was a bit of a shock that I didn't!'*

Darren thought going home would be a time of rest and peaceful 'daddyhood': *'Even before we left the hospital, on our way down in the lift, the nurse who was carrying the baby down for us was saying to Maureen, "Oh, it's lucky you've got your husband at home for a few days, that'll be a help," and I was thinking, "What can I possibly do to help?" I had no idea of the work involved. I imagined that Maureen would breastfeed, the baby would sleep a lot, smile at me from time to time . . . and I would help, I'd change the odd nappy or two. But that was all. I had no idea.'*

HOME MAY be the place you most want to be in the first few days, but even so, it can take some getting used to.

Naomi had been in hospital for quite a long time: *'Although there are compensations, like you get your medicines brought round, and the meals just appear, there are still so many constraints; like, if your baby's crying when the meal arrives, your dinner just goes cold – no one's going to pop it in the oven for you because there isn't an oven.'*

Rowena's husband began to long for some privacy, even at home: *'People were in and out all those first few days and it seemed like we'd never get any peace and quiet. People kept saying things like, "Oh it's so lucky you've got Peter here to help for a bit", and I was getting cross because all I was doing to help was making them tea.'*

David found himself impressed by Tina's growing knowledge and let himself be guided by her: *'We'd been living with Tina's parents and had only moved into our own flat three or four weeks before and there were still things in boxes that we hadn't got round to unpacking. We'd borrowed a cot from Tina's sister and put it up in the bedroom, next to our bed, and Tina put the baby in there when we got back from the hospital because the baby was asleep, and he looked so small and lost in there I wanted to take him straight out again. But Tina had put him in, so I didn't. She already seemed to know what was best because she'd been with him all the time in the hospital and I hadn't.'*

First days

YOU MAY BE new to the job and feel that you're dependent on 'experts' but no one knows your baby as well as you already do. It is surprising how quickly we learn to read our baby's signals, even when we may have had little to do with babies before. It is astonishing how much our instincts are right, and perhaps in itself this may give us confidence.

Philippa's baby's umbilical cord hadn't quite healed properly: *'So the midwife didn't discharge us at ten days like she was supposed to and I was really disappointed by that. I wanted to move on, and I felt this was holding us back in some way. I wanted the reassurance that everything would be alright, but I also wanted to take on the responsibilities myself.'*

With that responsibility, though, however much it is wanted and wel-comed, can come uncertainty, as Sally clearly knows: *'My brain has gone. It sometimes feels like a big empty space in my head where I used to do thinking. I don't even look at newspapers any more because they don't make sense. Or if I do pick up a newspaper, I always seem to find things in there that upset me, and more and more things upset me now. I end up crying over news stories. It feels much safer, in a way, just having me and Kevin in our little world.'*

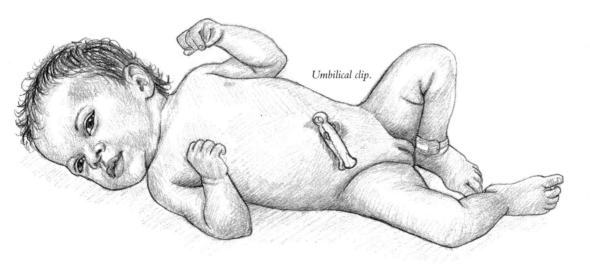

Umbilical clip.

THIS INSTINCT to nurture and protect, almost to make a 'nest', is very strong in many parents in the first weeks of their baby's life. For some people, this 'nesting' instinct began to manifest itself in late pregnancy with an urge to repaint the spare bedroom. If, during late pregnancy, your nesting instinct prompted you to do something slightly more practical, like freeze a month's worth of nutritious dinners, then you will be more thankful now than you could ever have believed. This is because, when your baby arrives, something odd seems to happen to time.

For Gillian the change was dramatic: *'Life is so slow now, that's the thing I can't get used to. It takes all day to do anything. It's ten in the morning and I'm still in my dressing-gown and the baby's having her third feed of the day and I'm wondering if I'm ever going to be able to get dressed and get to the shops. And yet, because there's never a moment to do anything or finish anything, it's all packed in so tight and the time rushes by. What happens to it? This is the thing they don't tell you.'*

The rhythm of life is very different in these early days. Some parents adjust to it almost at once; others find the change of gear much more difficult to accept. Rose felt nothing could prepare her for how she would feel: *'I found the first few weeks very difficult. Life was so different to how I imagined it was going to be, and so different to everything I'd ever experienced before, that I felt like I'd been thrown in the deep end and was going to drown, while all the time I smiled and everyone thought I was paddling along happily. I loved him, I loved him but I wasn't enjoying him.'*

As Yvonne points out, your daily pattern does change but sometimes it can seem slow to do so: *'At about three months I thought I'd start giving Andrée some carrots mashed up or something, potato, things like that, and I gave her tiny amounts on the end of a teaspoon and she would spit some out and enjoy others, and I liked that, watching her decide. But more than anything I liked having something different to do. It felt like every day was going to be the same. Baths, feeds, nappy changes, showing her books . . . apart from the baby clinic, where they had a mother-and-baby club afterwards, there was nothing to make one day different from another. I might do a trip to the shops one day, a walk to the woods another. But that was it. I needed to feel that we were going to move on, that Andrée wasn't always going to be totally depen-*

dent on me in this way, and I think those first teaspoonfuls of carrot were one way of reminding myself of that.'

For some parents, the surprise is how much they take to parenthood, as Rachel happily remembers: *'The one thing that I wasn't prepared for is how lovely it would be. And I didn't realise how happy I would be. People just don't tell you that. When you're a mother, you don't find yourself saying* to other mothers, "Isn't this wonderful?" You find yourself saying, "Are Pampers or Boots nappies better?" So I didn't know how absolutely wonderful it would be. There is a negative side, because I also didn't realise how much my life . . . well, how unselfish you have to become. You always have to put the baby before yourself. You stop doing things you enjoy doing because the baby comes first. But I enjoy feeling that she depends upon me. It makes me feel very special.'

Amanda likes parenthood too: 'People always seem glad to see you when you've got a baby. When you're out shopping, people come over and talk to you and can be really friendly. I enjoy the days, just me and the baby.'

OTHER PARENTS will be surprised at how unhappy they suddenly feel, often for reasons they cannot quite articulate.

Beverley had a difficult delivery, forceps, 23-hour labour, pethidine: 'It was really awful, and that did make a difference to how I felt afterwards, without a doubt. At least for the first, I should think the first four weeks, although I wouldn't have been considered clinically depressed, I was suffering from some sort of depression, shock, whatever. I just couldn't relate to Josh at all. People would say, "Oh, isn't he lovely? Doesn't he look great!" And I'd think, "Well, no." It wasn't until he was about four weeks old that I wanted to spend any time cuddling him, and then I did start to feel better. Also, because it was a traumatic birth, he was quite a whingey baby, and I didn't really like him. I kept wanting to put him down. I think my husband got very depressed around that time as well. He used to say, "I don't feel the way I thought I'd feel about Josh." And I'd say, "Neither do I." It was quite weird, and really horrible.'

DIFFERENT PEOPLE will tell you different stories about parenthood, but only you can know how you really feel: 'People kept saying to me when she was tiny, "Oh, make the most of it, this is the best time." And I thought it was the most dreadful time of my life. I thought, "If this is the best time, how am I going to cope when things get worse?" Then I met someone else who felt the same way, and her baby was slightly older, and she said to me: "This isn't the lovely time, this is the horrible time. Things do get better." And that was such a relief. Not everyone thinks it's good, that very early bit, though you get so wrapped up in it.'

Baby blues

BABY BLUES do seem fairly universal. That is to say, they have been suffered by women in all cultures and all times when their baby is very tiny – usually around three or four days after delivery, when hormone levels drop and milk production kicks in. They are often linked with a sense of physical and emotional anticlimax after the birth. Nurses will often dismiss your tears with the label 'three-day blues', which is of no help when you can't stop crying.

This is something Helen tried to explain: *'The day Jo and I came out of hospital was very exciting. I was so glad to be home, and so pleased to sleep in my own bed again. But the next morning my breasts were enormous and solid, Jo was fretful, and everything just seemed to fall apart. I started crying and crying and didn't really know why. I felt odd but I didn't feel sad. The tears just came out of nowhere.'*

THE FACT that these blues are so common, and always happen at around the same time, leads many experts to think that one of their causes is hormonal, though this explanation may not be much comfort.

'I was sobbing and sobbing, though if someone had asked me why I'd have been hard pushed to tell them, and the nurse said, "Oh, a lot of you go through this – you'll feel better tomorrow, believe me," and that just made it worse. I thought, "How do you know?" I felt so unhappy, I couldn't see myself ever smiling again. It all just seemed so pointless.'

Baby blues, whatever their cause, are usually all over by Day 10 at the latest. Few women find that this unusual sadness persists for longer. If it happens to you, it will help if not only you but your partner and perhaps other members of your family are prepared for the possibility. That way people will be able to reassure you that everything will be all right again, and with their reassurance and support, and patience, it soon will.

Helen has an extra remedy of her own, however: *'I was so sad, so sad and Kieron was flapping about not knowing what to do, so partly to get him away from me because I wanted to be able to cry in peace, I'd say, "Oh, I could just eat a Marks & Spencer prawn sandwich", and off he'd pop to Hammersmith to bring one back. And then he ran me a bath, and then he took Jo for a long walk . . . And none of it made the slightest difference at the time. It only lasted a couple of days, this weepiness, but it seemed eternal, and then it was gone, without me even noticing. But a long time afterwards I thought: what loving things to do. Everything Kieron could do, he did. And whenever I was feeling down with the baby, that thought would help.'*

Puerperal psychosis

WITHOUT WANTING to alarm people, it didn't seem fair to write a book about becoming a family and not mention this acute illness. Puerperal psychosis is an illness completely different in kind to the usual 'baby blues'. It is different to ordinary depression, too. Puerperal psychosis is an illness that makes its sufferers feel totally alienated from reality, as Denise explains: *'I was overjoyed when my baby girl was born . . . and the joy and excitement of those first few days did not wear off. Instead, I became more and more elated. For someone who is generally reserved, this was a change in personality. This powerful feeling of joy was one I had never felt before – nor have I since ever felt so happy. I literally could not stop talking – I felt that I had so much I wanted to say, so much to do, that I didn't feel the need for sleep. I lost all inhibitions and said whatever came into my head without pausing to think. My mind had gone into overdrive. I no longer had any control. I knew that something was wrong, and told the midwife who visited me at home that I was worried I was too "high" and might come crashing down. She just gave me a strange look. My GP thought it was good that I was enjoying motherhood so much. And I was. Being a mother was the most wonderful thing that had ever happened to me. And then everything fell apart. I began having involuntary thoughts about harming my baby – not so much thoughts as real pictures of causing her harm. What bewildered me was that I adored her...so why was my mind repeatedly trying to bash her brains out?'*

There is no mistaking puerperal psychosis – it is qualitatively different to other forms of 'depression' following childbirth. Its onset is rapid, there is no slow build up, and it seems to be a reaction to the sudden changes in hormone levels that occur after labour. It may help partners and supporting relatives to know that this is an illness completely outside the woman's control. She cannot 'snap herself out of it' and she cannot 'be reasonable'. She needs medical help.

Sadie saw visions and was more concerned to alert her friends and family to the meanings of these than to look after her baby: *'I saw God and then Jesus, who was telling me I had done wrong. And I knew my child would be taken by the Devil if I didn't protect her.'*

Most women with this illness will need to be hospitalised as they are unable to function effectively, and many take several months to recover as Denise continues: *'I spent four weeks on an Acute Admissions ward, then four weeks in a Mother-and-Baby Unit in the psychiatric hospital. By the time I went for my postnatal check with my GP at eight weeks, I was starting to get back to normal. I felt very vulnerable, sitting there in the waiting room. I watched another mother come in and very capably start to change her baby's nappy. The tears came suddenly and violently as it came home to me just how different I was to "normal" mums. I came home at ten weeks, but it took the best part of a year before I felt 'myself' again and not just going through the motions.'*

But women who have puerperal psychosis *do* recover, although it may take a long time and the demands upon partners and family will be very great. Often relatives will need to care for the child and, depending on the medication and state of mind of the mother, breast-feeding may not always be possible.

Research continues into the causes and the reasons why some women get this rare and distressing illness, and the most effective treatments, but there are no definite answers yet. The work done by Dr Katarina Dalton on the use of progesterone injections as a means of prevention is gaining coverage and acceptance. Although its preventive role cannot help a first-time sufferer, it can be of great reassurance to those who have suffered that they do not need to go through this again.

A 'ROUTINE'

CHANCES ARE, at least one health professional or relative will have advised you how desirable a routine is for your baby, although very young babies may not respond well to being 'put into' a routine. However, it can be helpful to establish an evening routine of supper, bath, story, bed (or similar). This sort of routine, if established early, can reduce bedtime problems in toddlerhood. Indeed, it gives most children a feeling of safety and security if roughly the same things happen at roughly the same time every day. It helps to give a sense of pattern and reassurance. And it can help you, too, if you're finding the demands of parenthood overwhelming: a routine can bring everything down to more manageable proportions.

Beverley felt she needed to get her new life into some sort of order: *'I think my idea of a "routine" came from my mum. Also, it came from me in the first three months trying* not *to have a routine. I remember thinking, "I want Josh to be a really flexible baby. I'm going to take him out with me whenever I need to go, feed him whenever he's hungry, put him to sleep when he's tired, and he's just going to adapt and be really flexible and it'll be great." And it was a nightmare. He ended up not having a sleep in the day, and then he wasn't sleeping well at night . . . it was just terrible. And I found that once I started doing things in this very strict routine – which I really resented, I didn't like having to do it at all – things got better. I thought, "Right, ten o'clock, he'll have a morning nap. Three o'clock, he'll have an afternoon nap," and I put him in his cot and he just started having them. It made a difference because I could say to people, "Oh, come round then because I know he'll be asleep", or whatever. I know where I stand, now.'*

YET, NO MATTER how desirable a 'routine' may be, one thing many parents resent is the lack of spontaneity in their lives. Whether you intended to carry on as before or not, you'll soon find you can't.

Deirdre's mental planning will sound familiar to you if you've already had your baby: *'I'd think, right, she's due for a feed in the next hour or so, and afterwards she'll probably fill her nappy, so if I change her then, we could go out after that and she'll probably have a sleep in the pram, but that means I won't have had my lunch . . . Okay, if I have my lunch now – it's about ten o'clock in the morning – that might do it. And if we spend longer there than I planned on, I'll be in trouble if I don't have what she needs, so I'll have to take wipes, nappy cream, dummy, bottle of water . . . And then I have to organise all these and then she wakes up and I still haven't had my lunch and this is all just to go round and have a cup of tea with a friend. How women go out to work every morning when they have babies, I just don't know. This is what I can't stand, not just being able to pop out and have a cup of tea when I feel like it.'*

Olivia's comments ring true too: *'There's a picture in a book of a father typing and this baby sitting in a bouncy chair watching him. It's got this cheerful caption like "Let the baby join in family life!" I can just see Beatrice sitting in her chair watching while Robert studies engineering. I think images like that can build up a false picture. Especially if your baby's not conforming to that image.'*

WHEN YOUR BABY arrives, images are what you have to forget. In the mother-and-baby magazines, those are models you are looking at, with their shiny hair and their designer outfits in their polished kitchens. They aren't real mums. Real mums have mysterious stains on their jumpers and a permanently quizzical expression, as if they've just forgotten which day of the week it is . . . which is usually because they have. And real mums have real babies.

Coping with that reality, with all its stresses and strains as well as its joys and delights, is what becoming a family is all about.

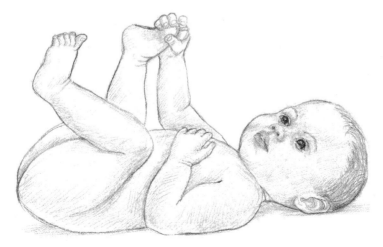

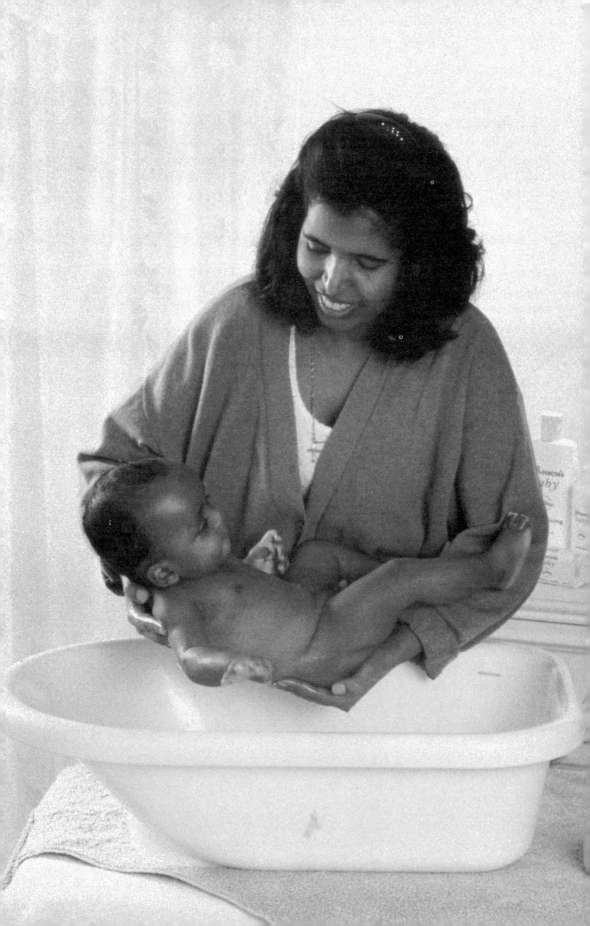

CHAPTER *two* Learning new skills

ONCE YOU'RE home, it often feels like people are relying on you to be the expert:

> *'How is he sleeping? Good or bad?'* What's 'good'? What's 'bad'?
> *'Are her feeds regular?'* What's 'regular'?
> *'Are his nappies normal?'* How can a nappy be normal? Should I be saving it to show them, perhaps? Then they could decide whether it was normal or not.

People look on you as the expert because already, even when your baby is very tiny, no one knows him or her as well as you do. You may feel you have an impossible amount to learn, but don't forget you have instincts, too, and these are for listening to, not ignoring.

Whatever is right for you, your partner and your baby, if it makes you all happy, then you're being exactly the kind of parents your baby needs you to be.

HOLDING

SOME PARENTS find it hard to get used to handling their new babies, feeling they're very fragile, others find it hard to put them down.

You will notice that your baby will respond much more cheerfully if you keep him held close to you and don't lurch him from one position to another very suddenly. It's an instinctive reaction in most of us to stroke and cuddle our babies, but keep it gentle. Save games when you hurl him madly through the air for later on in life. If it's a toddler saying: 'Throw me up to the sky, Daddy', you can join in the fun. But shaking or throwing a small baby is never fun. The baby will hate it and you could seriously harm him.

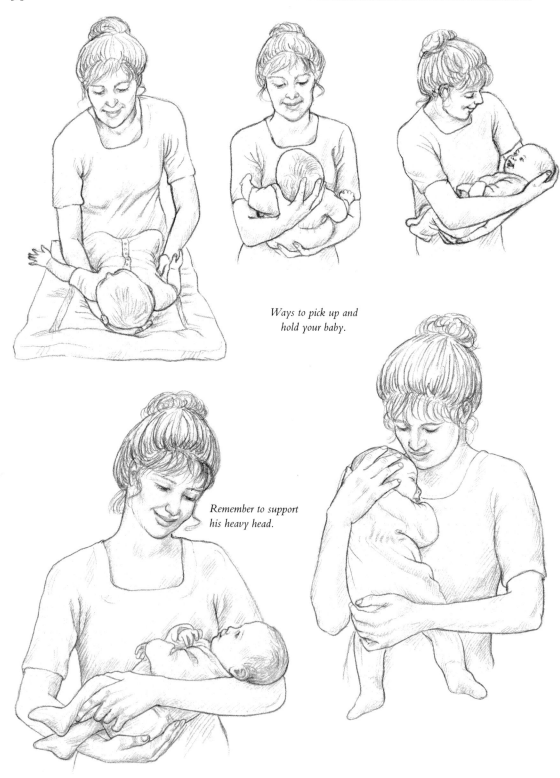

*Ways to pick up and
hold your baby.*

*Remember to support
his heavy head.*

Baby massage

As an extension of the stroking and cuddling that new parents find babies love, you might like to try baby massage as a way of soothing and relaxing your baby. A massage with a bath can be very beneficial – both for parent and baby, establishing a bond between them and allowing loving non-verbal communication.

If you're interested, you might find ads for baby massage courses in your local NCT newsletter or GP practice, as these will enable you to find out more about the techniques involved and the most soothing oils to use. Or try an introductory video as a guide.

BABIES LIKE TO BE HELD

- Close to you
- With their head and neck supported
- Upright, looking over your shoulder
- Cradled in your arms – perfect for talking
- In a baby carrier or sling
- Gently but firmly
- With your arm around his tummy and his back against your body – it widens his horizons
- A lot.

STEP BY STEP TO BATHING YOUR BABY

- A calm, warm environment is essential. Choose a time when you will not have to rush, when you aren't likely to be interrupted, and where you can get on with things in your own way and in your own time.
- Make sure it's the right time for your baby, too; that she has been fed so she isn't screaming with hunger, and definitely do not try a bath when your baby would much rather be having a nap: she'll scream with tiredness throughout, you'll both end up exhausted and your baby will probably be sick in the bath-water, she's so cross.
- Baths are meant to be enjoyable for all concerned. If your baby hates them, you can probably get away with topping and tailing for a week. If your baby loves them, you can give her one every day.
- Have everything ready beforehand:
  - warm dry towel
  - a spare warm, dry towel
  - sponge
  - baby shampoo if you like
  - a jug containing warm water to rinse your

baby's head – don't use the bath-water to do this – it could leave shampoo residue on your baby's scalp and this can cause irritation.
- You'll need a small baby bath. Prepare this beforehand, too, so that everything's ready when you undress your baby – make sure the water's not too hot.

  After a couple of months, when your baby's neck is stronger and she'll enjoy it more, you may like to take her in the bath with you. If you do this, have someone on stand-by to lift her out. Don't attempt to manoeuvre her and yourself out simultaneously with both of you wet and one of you wriggly. Again, the temperature of the water should suit the baby, not you.
- Most babies hate getting their heads wet, so the hair-washing part of the bath should be done as quickly as possible. If she starts to scream as soon as she feels the first drop on her scalp, don't persevere; just quickly wipe over her head with the dampened sponge and try again another day.

BATHING

YOUR NEWBORN will seem so fragile, you might well feel nervous handling her at first. Her head might be an odd shape if it has been moulded as she passed down the birth canal (for more information on this and other physical features of your newborn, see Chapter One) and you may be worried about touching the fontanelles. Nevertheless, you can't let this stop you washing her – you'll have to get round to this eventually and in many ways, once you're over the immediate aftermath of the birth, the sooner you do it the better it is for you and your baby. It will make her feel more comfortable if you can gently wash away any blood or dried fluids remaining after labour; and a

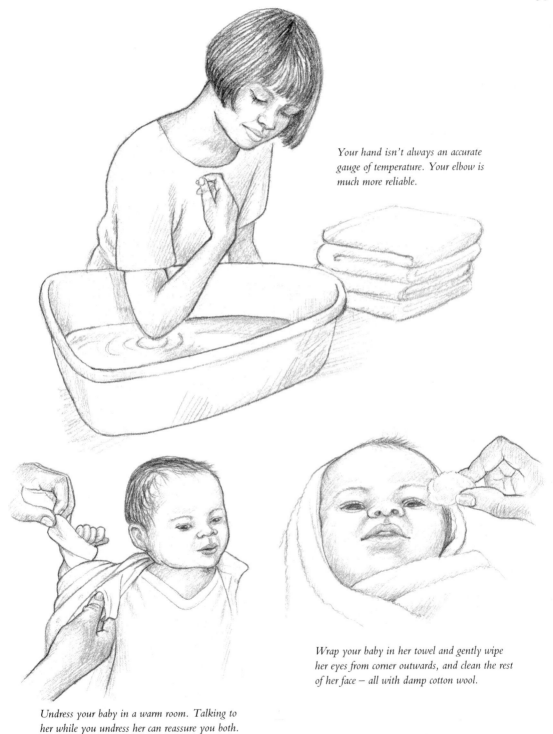

Your hand isn't always an accurate gauge of temperature. Your elbow is much more reliable.

Undress your baby in a warm room. Talking to her while you undress her can reassure you both.

Wrap your baby in her towel and gently wipe her eyes from corner outwards, and clean the rest of her face — all with damp cotton wool.

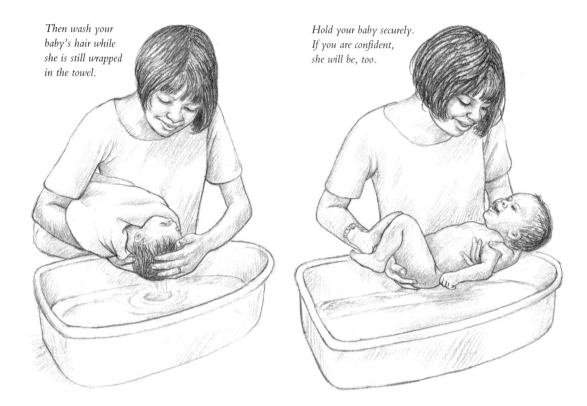

Then wash your baby's hair while she is still wrapped in the towel.

Hold your baby securely. If you are confident, she will be, too.

successfully washed infant, all fluffy and warm, will boost your confidence as a parent no end.

You don't have to jump in with both feet straight away and embark on a fully-fledged bathtime, unless this is what you want. You can just 'top and tail' her – i.e. clean only the bits that really need it. Ask your midwife or one of the nursing staff to show you how, and this will keep the baby happy and comfortable.

Washing your baby's hair

1. Undress your baby and wrap her in a towel, folded over at the back so you can easily cover her head with it afterwards.
2. Hold your baby firmly but gently. Hold her under one arm with her body against yours and her head over the water. Support her head with the hand of that arm. Tip your baby downwards slightly so that the water won't run into her eyes.
3. Use your other hand to wet her hair with a sponge.

Let her enjoy the warm water and freedom to splash.

Don't leave her in the water for too long. End the bath while you are both still enjoying it and you'll both look forward to the next one.

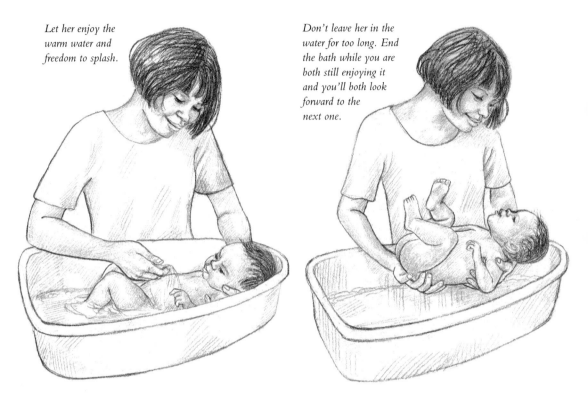

4. Rub in the shampoo gently then wash it off again.
5. Rinse with clear water left ready nearby.
6. Pat her head dry and wrap her warmly in the towel.
7. If you want to brush her hair, use a very soft-bristled brush.

Cradlecap

WHEN SHE IS between about a month and six months old, you may notice, underneath your baby's hair, a yellowish crust on her scalp. This is cradlecap, a condition so common almost every baby has it. It does your baby absolutely no harm whatsoever and, left to its own devices, will disappear completely as your baby grows. That said, if it is very thick or very noticeable, you will probably find yourself wishing you could do something about it. If so, don't be tempted into picking or trying to brush it off – you could pull the baby's hair out or cause an infection.

Some suggested remedies are:

- Massaging a tablespoon of almond oil or olive oil into your baby's scalp, leaving it for an hour then shampooing and rinsing thoroughly. You'll have to endure your baby smelling like a salad though

  (If you adopt this approach, you will have to keep the oil away from your baby's eyes while you're applying it, and make sure her fingers don't touch the oil, as she may then get it in her eyes.)
- Trying a bicarbonate of soda rinse: dissolve a teaspoonful in 500ml of warm water and dab it on with a cotton wool pad. Shampoo and rinse thoroughly. You will need to do this once or twice a week
- Combing her hair gently little and often – this will help to loosen the flakes.

No matter which recipe you try, cradlecap won't disappear overnight, but it will disappear.

Other things to check for:

IF YOU NOTICE patches of redness or soreness on your baby's neck or behind her ears, then it may be eczema; ask your health visitor for advice.

CHANGING

WHAT'S IT TO be? Terries or 'disposables'? Perhaps more importantly, who's going to do it? Especially when it's the middle of the night, your baby has completed an extraordinary performance, and it's a repeat show of the one she did two hours ago.

Nappy changing is one of the skills you will become surprisingly adept at over the next couple of years.

Disposables

Advantages

- Undoubtedly easier in general. This is why they are so popular.
- They are very absorbent and can see a baby through the night without you having to face a cotful of wet bedding every morning.

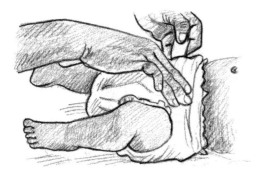

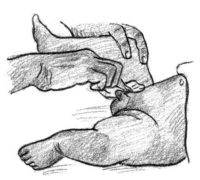

Remove old nappy on a waterproof surface. Accidents will happen.

Clean your baby thoroughly with warm water. Allow him to dry in the air if possible.

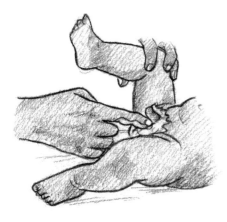

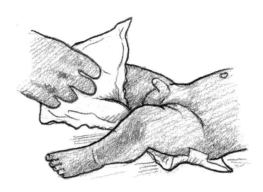

Barrier cream can help prevent nappy rash.

Lift your baby's bottom up, put the nappy underneath and then pull the nappy through to the front.

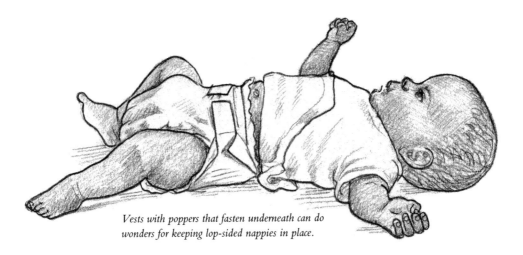

Vests with poppers that fasten underneath can do wonders for keeping lop-sided nappies in place.

Disadvantages

- You may have trouble finding some that suit your baby. Every baby has a unique shape and yours may not fit into one of the standard 'nappy sizes', so that you're always running the risk of leaks or pulling the adhesive tapes so tight your baby can scarcely breathe
- If you get cream on the tape, the tape loses its stickiness. This tends to happen at awkward moments
- Cost. Although the pence-per-nappy price might not be exorbitant, the amount that you will pay out in total over the years your baby is using nappies is stunning
- They are not earth-friendly; the raw materials they require, the processes used in their production, and the fact that they are not truly easy to 'dispose' of except in landfill sites, which are rapidly filling up, are not easy issues for new parents to ignore, if they are keen to preserve the planet for the next generation.

IF YOU ARE A committed disposable-user, you may find the new nappy-delivery services a great boon, especially in the early days when it's more difficult to get out with your baby, you're getting through the nappies at a great rate, and they are a very bulky item to carry home. Some shops will bring a month's worth, with no charge for delivery, direct to your door.

Terries

Advantages

- They are environmentally friendly
- They are comfortable, soft, and have no hard edges to irritate babies' skin
- Cheaper in the long run (see old editions of *Which?* in your library for comprehensive studies on this topic)
- Easier these days so long as you have a washing machine and preferably a tumble dryer.

Disadvantages

- Learning the origami necessary for successful nappy adherence
- Safety pins
- Soaking
- Buckets (smell)
- Washing
- Guilt – although the washing and drying of reusable nappies demands only a fraction of the energy used by disposables, the chlorine, bleach and washing powder may help to destroy the ozone layer.

ALSO (FORGET the stories of women taking their nappies down to the river – that wasn't in North London), you have to have a washing machine these days to be a sane terry-user.

There are now many cotton-nappy delivery and laundry services around. These involve 'fitted' nappies that don't require major folding techniques. You order up the correct size nappies for your baby – from newborn to toddler – which are then delivered to your door. You also get a bin with a liner, in which you place the used nappies until they are collected by the service, who simultaneously provide you with clean nappies. The laundered nappies are thermo-sterilised before being reused, so not only do you not have to wash them yourself, you can feel virtuous about not making any contribution to the landfill sites.

Or you could use terries to start with, disposables on holiday and cotton nappies later. The permutations are endless. Whatever you choose, make sure you're happy – those first few weeks can seem like nothing more than an endless round of nappy changing and feeding at times, so make it as easy and enjoyable as you can.

AVOIDING NAPPY RASH:

- Change your baby's nappy frequently
- Clean and dry your baby's bottom and all the creases thoroughly
- Allow your baby some nappy-free kicking time on the mat at as many changes as you can manage
- Use a barrier cream to help prevent the skin getting too damp
- At the first sign of redness, change nappies even more frequently
- Witch hazel and camomile creams are both helpful if a rash does develop. There is a variety available and you may like to try one or two before finding one that suits
- The best cure is letting your baby kick naked on a blanket on a waterproof mat for as long as he likes
- Severe nappy rash may be caused by thrush which needs suitable treatment. Consult your doctor or health visitor; if you are breastfeeding, you may need treatment too.

DRESSING

IF YOU HAVE infinite leisure and infinite ready cash, you can go round the shops ticking off those suggested 'layette' lists: three nightdresses, four vests . . . but you'll find that the baby can get through three night-dresses in one morning. And what sort of vest do you want? What sort of sleepsuit is best? Front opening? Back opening? Poppers down each leg or not?

If you're at all sensible, you will borrow twice as many newborn-size clothes as you think could possibly need. Babies are newborn-size for such a short time, the clothes hardly have a chance to get worn, never mind worn out, though some of them can develop rather startling stains. Also, what suits you and your baby may not be the sort of garments generally in use, as Lynn recollects: *'Somebody once told me that she'd used the tie-across-the-front vests for her premature baby in the SCBU and would recommend them to me. So when I was in Boots one day and I saw some, I thought, "Oh, well, they might just be the ones that suit", even though most vests on sale were the pull-over-the-head and button-underneath sort. And they were the best thing I bought. They didn't last long because they were small, but in those early days when I was frightened to touch him, practically, it was such a relief to be able to put him in clothes that I didn't have to wrench over his head. One arm in, roll over slightly, other arm in, fasten...and then he looked so sweet with this little bow! They were brilliant.'*

Another piece of advice from Hazel: *'Don't buy anything that comes off over the head for the early days. Not pleasant if there's a nappy leak.'*

OF COURSE, while you will want to buy clothes that are practical, express your baby's innermost personality, are well-made and yet relatively cheap, many of us hesitate before buying clothes when we are pregnant. It is as if we don't dare to tempt fate.

Yet, even though we might like to, we can't leave it all to chance. So when you're packing your suitcase for the hospital or filling the bottom drawer, you will need to make sure that you have a selection of the following items:

- Vests
- Nightdresses (useful in the early days as there aren't so many poppers to undo every time you need to change a nappy – not so useful if your baby is short-limbed and her arms keep falling out of the sleeves!)
- Sleepsuits (all-in-one stretch suits)
- All-in-one padded suit for the first outing (if you have a winter baby)
- Hat
- Mittens if you have a winter baby
- Cardigans for layering.

A shawl is also a useful item – you can wrap your baby in it for warmth and comfort. You will also need whatever sort of nappies you have chosen to use and a variety of sheets and blankets for the cot/basket/pram. Many of the blankets graduate to the higher role of 'cuddly' and will be trailed round lovingly for years.

Jennifer often thinks back to the first outing that she made with her mother to Brent Cross to buy all the baby's stuff in one fell swoop: *'I was about eight months pregnant, and it was a warm day, and I couldn't believe I'd ever need all the blankets and mittens she was handing to me. But I do remember picking up this yellow cotton blanket and saying: "What a beautiful sunny colour, I'm sure the baby will love this", and he did. He still takes it to bed with him at night. It's not quite so yellow now, of course, and not quite so fluffy, but I find it a useful connection between the world of when he wasn't here and I chose something for him, and when he was here and he chose it for himself.'*

DRESSING YOUR baby can feel at first like you're taking part in one of those competitions where you have to keep all the plates spinning in the air at once. If you choose a warm room so your baby won't become chilled, you will be able to take your time, and you will both be able to use the time for a chat.

Although dressing your baby is an art rather than a science it will soon become second nature – fortunately, as it will be many months yet before your baby can co-operatively manoeuvre all her limbs in the desired directions to make life easier for you.

DRESSING YOUR BABY

1. Place your baby on her changing mat or other comfortable surface. Put on your baby's nappy. Talk to your baby while you dress her, telling her what you're doing, the names of things, perhaps counting the poppers.

2. The vest. Gather up the vest around the neck opening. Stretch this opening wide and place it at the back of the baby's head.

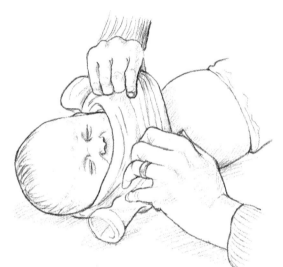

3. Use the fabric of the vest to gently lift your baby's head and slide the fabric over. Pull the fabric down at the back of the head first, and then, without taking your fingers from the neck opening, lift the vest over your baby's face. Stay calm if she starts to wriggle and don't try to rush – you'll frighten her more.

4. Gather up one arm opening. Reach through it, find your baby's hand, and enclose her tiny fingers in your own. With your other hand, pull the sleeve downwards over your baby's arm. This way, you won't bend or hurt her fingers. Settle the sleeve over your baby's shoulder. Repeat with the other arm.

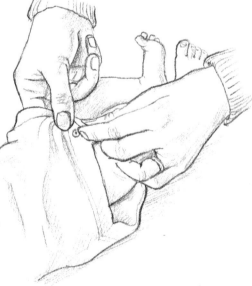

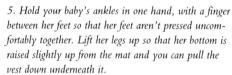

5. Hold your baby's ankles in one hand, with a finger between her feet so that her feet aren't pressed uncomfortably together. Lift her legs up so that her bottom is raised slightly up from the mat and you can pull the vest down underneath it.

6. Pull the vest down in front and fasten the poppers.

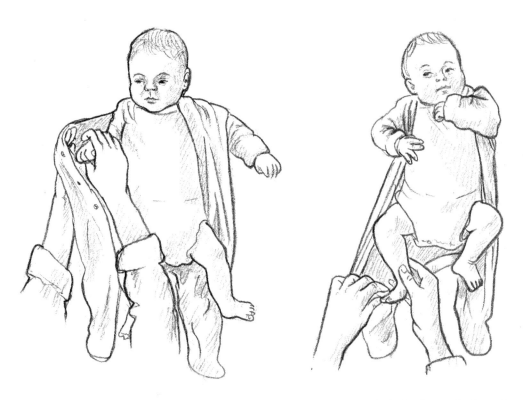

7. The sleepsuit. Put the sleepsuit down flat on the mat, open, with all the poppers undone. Put the baby on top of the sleepsuit.

8. Gather up one sleeve and open the cuff of the sleeve with one thumb and forefinger. Stretch the cuff wide and guide it over your baby's fist. Hold her hand in yours as you pull the sleeve up her arm. Repeat with the other sleeve.

9. Guide the first leg into the sleepsuit's leg opening and gently pull the fabric up her leg until her toes reach the foot of the suit. Make sure all the toes are comfortably in and not bent. Repeat with other leg.

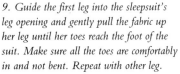

10. Fasten the poppers – either from the top down or the bottom up. If you start in the middle you can be guaranteed to have an odd popper left over at either end.

11. Smile. You've done it!

SLEEP FACTS

- Newborn babies do need a lot of sleep, 18 hours a day is not unusual. If your baby seems to be having less than this, it may be because she is having it in short bursts rather than long naps
- Sleep is good for babies. Growth hormones reach high levels while they sleep, and your baby needs time to rest and recuperate from the constant new stimulus of the world
- Babies need feeding at night. She needs food at frequent intervals, so you have to expect her to ask for it at least until she is three or four months old
- Babies' sleep patterns will change radically during the first six months of life. By the time your baby is six months old, she may well be sleeping between 10 and 12 hours each night (even if this is broken) with two or three hours during the day, often in two distinct naps, morning and afternoon.

SLEEPING

BEFORE YOUR baby was born, he could wake and dream and sleep at will, at whatever hours suited him. There was no one else to take into account. In the first days and weeks after the birth, your baby will try to persist with this individual pattern, sleeping whenever it suits him. This is why the subject of sleep is such a hot issue for new parents, because, as soon becomes obvious, a baby who sleeps whenever it suits him will come into conflict with the pattern adopted by most adults: namely, doing the greater part of their sleeping during the hours of darkness.

While you cannot expect your baby to adopt a pattern of eight hours of sleep every night from Day One, equally you do not have to let your baby dictate when you sleep *ad infinitum*. Playtime at 3am is bound to cause conflict with wider society eventually.

And sleep deprivation is so profound a problem that it has been used as a method of torture for centuries. If you don't get enough sleep, the whole family will suffer.

So, although you may have got through the first days or weeks in a fog, sleeping when the baby sleeps, what can you do to establish the pattern and routines that will suit everybody?

How much sleep?

THIS IS A burning question mainly for those parents who feel their child isn't getting enough sleep. If pressed further, and if they are being honest, those same parents might admit that in fact they are more worried about *themselves* not getting enough sleep.

Worrying about sleep can make matters worse, as it did for Hazel: *'I looked at a book and it said he should be sleeping around 18 to 20 hours a day – this was when he was about two weeks old. And he wasn't sleeping anywhere near that. And I'd read somewhere else that babies only grew when they were asleep so I thought he'd end up being tiny. I was trying to make him go to sleep all the time so he'd grow and this drove me to distraction.'*

A sleepy state can be perfectly natural for some babies, as Jennifer tells: *'I couldn't even tell whether he was asleep or not. He ended up in this permanent half-doze, especially in those early days when I was so keen for him to suckle and build up my milk supply.'*

YOU MAY FIND that one frequently asked question about your baby is: 'Is he settled yet?' This idea of the 'settled' baby is quite prevalent, and implies a magical transformation from the unpredictable bundle of the newborn to a well-organised, easily manageable baby with regular feeds and hours when you know she will probably nap. This magical transformation is expected to occur somewhere between six weeks and three months.

Some make this magical transformation a little later; some a lot later (although most parents find that by the time their child starts school things have been more manageable for quite a while). Some 'settle' spontaneously. Others will if you guide them in the right direction, providing them with stable and secure patterns that mean your baby can predict from one day to the next what will be happening.

When your baby is born, short spells when she is awake will alternate with sleeps which can be a few hours or only several minutes

---

Encouraging your child to settle

- Have a definite 'winding down' routine for the evenings; for example: looking at a book, bath, feed, change and donning of ritual 'nightclothes' (even if these are indistinguishable from the day clothes as your baby only wears sleepsuits)
- Don't get your baby used to falling asleep only in certain situations (like in the car or the pram or at the breast) as she will come to associate these circumstances with sleep and you will find yourself driving round the block at 3am
- Keep the room at a comfortable temperature: 18 degrees C (65 degrees Fahrenheit) is ideal
- Let your baby settle herself to sleep if she can; for example: don't rush to her and pick her up the instant her eyelids flutter open – she may want to gently drift off again
- Keep the atmosphere in the house as calm and relaxed as you can, but don't tiptoe round her and feel you have to stay quiet; the womb is one of the noisiest places on earth – heartbeats, gurglings, joint movements, hearing people talking – and your baby fell asleep there.

OWN ROOM/PARENTS' ROOM

Own room

Advantages
- Parents have their own space
- The baby starts off in his own room and won't have the trauma of transfer at a later stage
- The baby won't be disturbed by you coming to bed.

Disadvantages
- The fact that their baby is not near them can cause some parents to worry
- The baby can be lonely
- Further to go for night feeds.

Parents' room

Advantages
- The baby is close for checking and feeding
- It can be reassuring to parents, to have their baby close
- Breastfeeds can be achieved with both of you still half asleep.

Disadvantages
Your sleep may be disrupted by the little noises babies make. If your baby sleeps with you in your bed, be aware of the following:
- The weight and heat of the parental duvet may be too much for some babies and could be dangerous. A duvet is not recommended for a baby, even in their own cot. If parents take the baby into their bed, it is safer to use sheets and blankets rather than a duvet
- You can't sleep in the same bed as your baby if you've had a few alcoholic drinks, as you might not wake sufficiently to avoid rolling on top of him while you're asleep
- Nappy leaks mean washing large amounts of bedding instead of tiny cot-sized amounts.

long. Day or night makes no difference to your baby – sleep patterns are something we are socialised into. You may long for your baby to sleep 12 hours straight through at night, for example, but if you were living in Spain, perhaps, you might prefer her to have a long afternoon sleep during the heat of the day and only eight or nine hours at night. Whatever pattern you choose, that will be the one you will be trying to guide your baby into – and there is nothing wrong with that. Patterns make life easier for everyone. Therefore, if your baby hasn't 'settled' by three months of age or so, you may like to help her find a pattern of sleeping and waking that suits her, and whose hours and predictability suit you.

Where to sleep?

PERHAPS THE strongest statement you can make on the subject is where you want your baby to sleep at night.

In a separate room? Yes, you can try sleeping with one ear attuned to the slightest whimper of the baby in the next room. Or buy a monitor.

With you? Yes, but it's important that your baby does not get overheated. The Foundation for the Study of Infant Deaths recommends your baby sleep in a cot next to your bed for the first six months.

If you choose this option, but want your baby to be close, try leaving the side of the cot down so that he can sleep alongside you. You can lift him across for night feeds with the minimum of disruption.

Felicity felt very strongly, right from the start, that her daughter, Rebekah, needed to be with them: *'With us. That's where she was during the day – I wouldn't have dreamed of making her sit for hours on end in a cot by herself then – so why would I want to make her do that at night? So she was in our bed, plain and simple, from the beginning. There wasn't anything to get flustered over, then.'*

Jess tried to get her twins to sleep independently from her and Richard: *'I meant to do all the things that they said you should do in the books to get a good night's sleep . . . leaving them for five minutes and then for ten minutes, then for 15, but I just couldn't. I kept saying to Richard, "Let's try it next week, perhaps, when I've got a bit more strength", and next week would come and I'd be just as tired, and it was always less exhausting just to go to the twins and be with them if they cried, rather than battle it out in some contest of wills for however long it might take. In the end, when it came down to it, I just couldn't bear to hear them cry.'*

FOR SOME PARENTS, like Gwen, there was no question from the beginning: *'It didn't feel right, to let her dictate when she went to bed and when she had a nap . . . she was tiny! A friend of mine had said, "Put her down in her cot when it's bedtime, then go outside and walk round the garden or something – away so you don't have to put yourself through any anguish if she's crying." And it was a brilliant thing to have said. I'd put her down, walk round the*

> ### Things you can do to encourage your child to sleep well
>
> ● Help your baby to form a bond with a 'cuddly'. Muslin squares and terry nappies are great favourites. Place one against your baby while you feed her, perhaps, so that she comes to associate it with comfort and warmth. Some lucky parents find that by about two months of age they only have to present the muslin square to the baby to trigger an automatic thumb-in-the-mouth-time-to-drop-off response
>
> ● Let your baby fall asleep to a musical mobile. As the music slows (so the theory goes) your baby should slow and sleep, too. It doesn't always work. I know one family who had two mobiles and the baby wanted both and they played different tunes. It got worse when the boy got a bit older and wound them both up in the middle of the night
>
> ● Have a glass of wine. (This is for you, not the baby.) It may make you sleep that bit more soundly so that it's your partner who has to get up first and pace the bedroom floor and then you can be the one who leaps out of bed in the morning bright-eyed and bushy-tailed and saying, 'Did she sleep right through the night, then? Oh, really? I didn't wake up.'

Calming techniques for you

- Never lose sight of the fact that you need to wind down and relax, too. Practise some of those calming relaxation exercises that you learned when you were pregnant
- Join a yoga class and practise its techniques once or twice a day. The gentle stretching and deep breathing are an excellent way to dissipate physical tension
- Join any sort of class if it's going to get you out of the house for an hour every week – it will help ease your tensions and give you a constant reminder that there is a world beyond the four walls of your home
- Tell your health visitor if it's getting you down. She may know how to help and have some useful suggestions for you.

---

garden for five or ten minutes – she'd start off crying, but when I got back things were always quiet. It got us into a really good habit right from the start. She's always been able to settle herself, and I've never had to walk up and down for hours getting cross with her. It made life very predictable, very manageable, and I valued that.'

Establishing a pattern

ONCE YOU know where and when you want your baby to sleep, stick by your decision. Wavering will confuse the baby, render you even angrier because you've had to give in, and make everyone more irritable through even more lack of sleep. Don't expect miracles. This sort of predictable sleeping is a new skill to learn . . . for everyone.

Sleep problems

IF YOU ARE one of the lucky parents who can skip this section, you should be aware that you are an object of envy for most parents. Not every baby settles down into a predictable pattern quickly or easily, even though you may have followed all the advice from your mother, health visitor, GP and the other parents at your local NCT or Mothers' group on how to encourage a good sleep pattern.

A baby whose sleeping is causing difficulties for his parents puts the whole family under a great deal of stress. We all know that a good night's sleep will find us refreshed in the morning, while a night when we sleep badly leaves us irritable and bad-tempered the next day. And when we're irritable, we find it hard to relax and drop off to sleep, making the tiredness even worse. It is not unknown for whole families to fall into this sort of vicious cycle in the first weeks of their baby's life. That's why it's important to decide, if you have a problem, how you as a family want to set about solving it. Your health visitor can give you great support, so can friends. So can other parents who know what you're going through. Lean on them as much as you can and it will make life easier for all of you.

Cot death

SUDDEN INFANT Death Syndrome (SIDS), as it's officially known, is a rare event. Despite extensive research, experts cannot agree on its cause although regulation of breathing and temperature control seem to be important factors.

The fear of cot death is a worry that affects every parent at some time or another, and it is one of the most distressing events that can happen to a family.

It makes things worse when the people around you are unsupportive as they were to Karen: *'When my son died, I found the fact that the police came to the house very*

> ### MINIMISING RISKS
>
> - Place your baby on her back or her side to sleep
> - Don't smoke near her. Don't let anyone smoke in the house
> - Make sure your baby stays at a nice, even temperature – in particular, don't let her get too hot. Use blankets on her basket or cot that can easily be taken off or added to, rather than a duvet which is much less flexible and more likely to cause overheating
> - Put your baby at the foot of the cot to sleep so that she can't wriggle down among the bedclothes and overheat
> - Keep the bedding and mattress clean, dry and well-aired
> - If you think your baby is at all unwell, contact your doctor
> - Breastfeeding your baby may reduce the risk of cot death, but as yet there is no conclusive evidence to show why.

upsetting. I got the feeling that because they were there I must have done something wrong. One of them, a policewoman, told me that because the doctor did not know the cause of death he had to, by law, call the coroner. The coroner's officer was asking for information and I felt like a criminal. This was made much worse later when people would make remarks to me like, "Breastfed babies never die from cot death", when they knew I was bottle-feeding Leila. Some of the people I had thought would be very supportive just weren't. It's like they thought it was catching.'

SOME PARENTS don't even want to read any information about it, somehow worrying that if they read about it, it might happen to their child. Deep down, you know that's not the case, reading never made anything happen. Doing things makes things happen. And there are things you can actively do to *minimise* the risk of cot death as shown in the box above.

FEEDING

BEFORE YOUR baby was born, he did not know hunger. Every single nutritional need was met before he felt it. It is only now, out in the world, that your baby knows what hunger is. For the first time, he feels an empty stomach. No wonder he cries.

From the moment you hear that cry, there will be a series of decisions to start considering:

- Are you going to feed him breast milk or 'bottle' milk? ('Bottle' milk is formula milk specially designed for babies – cow's milk – your doorstep pint of milk – won't be suitable for your baby until sometime around his first birthday. It's too low in iron and the vitamins that he needs to grow, and too high in salt and saturated fat)
- Are you going to leave him to cry a few more minutes because your mother-in-law says it's a good way to teach babies patience, or are you going to feed him straight away because that's what your instinct tells you to do?
- And, if you do start breastfeeding, how long will each feed last?
- And how long will this breastfeeding business go on? Until you go back to work? Until the baby hits three months? Until he's a toddler? Until he goes to school?
- And, if you're bottle-feeding, just how many bottles a day is this child supposed to have? And what goes in them?

ONCE, THERE wasn't this much choice. If you had a baby, you gave him breast milk. (You could, if you were either one of the very few women who found it impossible to breastfeed, or you were a member of the royal family, find a wet nurse – a profession that has fallen out of favour – but, on the whole, you got on with it.) There were no other options. In the days following the birth of your baby, some of you may long for the simplicity and certainty of bygone times. Already your life has been turned upside down – you don't want to waste time worrying over whether you've made the right decision.

Breastfeeding

MOST WOMEN have already decided how they're going to feed their baby before their baby is born. And these days many first-time mothers decide to start breastfeeding, because of the proven health benefits to both baby and mother.

There was never any question for Lynn: *'Breastfeeding was best. I was going to breastfeed. That was that. Nobody hinted that I might not be able to, or might have problems doing so. Good thing, really, because if they had, I might have thought twice.'*

Kay received plenty of encouragement at just the right time: *'Really, the breastfeeding counsellor led me to believe that most women could, so I could, so why didn't I?'*

A GREAT DEAL of research has gone into finding out exactly what nutrients babies need and in what proportion. Breast milk provides just the right amount of nutrients: proteins, fats, carbohydrates, vitamins and minerals for optimal feeding. Formula milk manufacturers, therefore, have spent a great deal of time aiming to produce babymilks that are as close to this perfect breast milk as possible, although there will always be some things that they simply cannot reproduce at all. In particular, your body will always produce milk that is perfectly suited to your baby and her individual needs – a feat so close to magic that you cannot hope to achieve it with powder.

Research has shown that one of the biggest factors that influences whether a mother breastfeeds successfully or not is the support – or lack of it – shown by her partner. This makes sense. How many of us would persevere with any activity that was slightly difficult if we got the feeling that no one really wanted us to do it anyway?

Helen's husband Chris just assumed that she was going to breastfeed: *'If he'd shown any hesitation or if I'd got the feeling that he didn't like it, then I wouldn't have felt supported, and I needed support, because it was a lot harder than I'd been led to believe it was going to be. The fact that he felt it was natural and right, and that he was so helpful in other ways because I was doing all the feeding made the first few weeks much easier for me.'*

Going out

YOU NEEDN'T be 'tied' to your baby if you're breastfeeding. Expressing extra is useful on two counts once breastfeeding is well established:

- It may help to build up your milk supply
- You can leave a bottle with a babysitter while you pick up the threads of your 'outside' life again.

Not that it's always so simple, as Louise explained: *'Great, I thought. Freedom. So I expressed for two hours, got an ounce of milk and was able to go to a meeting which lasted an hour and a half.'*

Useful tips for expressing come from Jennifer and Yvonne: *'I used to use breast shells – place one over one nipple while the baby fed from the other and I might have two ounces of milk at the end of a feed – an easy way of getting together enough milk to leave a spare bottle for the babysitter on the (rare) occasions that Gordon and I wanted a night out.'*

'I used a hand pump on one side while the baby fed from the other when I wanted to express extra. Solved the problem of the let down reflex in no time.'

Bottle-feeding

YET NO MATTER how much support they get, or how much they know it is the best thing for their baby, there are some mothers who decide that breastfeeding is not right for them, or at least not all of the time.

Jane didn't enjoy breastfeeding during the day: *'There was always someone there who made me uncomfortable, or Lyle would start screaming while we were in the middle of Sainsbury's and I'd have to spend half an hour in this little dark room somewhere, or in a Ladies' toilet, or I'd have to abandon the rest of the shopping trip and go home seething with resentment that we'd have to come out later in the day and try again. But nights were different. Lyle would come in the big bed with us, and make these little lapping sounds and go so quiet and content, it was like being on a tiny island in the dark all on our own and so safe and warm. He'd drift off to sleep, and I'd drift off to sleep,* and it was all so soothing. And every single time I'd think to myself, "Thank goodness I don't have to go down to a cold kitchen and warm up a plastic bottle." During the days, I thought a bottle would have been ten times as easy. But not at night.'

Virginia never wanted to breastfeed: 'I came under a lot of pressure to, from midwives, from my family — my own mother had fed us and was horrified I could contemplate doing something different. But I knew I'd be going back to work when Edie was about eight weeks old, and I also knew it would be much easier for both of us if she fed the way she was going to feed right from Day One. My breasts were very, very sore and engorged for a couple of days, and I resisted all temptation to express or let the baby have 'just one feed'. And gradually it faded. Edie thrived, and we had no problems making the transition from me-at-home to me-at-work.'

> ## BOTTLE BASICS
>
> If you decide you want to bottle-feed, you will need:
>
> - Around six or more 200ml size bottles
> - A bottle brush for cleaning
> - A steam sterilising unit or a tank and steriliser tablets
> - Formula milk – if you're not sure which one to choose, ask your midwife for advice.
>
> You may also need to try a variety of teats. Most bottles are supplied with standard-shape teats, but there is a wide range available, with holes of varying sizes, and it may take some experimentation to find the one which suits your baby best.
>
> You will also need some way to warm the bottles. Nifty little bottle warmers are available, but if you're on a budget, standing the bottle in a bowl of warm water will do. Formula should never be heated in a microwave: it can heat unevenly and, even though it feels okay to your touch, can still burn your baby.

Feeding difficulties

SOME PARENTS find that, with the best will in the world, they cannot go on as they started out, as Chloë relates: 'When my Jack was born, he weighed nearly 9lb. We started breastfeeding quite happily as I really wanted to, and persevered through the sore nipples, the sleepless nights . . . and the crying. Jack just wouldn't put weight on. He got thinner and thinner and cried all the time, and I got more and more exhausted. I tried to take the advice of my breastfeeding counsellor and fed him on demand nearly every hour, but he still didn't put on any weight. At ten weeks, Jack was dehydrated and I was desperate. I had done everything I had been advised to do but he was taken into the children's ward at the local hospital and they told me to stop breastfeeding him. I was very sad, but there was an immediate response: in a month, Jack had gained weight. Now he is on the top centile, and a big, thriving boy.'

Deirdre breastfed and bottle-fed her daughter for six weeks: *'When we switched to bottle feeds, she became more happy and contented, started sleeping better, and my partner and I were both getting more rest. At first I kept quiet about this whenever I talked to other NCT mothers but gradually it became clear there were lots of us in our group doing it and not letting on!'*

Weighing

IT IS ALL TOO easy, especially with your first baby, to become anxious about the weight gain he or she may or may not be achieving from week to week. Weighing is not meant to be a source of worry but of reassurance, and most times it is. Most babies pursue an upward path along the graph, but at varying rates of speed. Some parents have been made to worry unnecessarily if, for example, their baby is weighed complete with one wet terry nappy by one health visitor one week, and in glorious nudity the next. Such circumstances may conspire to make it look like the baby has actually lost weight. This sort of event can be a particular cause of worry if you're breastfeeding and not very confident in your milk supply, or if the health professionals are not sensitive to your concerns.

Sometimes weighing your baby if you're breastfeeding can be reassuring: *'The thing about breastfeeding is that I could never see how much was actually going in. Bottle-feeding mothers would swan around saying, "He's had a whole six ounces this feed . . . and he still wanted more!" and I'd never know — all I could say was, "Well, he's fed for thirty minutes but I think half that time he was actually asleep." We like the security of those little numbers adding up. It was such a thrill to see him clock up a steady half a pound a week at the clinic, therefore, as it seemed like I was being vindicated. I can see, though, that if they'd said he wasn't measuring up to their little graphs, I might have given in and put him on the bottle.'*

Faith's baby, Tony, was big — a big baby, long and solid: *'Everyone used to look at me as if I was feeding him too much, letting him become fat. It was actually quite reassuring to see that if you started off with his birth weight, he was exactly where he was supposed to be on the charts.'*

SOME BABIES are bigger than others. Some babies grow faster than others. If there is a long-term developmental problem, it will become obvious to you and the medical staff, and if your baby is not getting enough from breast milk, then this will also be clear for all to see as your baby will be thin, listless, tired and will actually lose weight over the course of more than one or two weeks. Talk to your breastfeeding counsellor about ways to build up your milk supply.

If there is something worrying you, then voice your concern, but don't be swayed by weight charts alone.

WIND

THIS TOPIC deserves a section on its own because for some new parents, the first weeks of their baby's life are completely dominated by wind – its going in and its coming out and how and why and whether it is mixed up with feeding.

Wind is what happens if a baby swallows some air while feeding. Breastfed babies can get wind, too, but they usually suffer from it less. Wind is only a problem if it seems to be causing your baby stomach pains. If she efficiently expels the wind with a burp of her own accord after every feed, you probably have no worries.

If your baby falls asleep comfortable after a feed, winding is probably a waste of time. On the other hand, some babies can be 'winded' for hours and still have a disturbed sleep.

Chloë said: *'Wind is making my life miserable. And the baby's life, too. We spend all our time soothing him after a feed, getting the wind out so he can sleep, but he can't settle and rolls around, then he drops off and we wait on tenterhooks because we know he'll start squirming again and we'll have to pick him up and walk him around until the air comes out and then he's hungry again. If someone could invent a miracle cure for this, they'd make a fortune.'*

Felicity also feels defeated by the problem of her baby's wind: *'It's just not fair. We spend hours every day trying to soothe her and nothing works. It dominates parenthood if you've got a problem like this. I went to see the*

Things you can try to minimise wind

- Feed in a more upright position
- Ensure your baby is latched on properly before letting her suck
- Try a different shaped or different sized teat on the bottle
- Try shifting positions mid-feed – a move to a more upright position can help your baby burp – and then she has more room in her stomach for the rest of her feed.

health visitor at the clinic and said, "Do you mind if I just ask you some-thing?" and almost before I could get the words out she said, "It's about wind, isn't it?" It seems so unfair that tiny babies should have to cope with some-thing that makes them so uncomfortable and that can't be fixed.'

WEANING

When to wean

WEANING IS the term that covers the process of moving your baby away from a milk-only diet to a diet containing a variety of solid foods. There is an initial transition period, called 'introducing solids', where you are combining breast or formula milk and solids. This period may take several months. There's no hurry.

Ideas on weaning vary. Recent advice from the Department of Health is that solid foods in any form – homemade, baby jars, cereals or rusks – should not be given before your baby is four months old at the earliest as the digestive system is not sufficiently mature to cope with it until then. Also, some foods, such as wheat, eggs, nuts and dairy products can cause allergic reactions in some babies, so they should only be introduced towards the end of the first year and then in tiny amounts. Many mothers favour delaying weaning until about six months but continue to breastfeed as breast milk is such a perfect food.

Be guided by your baby. There's little point trying to keep her on a milk-only diet if she's seven months old, crawling about and steal-ing biscuits off plates. Similarly, it is pointless forcing spinach down the unwilling throat of a five-month-old if they're not ready for it and just want milk.

Until as recently as 1994, three months was officially judged to be a good age for weaning, and mothers were sometimes encouraged to put cereal in their baby's bottle to help them sleep through the night. Cereal in the bottle will not help any baby sleep through the night, though it might help wake him up with wind. However, these are facts to be aware of if you have a well-meaning older person advising you to introduce solids early. Forewarned is forearmed; you can work out some lines of argument explaining why you're not going to give him a rusk quite yet, and when you do it certainly won't be one of those with sugar in it.

Do not be misled by the labels on baby food jars that say 'Suitable from three months'. It's in the manufacturer's interests to get every mother in Britain weaning a whole month earlier than they need to.

When you do introduce your baby to 'household' foods, don't feel that you have to lovingly purée every turnip by hand. Any soups or stews that you are making can be readily adapted if you remember:

- Don't add salt – food has enough natural salt in it without extra
- Don't add sugar. It's a slippery slope.

AND DON'T feel that every meal your baby eats has to be a model of wholesome eating. Naturally, you want to promote a wide and varied diet, high in nutrients and vitamins, but that doesn't mean there aren't times when you'll all be happier having beans on toast.

Rice-based cereals can make an excellent introduction to solid foods for your baby. Gluten – found in wheat products like bread – can cause an allergic reaction in a young baby, so cereals containing gluten are best avoided at first. Many manufacturers make pure rice cereals in boxes and you can mix a teaspoon or two of this rice with expressed breast milk or water for first-food experiments. Boxed baby-food has the advantage over jars in that it is less expensive – you use what you need when you need it.

> **Remember:** when you first start introducing your baby to solids, she's not going to eat more than a teaspoon or two from the jars. What are you going to do with the rest of it? Why not try giving her a bit of your own mashed potato instead?

Home-prepared food is right for some mothers, but not for others, like Diana: *'I know some people who were very organised – they seemed to be puréeing cabbage and freezing it in ice-cube trays all the time. I envied them their organisational abilities more than anything.'*

Reading about weaning can make things more confusing, as Hazel discovered: *'There were some highly alarming "weaning guides" around*

BABY FOODS

Instant baby foods from the family table:

- A few teaspoons of puréed or mashed vegetable
- Fruit purée – from about five months
- Natural yoghurt with a spoonful of fruit purée
- A wedge of celery or apple to gnaw on as the teeth come in.

With all finger foods, there is the possibility that your baby will manage to slice off a sliver with his newly emerging incisors and this can catch in his throat, alarming everybody. Many parents worry over the dangers of choking at this stage but that can't mean that you keep your children on runny foods for ever. Babies and their teeth need to get to grips with some solid nutrition and there will be the occasional coughing fit. To put your minds at rest, however, follow these two simple rules:

- Never leave your baby alone when eating.
- Find out just what you should do if a baby begins to choke. The techniques needed

are different to those required by an adult. There are many excellent manuals you can turn to for reference, and for practical help, contact your local branch of the St John Ambulance as many run first-aid and emergency courses for parents. Knowing what to do in an emergency will mean that you won't panic every time your baby splutters – and they can splutter over everything from a wisp of apple peel to a spoonful of custard.

Instant foods for the older baby from the convenience shelves:

- Baked beans on toast
- Breakfast cereals that don't have sugar coatings
- Vegetable soups (although some are very high in salt levels)
- Bagels
- Hard cheese (like cheddar, not unpasteurised soft cheeses) grated finely
- Fromage frais
- Avocado.

when I was starting Ben off on solid foods. They said things like "Your baby may be ready if he has doubled his birthweight," but he'd been tiny at birth so had doubled his birthweight at around two months, which was much too early. And then there was, "Replace the fifth feed with some cereal." Well, to this day I don't know what that meant.'

THERE ARE many excellent recipe books on the market that will help you to provide an imaginative and well-balanced diet for a baby who is just learning how to eat solid food. You can browse through them as you need them. Be open minded – just because you don't like lentils, it doesn't mean your baby won't.

This piece of advice served Hazel well: '*One of the most valuable pieces of advice I ever got was to remember that foods don't have to be served plain or just boiled to be nutritious. I used to feel Ben had only eaten an egg if he had eaten a hardboiled egg all at once, out of his eggcup. But it was still the same egg if I whipped it up with a bit of milk and flour and served it as pancakes, which he would eat without fuss. Unlike the egg.'*

AND BE FLEXIBLE. There are days when you don't feel like eating much, and other days when you seem to be ravenous every five minutes. There's no reason why your baby shouldn't feel the same.

Cultivate a catalogue of healthy snacks: apples, cheese, wholemeal rolls; and don't forget: babies weren't created with a need for fizzy drinks. If they're thirsty, water is perfectly adequate. That way you can save the very diluted fruit juice for the occasions you want to convince them it's a treat. And it's a drink in a cup, not a bottle, not if you value their teeth.

CRYING

ALL BABIES cry. If your baby didn't cry, there would probably be cause for concern. Some babies, however, aren't easily placated. They are often called 'crying babies' because it seems, especially to the harassed parent like Louise, that crying is all they do.

'David had cried a lot in hospital and the midwives and nurses would look at me and shake their heads sadly and say, "Oh, I think you've got a crying baby there." Then, as my heart sank, they tried to soften the blow by saying briskly, "Oh, but you'll cope." As the days went by, my list of reasons for the crying grew: Breastfeeding: Not enough? Too much? Cold? Hot? Lonely? Bored? Frightened? Yes, I was all of those. But what about the baby?

It's easy to smile now, I'm through it, out and on the other side, but then the words "Not waving but drowning" had a terrible reality.'

CRYING IS your baby's way of telling you something . . . unfortunately, it's up to you to figure out what this message means, and for every baby the message is different. Sometimes it's impossible to tell and we have to go through a series of guesses.

Something to do with feeding? — This is possible reason number one on everybody's list. Either:

- The baby is hungry, or
- The baby had too much at the last feed and now has a stomach ache.

There are other variations on this theme:
- The baby has wind
- The baby has had different milk to the usual
- The baby's mother had cabbage/red wine/sour grapes for tea last night and that's what has upset the baby's stomach.

NINE TIMES out of ten, if your baby is hungry, she will feed. If she isn't, she won't. Your baby may want to spend what seems like a whole day attached to your breast, but that may be because she is going through a growth spurt and needs to build up your milk supply. If you can find a day to do this, then give it a go. Nine times out of ten, too, if your baby is feeding, she won't be crying.

When your baby won't stop crying

IF YOUR BABY cries persistently beyond the first couple of weeks of life you will probably try out any theory to help make him feel better. A baby's crying is so sad and so piercing, it can make parents despair. All they want is for their baby to be happy, and here he is so obviously miserable.

Gwen found she had nothing but sympathy for those parents whose baby cries all the time: *'Ellen cried from dawn till midnight from about two weeks old. It's not just the crying that's so disheartening – though that in itself, day after day, is dreadful – it's the fact that all your dreams about parenthood are so suddenly and completely shattered. I had dreamed of, oh, I don't know, lying in a sunny room with Ellen, gazing at her fondly, bonding gently with her, and when she was six weeks old I went to the chemist to buy earplugs to shut out the noise of her screams. That was the difference between dreams and reality.'*

A common feeling is expressed by Louise: *'People would say, "Oh, it'll pass. He'll grow out of it," and I'd say, "When? When?"'*

MOST PARENTS find the crying almost impossible to ignore – hardly surprising as nature's designed it specifically at the pitch and tone that will attract the most attention. In a quest to calm their baby and rest their own shattered nerves, the lengths to which some parents go is truly amazing. I have listed a few of them in the box on the right in case you're one of those parents who's looking for something new to try. Some of them may provoke a smile, but do not laugh. They are all evidence of how far some parents will go to make their babies happy and, as such, in the end are nothing more than a proof of love.

Colic

IF IT HELPS, you can call your baby's crying colic. It won't stop the crying but it may help to convince you that the crying isn't your fault. 'Colic' is an accepted phase of babyhood that some babies go through somewhere between three and 12 weeks of age. The classic symptoms are prolonged and persistent crying, usually in the evenings, perhaps with the baby drawing his knees up towards his stomach as if in pain. Whatever you try, it does not stop the crying. The crying may go on for several hours until you are all exhausted.

If this happens to your family, the experience will probably feel far worse and more distressing than any book could prepare you for, though perhaps it may help a tiny bit if this book reminds you that 'phase' means just that: there was no baby ever who had colic who did not grow out of it.

Kay sums up her feelings on this subject: *'Colic. Such a little word. Do doctors have any idea what it means? Just as Geoff returned from work each evening at around six o'clock, when he was tired from work and I was des-*

CURING CRYING

If you've tried all the obvious – hunger, cold, thirst, boredom, desire for a cuddle – and you've checked with your health visitor or GP that your baby's not ill, try:

- Letting your baby listen to the vacuum cleaner
- Swaddling
- Sitting your baby in front of the washing machine
- Walking him round the block in his pram (take a guard dog if it's 3am)
- Singing to her (she has no preferences as to repertoire at this age)
- A baby sling
- Getting a grandparent, relative or friend to take over for a couple of hours
- Music – whatever's your favourite
- Womb music tape
- Give him some gripe water – it probably won't make a blind bit of difference, but there's always a chance…and washing the spoon will take your mind off the crying for a moment.

perate for adult conversation, the five hours of screaming would start, and with it started the horrible, sick feelings in my stomach. My maternal feelings urged me to help my baby, to make things better – as Guy screamed, his face was plastered with sweat, it ran down his face; his cheeks were white and his lips blue. We watched this and Geoff and I would hate our helplessness. And sometimes we'd hate each other for not being able to stop this. "Oh, it'll stop of its own accord at around three months," they said, glibly.

And it did. But that didn't take away the memory of the nightmare.'

You may feel you are to blame yourself, as Parveen did: *'I would casti- gate myself over and over. It was my fault that she cried – I wasn't caring for her properly. I should play with her more, take her out more, feed her more, and so on. I had, in my imagination, my own idea of the perfect, kind lov- ing mother – and I was failing miserably. I have never lived with so much guilt.'*

IF IT HELPS, remind yourself that second and third babies can get colic just as much as first ones – it is in no way a reflection on your skills or experience. It may also help to remind you that, surpris- ingly, colic doesn't run in families, so if your first baby does have colic, chances are, your second one won't. Mind you, nothing is of much comfort when you're in the thick of it as Callum comments wryly: *'Nothing anyone said or did made the slightest bit of difference or made us feel any better. The only thing that would have made us feel better was for the crying to stop. And one morning she woke up smiling. That quickly. It was over. It had gone and it was like we had a different baby. At last we could be real parents instead of just parents trying to stop their baby crying all the time.'*

IF YOUR BABY has colic, enlist as much help as you can. The crying will wear you down quicker if you are alone, so try to get your moth- er, friends, sister, distant relative, neighbour . . . anyone willing to lend a pair of arms to come. It will give you a much-needed break, and a change of 'rocker' may soothe your baby for a while.

There is still little understanding of why it occurs and no one proven cure for colic. What helps one baby may make no impact at all on another. Because colic often fades at around 12 weeks of age, a popular theory is that the stomach pain that was its cause disappears as the digestive system matures. This doesn't offer you any relief though.

Another idea is that your baby has been overstimulated and needs to 'let off steam' in the evenings. Proponents of this theory are a little vague as to why half an hour with a wind-up mobile can result in three hours of screaming several hours later, however, so you might as well continue to keep your baby happy in the best way you can during the day.

There has been much interest recently in a theory that babies who persistently cry may be suffering residual effects from birth trauma – perhaps a difficult passage down the birth canal has left skull bones out of alignment. Treatment is through a technique called cranial osteopathy, where an osteopath will manipulate the bones of your baby's head. Those who've seen good results, naturally, swear by it; so if you feel your baby's got a persistent problem you can't quite put your finger on, why not search out a qualified practitioner?

If the crying gets too much

MANY PARENTS get close to breaking point with a persistently crying baby and feel overwhelmed by a frightening urge to do anything, anything to stop the crying.

If you reach the point where you can't bear to listen to your baby's crying any more:

- Put the baby down gently and go into another room
- Do this before you do anything else
- Take a deep breath. Sit down on your own for a few minutes and try to let some of the anger and tension dissipate.

In moments of calm, we all know that it is pointless to get angry with our babies. In moments of emotional tension, though, that is exactly what we do. It is very hard to listen to constant and repeated accusations as to what failures we are as a parent – which is just what the baby's crying seems to be – without being provoked into retaliation.

Worse, the baby will respond to your shouting and anger by crying all the harder.

So, don't let things get desperate; ask for help. During the day, ask your health visitor or GP to call, or go to them. Contact your local Social Services Department; they may assess you as needing help and support if your family situation is becoming too much for you to cope with. At night, try one of the 24-hour helplines run by some voluntary organisations (and listed in the **Directory**). They are often staffed by parents who know exactly what you're going through because they have been through it themselves.

Call the hospital A&E department if all else fails. If either you or your partner is going to hit your baby, it really is an emergency.

TEETHING

IF COLIC DOES not seem the right label for your baby's crying, what about 'teething'? (This is the one your author solaced herself with for a year.) Yes, dribbling, gnawing and finger sucking are all harbingers of the first tooth.

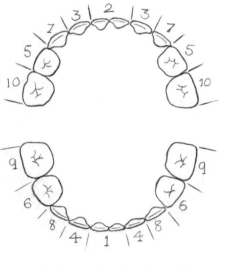

This diagram shows the order in which your baby's teeth are most likely to emerge, though the age at which they do so can vary enormously.

TEETHING – MYTHS AND FACTS

Myth: First teeth don't need cleaning

Not true! To keep your baby's teeth white and healthy, you will need to brush them from the moment they emerge. Get a baby toothbrush, specially formulated baby toothpaste and be gentle but firm: brush every day to encourage good habits. Baby teeth do matter. They serve as a guide for the permanent teeth and, if the milk teeth are lost, the adult teeth may end up overcrowded or badly positioned. They will have to last your child until he is six at the earliest, so protect them.

Myth: All babies need extra fluoride

Some dentists recommend giving fluoride supplements. Fluoride helps to make tooth enamel stronger and so can minimise decay. However, before leaping ahead, check with your health visitor or regional water authority whether there is already fluoride added to your local water supply. Some toothpastes contain enough fluoride to protect growing teeth if they are used regularly, and too much fluoride can cause discoloration in the enamel. So get expert advice from your own dentist for your own particular situation.

Fact: Babies can chew long before their teeth come through

If you wait until teeth appear before giving your baby things like carrots or apples to soothe red gums on, you will have denied her a pleasurable comfort. And if you wait until the molars come through before giving your baby 'real' chewable food (like lamb chops and potatoes or chicken and rice or cheese and broccoli pie) you will still be feeding her mush long after she's helped herself to a packet of crisps and a biscuit.

Fact: Teeth come through in the same order for all babies

Strange but true. The age at which that first tooth comes through, however, will vary widely. It's around six months, but can appear by three months.

Myth: You have to stop breastfeeding when the first tooth appears

The first tooth is usually a sign that the baby is getting ready to move on to gnawing crusts and carrots, but he will still be getting his nutrition from you.

The first tooth, however, may be several months down the road. Some babies seem to moan about it for every single one of those months, others do two minutes' grizzle and delight their parents with that lop-sided grin and pearly whiteness.

And don't forget that your own dental care is free up to the baby's first birthday, so make the most of this opportunity to keep your teeth in good repair.

GROWING

THE CHILD YOU will be putting a first birthday cake in front of is a very different child to your new baby: sure, you know it's the same child, but a passing stranger might be hard put to find any resemblance. The tiny newborn who could just focus his eyes on you will learn, over the course of his first year, to roll, sit, stand and shout, not necessarily in that order.

BY THE AGE OF FIVE MONTHS...
your baby will know when you are calling his name and respond by turning to you. He will reach and grab for toys – though he sometimes misses – and often put them straight into his mouth for detailed exploration. And...

MAJOR MILESTONES

Your newborn can:
● Make eye contact with you
● Hear: you may notice him trying to turn his head towards a sound, especially speech
● Distinguish his mother's milk from anyone else's

Between a month and two months old, your baby will:
● Turn his head from side to side
● Open his hands
● Smile
● Be able to hold a light rattle . . . though he may not realise that it's him who's got hold of it

Round about three months, your baby will:
● Turn his head towards sounds
● Focus on pictures and books
● Develop hand–eye co-ordination by watching his hands as he moves them about
● Push himself up, raising his upper chest off the ground if you place him on the floor

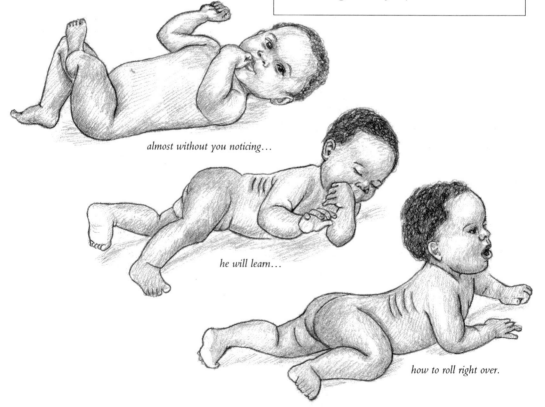

almost without you noticing...

he will learn...

how to roll right over.

PLAYING

ALL THE EXPERTS and manuals seem unanimous on one point: the value of early play. For some tired parents, the idea of trying to 'play' with a tiny baby seems strange, and makes them feel uncomfortable. Yet rest assured: your baby does not need to know the rules of Scrabble or how to bluff his way through a hand of poker quite yet. It is watching, listening, talking and exploring with his hands that are his main entertainments.

Some parents, caught up in this sort of interaction, may not realise they are 'playing' at all. Perhaps this is because play is very much a baby's 'work'. It is a serious matter. He needs to play, exploring objects, hearing sounds and babbling them back to you, in order to make sense of his world.

> ### Things you can do right from the start:
>
> ● Try to hold your baby's gaze; look into her eyes and tell her what you're thinking.
> ● Show her examples of different shapes and colours, either from books, or in wallpaper patterns, or in the cupboard in the kitchen
> ● Talk to your baby, tell her all the time what you are doing, so that she can begin to marry up your words with your actions
> ● Sing to your baby; the repetition of rhymes and songs will help her anticipate sounds and learn her language
> ● Rock your baby: the experience of tones and rhythms can soothe and reassure, as well as lay the foundations of a response to other forms of music.

You don't need lots of toys: your baby's favourite playthings will be her parents. And you don't have to be bound by convention: you don't need to wait until a child is ready to read before showing her books. There are valuable things you can do from Day One.

Patty describes what she used to do: *'There were all these things I used to do that I didn't realise were "playing", like tickling her tummy when we were drying her after the bath, or singing her songs as we walked up and down. I had this idea in my mind that playing was very formal, like we were all going to sit down and teach her how to play Monopoly. I was a bit frightened by the prospect.'*

Ideas for playing

WHEN YOUR baby is about a month old, he will find it easier to make eye contact as his ability to focus his eyes will have improved enormously. The easiest distance for him to focus is 21 to 26cm from his

AROUND SIX MONTHS...
your baby may start to sit unsup-
ported for a short time – making
playtime much more fun...

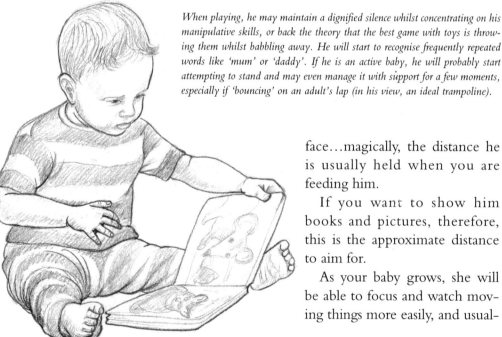

When playing, he may maintain a dignified silence whilst concentrating on his
manipulative skills, or back the theory that the best game with toys is throw-
ing them whilst babbling away. He will start to recognise frequently repeated
words like 'mum' or 'daddy'. If he is an active baby, he will probably start
attempting to stand and may even manage it with support for a few moments,
especially if 'bouncing' on an adult's lap (in his view, an ideal trampoline).

face...magically, the distance he
is usually held when you are
feeding him.

If you want to show him
books and pictures, therefore,
this is the approximate distance
to aim for.

As your baby grows, she will
be able to focus and watch moving things more easily, and usual-

ly by the age of three months will watch you from her baby chair as you move around the room. Mobiles and other moving toys also become more attractive around this point.

Repeat words, games and actions as often as you can. Repetition helps a baby to remember and remembering helps him to learn.

There are some toys that are useful from very early days. A sample is given right but remember, what turns one baby on may leave another cold. If possible try – at mother-and-baby groups or toyshops with samples – before you buy. Don't forget the usefulness of Toy Libraries. You join and pay a small sum each week to borrow a toy. That way you can introduce your baby to a wide range of toys, take home those that capture her attention, and ensure that you are providing toys that are exactly matched to your baby's developmental abilities: bold and striking mobiles for the very tiny ones, multi-textured rattles when her manipulative abilities are improving and she is learning the contrasts between rough, smooth, hard, soft.

A word of warning: there is a mysterious toy-related syndrome that affects some babies: whatever they coo over delightedly in the shop becomes an object to shun when at home. What they only hours ago

BABY TOYS
● Playmat
● Patmat (with water in)
● Soft ball with a bell in it
● Activity centre
● Mobile
● Friezes to look at together.

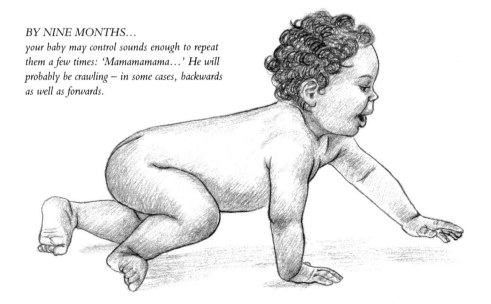

BY NINE MONTHS...
your baby may control sounds enough to repeat them a few times: 'Mamamamama...' He will probably be crawling – in some cases, backwards as well as forwards.

He may well start pulling himself
up on the furniture to a standing
position and then progress to
walking, using the furniture as a
support...

...*or he may hold out his hands as a sign that he wants you to help him walk.*

BY THE FIRST BIRTHDAY...
By this stage, the differences in progress will be marked: your baby may well be walking unaided, or quite possibly he won't have even bothered with crawling yet, having enough to occupy him immobile. You may find he wants to blow the candle out on the cake himself, and that he can say 'mama' and mean it.

The golden rule is to encourage the next stage in development or learning but not push your baby towards it. If you push him, he might reach it a week earlier than he might otherwise have done, but have an exhausted parent into the bargain.

gasped with amazement at, they now ignore. There is no cure. Your best hope is to put the offending item away for a month then try again.

As your baby grows, the number of toys that will occupy her increase, and become more wide ranging. At around nine months, you could introduce a baby bouncer, for example as Agnes did: *'It was the only peace I ever got. I'd hang Sam up in the doorway, run to the phone and make a few urgent calls, with him going up and down non-stop.'*

Remember: with all toys: no matter how wonderful it is, it is no substitute for your attention. If your baby was honest, he would like you to play with him all the time. If you were honest, you'd probably admit that you don't *want* to play with your baby all the time; for a start, you've got the next meal's menu and the last meal's dishes to worry about.

Between you, you will have to strike a balance. If you never give your baby any attention, you will end up with a very unhappy child. If you don't give yourself time to catch up on things you want and need to do, you will end up a very unhappy parent.

Talking to your baby

THIS IS ONE of the most vital things you will ever do. It does not appear to matter whether you follow the 'woof-woof-doggie' road or launch straight in on the 'canine quadruped' level. If you'd rather do the woof-woofs in private, do so, but do them.

- Talk to your baby in short, simple sentences
- Talk to your baby about what's going on around you – words always make more sense in context
- Use lots of repetition
- Have fun reminding yourself of every nursery rhyme you can remember from childhood . . . and remember that your baby will not mind if you sing out of tune
- Give your child a rest from a noisy background – radio and TV won't help your child to sort out meaningful from meaningless language

- If your child is happily babbling imaginatively and alone . . . don't interrupt her − she is exploring language on her own account and needs to be encouraged to do so
- Your child may have more trouble getting the hang of his or her own name if it starts with a vowel: Emily = Lemily or Nemily; or if the accent is on the second rather than the first syllable: Simone = Mon.

SPEECH AND language are unfortunately one of the main areas of parental competitiveness. If your friend's child is singing, 'Twinkle, twinkle, little star', complete with actions, at the age of 18 months, and yours is still shamingly at the 'Uh?' stage (you may detect a note of personal recollection from your author at this point), then you may well wonder just when it is you have to start to worry. Luckily, the answer is: hardly ever.

Just as children master all their physical skills at different ages, so talking, with its unique mix of physical accomplishments (can I get that tongue into the right place behind the teeth?) and mental abilities (now what are those things that say miaow called again?) is a skill that can withstand wide degrees of variation. That is to say, your child will talk when he is ready and not a moment before.

Speech development is linked with your baby's hearing, and indeed, it is when a baby does not babble in the usual patterns that early deafness can be diagnosed. Your baby will have regular hearing checks, but if you are concerned about this aspect of your baby's development, ask your health visitor for time to discuss your worries and perhaps run an extra test.

Hilary found that it all happened without her noticing that things were moving forward: *'You just take it for granted that they'll talk and then the next minute they are. "More juice", or "Daddy gone", or "Bye bye". I did talk to her a lot, and it was always about things that were around, and I think that must have helped. And you always knew that she understood far more than she could say, like waving when we were leaving someone's house: she did that without saying anything at first, when she was about eight or nine months.'*

Agnes describes her experience: *'I was lucky because although Sam was*

TIMES FOR TALKING

In the first month

Babies make noises from birth. No matter what language their parents speak, their first sound will probably be something like 'uuu', coming from the back of the throat.

Around three months

This may be when your baby starts to 'babble'. Babbling is exactly what it sounds like: a string of experimental sounds. You may find that you can have a short 'conversation' with your baby: When she is quiet and awake, come close to her so she can see you. Does she make a sound? If not, say something clearly and deliberately to her. You may well find that she 'replies' with a sound of her own. If the results are uncertain, try again in a couple of weeks' time.

Around four months

If you try the 'conversation game' with your baby now, you may find that if you make a clear and delivered sound to her, like 'mmm' or 'dudu' that she will try to imitate it. If she can't make the sounds, you may see her tongue and mouth trying to move into the right positions. Give both of you a pat on the back: this is a great achievement for such a tiny baby.

Around six months

Around this age, many parents notice a change in their baby's babbling. They stop making so many strange sounds – often sounds that are found in other languages – and start to concentrate on the sounds found in their own. That is, they start to imitate more and more in their babbling the sounds they hear all around them, the sounds they hear you say as you talk. Imitating what they can hear is such an important part of learning to talk that she deserves another pat on the back. Some parents manage quite long 'chats' with their babies now, with each trying to imitate the other.

Around ten months

Babies start to string babbling sounds together as they approach the end of their first year. They may have quite long monologues in 'babble'. You can encourage language development by treating the babble as if it really is part of a sensible conversation: 'Oh, does that mean you're a happy baby then?' Your baby needs a response from you at this stage, and if she is lucky she will have managed to string two random bits of babble together in such a way that they sound remarkably like 'Mama'. This will have produced such a delighted reaction from her audience that your baby will be keen to try to achieve this effect again: the smiles and cuddles it brings are just what she needs. And then she can do the same trick with 'Dada'. Or the other way round.

"late" in talking. I had a friend whose baby was just as late. So we kept each other's spirits up! And it's true – whatever big differences there are at 12 months, they're all evened out by the age of four, which is where they are now. Now you can't tell who talked fast or slow, they all yell as loud and you spend most of your time asking them to keep the noise down!'

TIMES FOR TALKING

Around one year

Your baby may well have sentences of babble and one or two distinct words, often 'Mama' or 'Dada' or another care-giver, or something that has caught her attention, like 'ba' for ball. You may find that she uses the same sound to mean a lot of different things: 'Da' can mean Daddy, any man who comes into view, her blanket and 'Pick me up, please'. Accept the sound in its context but do not try to force her to say something different for all of these things. She will when she is ready. You can often tell from the intonation whether something is a question or an exclamation, even though there are no recognisable words in it. She may well shake her head for no, shout for attention and 'sing' along to your songs. On the other hand, it is just as likely that you have the strong, silent type.

By 18 months

During your baby's second year, you will lose track of her language accomplishments. She will move from two or three recognisable words to a vocabulary of around 200, and will be able to understand even more. She will be putting more and more words together, in sentences of her own. 'Ball there', 'juice now', and 'more dolly' mean that your child is communicating with you on her own terms. Don't forget: one of the earliest words every child learns is 'no'.

IF YOU HAVE a 'slow' talker, comfort yourself with the old chestnuts that Einstein didn't talk until he was four, and neither did Schopenhauer, whose first sentence was allegedly: 'The soup's cold'. And when asked why he had declined to display his linguistic achievements before this, he pointed out that the soup had never been cold before.

So, if you're at your wits' end, you can try cold soup, but I won't promise anything.

If your child does have a problem that would benefit from specialised help, this will not usually be apparent before two or three years of age. At that point, your health visitor will probably note any cause for concern at one of your baby's regular developmental checks, and will refer you to your local Health Authority's Speech and Language Therapy services.

If your child will benefit from intervention, he (and for reasons no one is entirely sure of, more boys than girls need help with their speech and language) will be given an appointment for an assessment with a speech therapist, who may then advise you on things you can do at home, and ask to see the child on a regular basis to give him help with special exercises that can strengthen the muscles he uses for talking, or help him to form sounds in different ways.

Call your doctor if your baby:

- Has a fever with sweating
- Takes less than one-third of his usual fluid or passes much less urine than usual
- Vomits green fluid
- Grunts with each breath
- Passes large amounts of blood in his nappy
- Is unusually quiet, still or floppy.

NURSING

THE LIST OF illnesses that can affect a new baby is alarming: asthma, conjunctivitis, coughs, croup, ear infections, hernia . . . In every case, they can panic first-time parents. However, in their first couple of years of life, babies can develop plenty of minor illnesses and come out none the worse, and with their immune system actively stronger.

Christine's behaviour was not unusual: *'I wanted to phone the doctor every time the mucus from his nose turned green, or if his poo was a bit runnier than usual, if the truth be told. No, what I would have really liked is a paediatric consultant on call in my home 24 hours a day. However, I had to restrain myself, and I knew I had to, because when I called the health visitor out once, when Stephen was about three weeks old, as I was worried about the fact that he kept being sick after feeds, she took one look at the tiny amount of milk he was bringing back up onto his bib and said very patronisingly, "That's possetting, dear." Well, how was I supposed to know it was normal? I thought he had a major stomach problem.'*

Special 'fever-scan' thermometers can alert you to rises in temperature.

DESPITE THE fact that many of us worry that we're consulting the doctor on nothing more than a vague 'something's-not-quite-right feeling', doctors would much rather see you in the surgery and reassure you that all is fine, than risk a serious problem going unnoticed. Health visitors would rather have the opportunity to put your mind at rest if it means you can stop worrying.

Sponging with tepid water is a tried and tested way of reducing your baby's temperature if a fever is making her uncomfortable.

If a doctor prescribes eye drops for your baby, which may happen if your baby gets a relatively common infection like conjunctivitis...wrap him securely in a towel (easy for washing if there are any spills).

Hold him firmly against you.

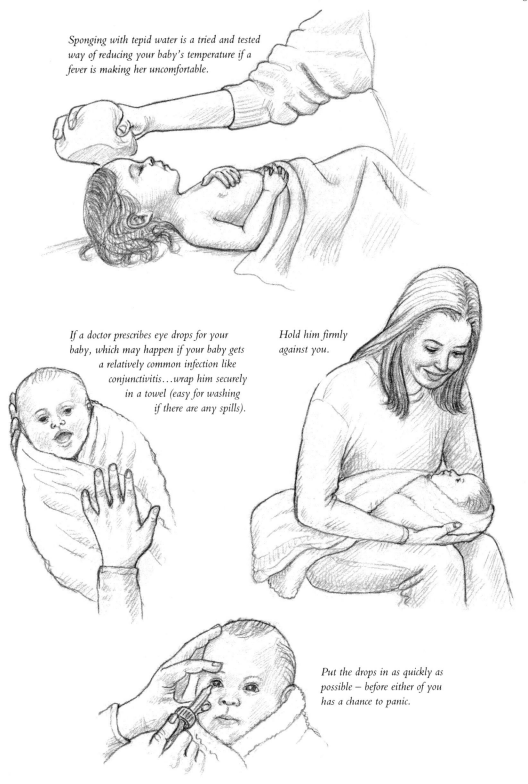

Put the drops in as quickly as possible – before either of you has a chance to panic.

Asthma

ASTHMA IS AN allergic condition which results in your baby having severe breathing difficulties. Whatever your child is allergic to – a particular kind of pollen, or the dust mite, for example – there will be a reaction to it in the breathing tubes of his lungs, and it is this which produces the characteristic asthmatic wheeze. Breathing can become very difficult for your baby and he may need hospital help.

If you think your child is having an asthma attack, call the doctor - there are other reasons why a baby may become breathless and the GP will need to rule them out. While you wait, sit your baby up and calm him as much as you can. He will usually get enough air, however much it feels like to you and to him that he won't.

If asthma is diagnosed, you will receive specialist help from health workers and will be trained in how you can reduce the propensity to attacks and how to use the medication that can cut short an asthma attack.

Eczema

THIS IS A problem which, together with asthma, seems to be affecting more and more babies. Rowena's baby began to develop eczema: *'Neither Peter nor I had ever had any problem with eczema, so when it started we weren't even sure what it was – these red patches behind Robert's knees and ears. We treated them occasionally with a little hydro-cortisone cream, but really, thought no more of it than that he had dry skin. But when I stopped breastfeeding him at around five months, the problem suddenly rocketed. The patches began to spread and became very itchy, raised and red, and the doctor prescribed steroid cream. I wasn't happy with this, the thought of him being so small and wondering what possible side-effects such a powerful cream could cause, that we began the quest for alternatives.'*

ECZEMA

Eczema: some things to try are:

- A cow's milk-free diet (use pasteurised goat's milk instead of cow's milk as a drink or mixer). Do not try putting your baby on a totally dairy-free diet without medical supervision as it is much more difficult to ensure that she is getting all the right nutrients from other foods
- A couple of handfuls of sea-salt in the bath
- Use of an oil-based or moisturising soap
- Emollient creams.

MANY PARENTS feel like Rowena; when it comes to conditions like eczema, they do all they can to check whether there is an allergen in the diet or the home causing this reaction and many parents have found some help in homoeopathic or 'alternative' remedies.

Coughs and colds

DO NOT EXPECT your GP to prescribe antibiotics at the drop of a hat. If your baby's illness is caused by a virus, antibiotics will be worse than useless: they will actually mean he could become less resistant to future bacterial infections.

Amy describes how she nursed her babies through minor illnesses: *'The worst times these last few months are when the twins have got something – a cold, a cough. One time, they got a bug and had terrible diarrhoea and vomiting. I went through sixteen changes of clothes in one day – I think ten sleepsuits for Alice and six for Bethany. Then the following week they got ear infections. You just have to say to yourself at the end, "We got through it. What a wonderful achievement. Well done!" And then you keel over into bed, absolutely drained.'*

ALWAYS CONSULT your GP or local hospital if you are worried about your baby. This is especially the case when your baby is very young as illnesses and infections can take hold in tiny bodies frighteningly quickly. In particular, if you suspect your baby has a severe pain in the head, neck or stomach, do not waste time wondering what to do. Even if you are a firm believer in alternative therapies, only use these after you have made sure there is no serious problem requiring urgent medical intervention.

Hospitals

There may be times when your baby needs more nursing care than you can give him at home. Raisa describes her experience in hospital: *'I laid her down on what seemed like a huge trolley, flat, with no pillows. Up till now I'd felt really safe and cared for but now I felt suddenly very vulnerable. This was it, where I had to say goodbye. I couldn't go through those doors into the operating theatre with her. I held both of her hands in both of*

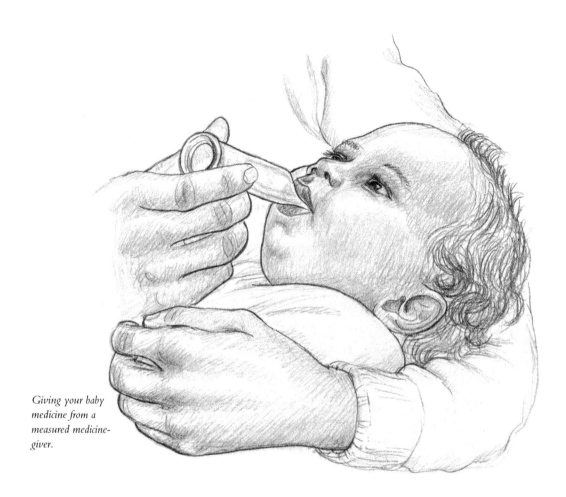

Giving your baby medicine from a measured medicine-giver.

mine and the anaesthetist placed this tiny mask over her mouth and nose and she just stared at me, already not really awake. After only a couple of seconds, her hands went dead. That was the worst thing. That was really scary. It was like the life had gone out of her and would never come back. And of course they had to hurry once she was under, so they whisked the trolley away and I just had to go back to her room and wait for her. I was sobbing and sobbing, even though I knew there was no other option. It was as if I'd been smiling for her all this time, smiling so she didn't get scared, and now I let all the scared-ness come back. It was three hours before they brought her back. The longest three hours of my life. She woke briefly that first day, then almost straight away went back into what the nurse called a "proper" sleep. It was the next day she opened her eyes and looked at me and I knew I'd got her back.'

IF YOUR BABY DOES NEED TO GO TO HOSPITAL

- Tell the nursing staff if you're breastfeeding; if necessary, ask for a breastpump. (If your hospital does not have one, contact your local NCT branch – many branches have pumps immediately available for mothers of hospitalised babies)
- If you are bottle-feeding, take along some of your baby's usual formula
- Also take blanket/dummy/teddy. Your baby may not be able to have these things at first, but they will certainly help to make the hospital less strange and frightening as he recovers

- Be prepared to spend as much time as you can with your child throughout his stay
- Don't listen to any nightmare stories from friends or relatives…your baby is an individual case
- Ask the medical staff for as much information as you need. This may help you to…
- …stop worrying unnecessarily. Your baby is sensitive to feelings and will pick up on your anxieties, so keep them as few as possible.

DEVELOPMENTAL DISABILITIES

SOMETIMES AS babies grow, it becomes apparent to the parents that they aren't developing in quite the way they should. Sometimes they don't hit the major milestones of babyhood – smiling, rolling, sitting – in quite the same way as other babies. Sometimes it's just a sense that parents have. If you have worries, get them checked out. You may be frightened by what you might hear, but the benefits of knowing outweigh the pain and uncertainty of *not* knowing.

When Deirdre and her husband were told that Alice definitely had learning disabilities, they were devastated: *'No – that's not the right word, because there isn't a right word that can convey what we felt. This wasn't the sort of thing that could happen to us – this was the sort of thing that only happened to other people. I didn't like being the "other people". But we made contact with the local support group and we were able to talk to parents who'd been through exactly what we'd been going through. So, although there was a part of us that wanted to deny it, as soon as we started talking to other parents, all the jigsaw pieces fell into place and everything made sense at last. It was true, and we were going to have to come to terms with that.'*

IT CAN BE a devastating time for parents, like Lily and Mike: *'In that instant, when he was diagnosed, the slate was wiped clean. Every expectation and every hope we had ever had for him were gone. There was no question now of him "achieving" things in the way we might otherwise have pushed him to. We knew from then on that any normal thing he did – like feeding himself or talking to us – would be an achievement. You readjust your levels of expectation downwards. That's the hardest thing to do. But once you've done it, you're starting from zero and can only go up.'*

LOVING

LOVE CAN BE instant, or love will grow. Because the love for your baby is bound up with so many other emotions and physical changes, it is one of the most complex loves anyone can experience. Furthermore, the love felt by a mother may be completely different to the love a father feels for his newborn child. Although he won't be suffering the physical effects of pregnancy and giving birth, he may well feel overwhelmed by responsibility and the need to provide for and protect his new family. Some new fathers may appear not to love their new baby, to the extent of rejecting her – this can be a hurtful phase, but time and patience are usually all that is needed. The love that grows may well be all the stronger for the difficult start.

Tony and Geoff remember the helplessness they felt on the arrival of their sons: *'The nurse gave me the baby to hold while they were still stitching Louise up and I wanted to tell her she was making a mistake. Before he was born, I hadn't thought what it would be like, what it would feel like to hold a baby, and I wanted to tell the nurse that I wasn't qualified, that she should find somebody else if she needed to put the baby down somewhere while they were busy. The baby was so small and I felt so stupid, not knowing what to do.'*

'I'd been standing there helpless all day and all night, it seemed, and at last I had something positive to do. That was my first thought. The next was that I had a son, which was the first time I'd thought about it. Here was a baby, but he'd be a little boy one day.'

And Alan remembers the feeling that this couldn't be real: *'I was relieved. No, I was knocked sideways. I kept looking at him and touching him because I couldn't believe it. I felt very proud of the whole thing, that this was my baby, and proud of Vicky because of the way she'd come through it. So there was relief that it was over, because Vicky had been in pain, and there was relief that it was over because we now knew that the baby was alright – because there is always that wondering, right to the last moment – but really, I was just wandering around in a daze. I hadn't thought about what would happen after the labour because I'd never really believed it was going to happen.'*

FOR MOTHERS, there are the added physical effects of having carried a baby for nine months, the trauma of giving birth, the physical and mental exhaustion of early postnatum and the realisation of the hard work to come! To balance these rather negative effects, a mother has the unique privilege of being able to look at her baby and know that it was her body that nurtured him from a single cell through to this newborn state, and it can be her body (if she chooses) that will continue to nurture him for however long they both wish. It is not surprising that her love for her baby will change, develop, grow as the weeks, months go by. No mother need feel guilty if she experiences moments of not loving her baby, especially in the early days: you are still adjusting to your new state and role.

For Cathy, it took some time: *'I wasn't all that bothered about the baby for the first few days. I know it sounds very selfish to say so, but I was a bit peeved with the way things had turned out. I had to sit on an inflatable cushion because my perineum was so sore, my nipples were raw and after every feed I'd dab them with a bit of breast milk and leave them exposed to the air. So there I am sitting in state all the time and wondering if the laxative the midwife has just given me to relieve my constipation is going to work yet…and I'm supposed to bond with this baby. It wasn't quite the angelic gazing-into-each-other's eyes process that I'd imagined when I was pregnant. I thought – I'll let my stitches heal and then I'll get on with the bonding.'*

For a mother of twins, like Jess, it can be more difficult: *'I love them both, dearly, but splitting myself in two to love them both equally in their own right has been hard. Mind you, I don't know if it would have been any easier if they had come along one at a time instead of both together. I just know that when I think of them, I still lump them in together as "the twins", and I don't know when or if that will change.'*

SOME PARENTS find 'love' elusive at first, as Louise discovered: *'I tried so hard to love him. I'd loved him with such a passion when, warm and slippery, they had laid him on my tummy seconds after his birth. I would gaze at him in wonder as he fed from me in those early days. But as time went on and the screaming started and never stopped I began – and even now it is hard to admit this – to hate him. I would lie next to my husband in the dark and ask, "What if I never love him? What if he never loves me?"'*

Other mothers, like Madeleine and Parveen, experienced love through a heady mixture of relief and confusion: *'Do you know what I felt when he was born? Relief. The end of the pain was just so wonderful. And I felt…I felt… "God, I've actually done it." It was amazing because through all of this I never really believed that I was going to have a baby at the end of it. When I was getting ready – I mean, I did make some clothes and things – but I kept thinking I ought not to count my chickens. So when he was actually there, I thought "I've done it! This is such an achievement!" So there was achievement and relief and also slightly a feeling of, "Oh, what do I do with it?" They'd given me this baby and expected me to know what to do with it straight away. Same for Ross. We were fumbling round trying to do something with this little slimy thing.'*

'*I felt very strange. I was so happy and yet somehow I was so sad as well, and when I started crying I didn't know which had caused it: the joy or the sadness. We were so glad to have her here, especially after the long labour when we thought she might never make it at all, but now that she was here I felt such a weight of responsibility. I knew how hard life could be and she didn't, and she had it all before her, to learn about. I felt this fierce desire to protect her, yet I already knew I wouldn't be able to protect her from everything.*'

SMILING

MANY PARENTS maintain that their baby can smile at them right from Day One. Lesser experts dismiss this as wind and draw complicated graphs to show that your newborn can't possibly be focusing his eyes yet, much less recognise you, much less co-ordinate his muscles for a smile.

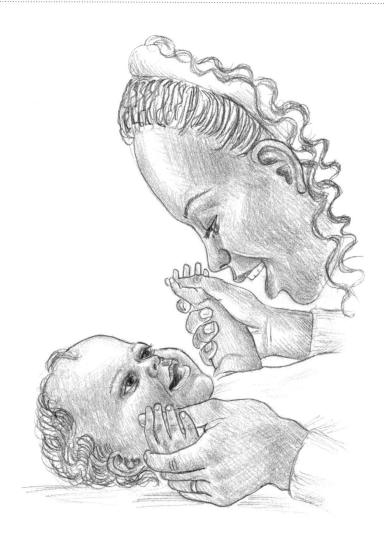

Joanna explains her baby's smiling: '*When he cries, I pick him up and he puts his head on my shoulder and sometimes he turns his head slightly and beams at me. Yesterday I said this to my mum and she said, "Oh, all babies do that, it's just wind. He can't be smiling yet because he's only three weeks old." But I don't believe that. I think he's getting to know me and he's smiling because it's me, or trying to smile, making these sort of odd crinkles with his mouth. And his cries are real so why shouldn't his smiles be real as well?*'

THE SMILE IS the beginning of sociability: your baby has an innate desire to relate to other people. Eventually she will have a circle of relatives and friends, all of whom have earned that smile. But for now, it's yours.

Perhaps Phoebe sums it up: *'I know in these books they say babies don't smile for about six weeks but I think that's just because they don't smile at the people who write those books. They smile at their mums.'*

IN THE MIDDLE of the nappy changes, the feeds, the stress and the worry over our small, vulnerable babies, when we see that smile as they turn trustingly towards us for protection, we remember why we wanted to have a baby in the first place.

CHAPTER *three* Your new self

PREGNANCY IS over. Your baby is here. But that doesn't mean you can now return to the state you were in, physically, socially or psychologically, before the baby was born.

Physically, your body will not immediately snap back to its pre-pregnant lissom shape. Chances are, you will have to go home from the hospital in a maternity outfit. Stretch marks, a sagging tummy and tender breasts may be the least of your burdens if you have stitches, (episiotomy or caesarean), to cope with as well. Don't rush yourself to get back to normal: it took you nine months to reach that shape, nine months might be a good time-span to consider for recovery. Crash diets will make you feel tired at a time you need all your energy and may interfere with breastfeeding.

And it goes without saying that a newborn has quite an impact on most people's social lives. You may find new friends, you may rediscover old ones, you will certainly have different topics of conversation.

Psychologically, you have made the transition from being an individual in your own right, pleasing yourself, accountable only to yourself, to being an individual with responsibility for another human being. You may find the physical alterations much easier to cope with if you can look at the changes to your body in these terms: instead of bewailing the fact that your new shape is less elegant, that your nursing bra and breastpads prevent you from wearing the latest string bikini, or that your varicose veins mean you're going to be sticking with leggings for the best part of the next year or so – celebrate the changes and transformations of your hard-working body doing the job for which it was designed: carrying, nourishing and caring for a new life.

RECOVERY

SOME WOMEN really do seem to bounce up off the delivery bed and leap right into parenting with scarcely a twinge. Others find that the emotional hurdle we have leapt over into being a parent is as nothing to the simple physical legacy of childbirth.

Harriet feels very little difference: *'I can't believe it, I spent all that time getting ready for the birth and now I've just forgotten it.'*

Eileen concentrated on ensuring her caesarean stitches healed: *'For the first couple of weeks, just getting on and off the bed was agony. I was so scared of pulling the skin because the scar had come open on one side on my second day back and I was terrified of making it worse because I could already see that it was healing all lumpy and lop-sided.'*

One of the major concerns at antenatal classes is often stitches and tearing of the vaginal wall or perineum (the area between your front and back passages). Chloë had hoped she'd avoid them: *'I tore, so I had stitches, and I tore in a funny place, so it's still sore and Jack's eight weeks old now. And I had an infection . . . so did a lot of my antenatal group so we wondered whether it was something at the hospital. I'd been doing everything I could to help them heal. They tell you to bathe a lot, and after a bath I would dry them with a hairdryer, and that really seemed to help. And I used witch-hazel on them which helps to dry them out. I thought about nothing else in those first few weeks except my stitches.'*

HELPING STITCHES HEAL

- Take frequent baths or showers – this will keep the stitches clean
- Do not put 'bubbles' in your bath, they can cause irritation
- Wash yourself after going to the loo – again this helps to avoid infection
- Dry your perineum thoroughly – with a soft towel or, if you are too sore, a hairdryer on a cool setting
- Eat well. Good vitamin intake aids skin repair. In particular make sure that you get enough iron and vitamin E
- If you notice any burning or swelling, or any unpleasant discharge, tell your midwife. If an infection is caught straight away, antibiotics will usually clear it up pretty swiftly.

IF YOU have stitches, they may well feel uncomfortable in the early days but they shouldn't feel unbearably painful. Your midwife will check your perineum and make sure that the stitches are healing as they should. If you have any worries, ask her for reassurance.

The stitches used these days dissolve; you will not need to have them taken out. If yours don't seem to be dissolving as quickly as you'd expected, ask the midwife to take a look for you.

Even after your stitches have healed, and your blood loss (the lochia, it's technically termed, though it can seem like just a long period) has ceased – usually by about six weeks, there can be physical repercussions to deal with that go beyond the tiredness caused by having a newborn baby to take care of.

Alice describes how she feels: *'I still can't bend over very well, and I can't use the baby bath which my sister lent me because when it's full of water I'm not strong enough yet to carry it. Still, it's better being home than being in the hospital because there if I wanted to give him a bath I had to do it in a room with a very hard floor and he was a wriggly baby and I spent the whole time being petrified I was going to drop him, and then I wouldn't be able to bend down far enough to pick him up!'*

Fiona followed a traditional remedy during pregnancy and was disappointed when it didn't work: *'I'm very cross. I drank gallons and gallons of that horrible raspberry leaf tea when I was pregnant, hoping for an easy labour, and I ended up having pethidine and forceps because he was facing the wrong way. I feel wretched. I look at him and think, "Why couldn't you have just turned round?"'*

Sushma found other physical effects more inconvenient: *'I hated the fact that my digestive system just couldn't get back to normal. Everyone had advice. I kept drinking loads of water. Even casual visitors would pop round with some fresh fruit. It seemed like the whole world was concerned with the state of my bowels. Bowel trouble didn't fit with my image of motherhood at all.'*

AT THE HEART of the way many of us feel is this mis-match between how we think we're supposed to feel and how we actually feel. We see images of motherhood that don't take account of the tiredness or the stitches or the funny lop-sided way our caesarean scar is healing.

Philippa describes another physical side-effect: *'I was losing hair in handfuls. Everyone kept saying it was normal and to be expected, but every time I washed my hair, I felt like I was washing away a bit more of this healthy bloom of pregnancy and all I was being left with was this thin, raddled, dull creature.'*

YES, WHEN WE were pregnant, many of us bloomed, and many of us will exchange that bloom for the characteristic vacant stare of new parenthood – a stare that owes much to disorientation and lack of sleep. We will lose the extra hair we managed to hold on to, we will find our bodies radically different – but we have gained a baby.

It took nine months to get to this point – if you try taking nine months to get back to normal, you may begin to look and feel the way you did before physically, but psychologically you've reached somewhere a lot further away.

DEBRIEFING

MANY WOMEN feel a deep need to 'debrief', to go over and over the events of their labour, to remember what happened, to make sense of what happened, and sometimes relive any events which were traumatic or confusing. If you can talk over your labour with your midwife, antenatal teacher or a friend who's good at listening, with your obstetric notes if necessary, it will be one of the best ways of dealing with experiences that you now want to integrate and put behind you so that you can move on.

Even the most normal and straightforward labour – in the eyes of the health professionals involved – is a huge, life-changing event for the parents. Ask for some time to talk about what happened if you want it. Having your questions answered now can save you much worry and heart-searching later.

Benefits of talking over your labour:

- You can have your questions answered
- You can come to terms with events and move on
- You can fill in any 'missing pieces' from the birth
- You can get rid of any 'blame'
- You can stop worrying.

Roisin went back to the hospital and asked for some support: *'I'd been having terrible nightmares about the haemorrhage. I would wake very frightened, thinking that it was going to happen again somehow, and that the baby would die and it was all my fault. Awful. Just awful. I wrote to the hospital and asked if I could sit down with someone and go through all my worries, and they gave me an appointment. I wrote down all my questions in advance to make sure I didn't leave anything out. And I came out with a much lighter heart.'*

CAESAREANS

THE LONG-TERM emotional aftermath of a caesarean can be very strong for some women. Even when your scar has healed and your body is feeling stronger, you may feel as if you have not come to terms with what has happened.

Katharine's son, Max, is six months old and she is still disappointed that she had a caesarean: *'I don't really know why. Perhaps if there'd been one particular reason, one definite thing which had made the doctors say, "Right, you've got to have a caesarean," then I could have come to terms with it better. But it was a combination of factors: long labour, the fact that his head never engaged, and his heart-rate kept dipping, that made them say, "Oh,*

*well, we think we should . . ." And that means I go over the whole thing
again and again in my mind and wonder, "What if they hadn't?"'*

IT WAS ONLY early in the twentieth century that caesarean operations
began to be successful – and even then the risks were high. The incisions were large and vertical, infections tenacious, and often fatal in
the days before antibiotics. Caesareans were a last resort.

These days, the operation is far safer and far less to be feared.
Epidurals and spinal blocks mean that those of us who are brave
enough to stay awake while the incision is made can be there to greet
our baby. Sushma and Eileen chose to do this:

*'I was very nervous. I said "When are you going to start cutting?" And the
surgeon said, "About two minutes ago." '*

'We were invited to have a peek over the curtain when he was actually delivered, Mick did, but I couldn't look.'

THE OPERATION can often be a swift and safe option that allows for
the optimum outcome for all concerned, and no mother does not
want to do the best for her baby. This is what makes it very difficult
for many caesarean mothers to talk about the disappointment they
might be feeling if they have had a surgical delivery.

How can they express regret when the alternative might have cost
their baby's life? It may not be very natural for a baby to emerge
under the bright lights of an operating theatre, but does that matter?
Many mothers feel that it does, or at least that they have to be given
the opportunity to express their mixed feelings about the birth.

Interestingly, the mothers who seem to recover the most quickly
are those whose caesarean was planned. It is usually the mothers who
have emergency caesareans who find recovery hardest, perhaps
because they were psychologically unprepared for the event and
have to come to terms mentally, as well as physically, with what has
happened.

Erica felt very distant from her baby for the first few days: *'I didn't feel
as if I'd had a baby, I felt like some kind of fraud and didn't know what I was
doing up there on the postnatal ward. My stomach was all sagging and horri-*

ble, and red around the scar and when I looked at it, I felt sick. I kept getting *the most terrible fear that they'd somehow missed my real baby when they'd done the operation, that they'd left it still in my stomach. This was made worse because of the awful wind pain I got. I was full of these bubbles and pains that, to me, were exactly like a baby kicking. I remember lying in bed in this half-awake state thinking that the baby was still inside me so I'd been given the wrong one to look after.'*

Alice had had an emergency section with her first son, Matthew, so she was expecting the few weeks after the birth of the second one to be equally unpleasant: *'But it was much, much easier. I had a spinal, we knew when we were booked in and could arrange childcare for Matthew well in advance, and afterwards I was up and walking about sooner, I didn't need so much in the way of pain relief, and I felt altogether happier, more cheerful.'*

Recovery from a caesarean

WHILE CAESAREAN mothers are relieved to have their baby safe with them, they do have a myriad of physical hurdles during the recovery period.

Feeding your baby with both of you lying down can be one of the most comfortable options if you've had a caesarean.

Breastfeeding your baby on a pillow can take some of the pressure off your scar.

Katharine hated every minute she was on the postnatal ward: *'I had no idea how to care for a baby, I couldn't move, I was in terrible pain, and it was the noisiest place on earth. All the side wards were full so there was nowhere else to go, and Michael had to go home every night and I couldn't be with him when I really wanted some comfort and love. I got constipated because I was so frightened of pushing and bursting the stitches; my milk came in late and Max spent the third day of his life screaming with what I took to be hunger and when I burst into tears the nurse said it was the baby blues and everyone got them and I'd probably feel a bit better by tomorrow. It took me weeks. Weeks and weeks before I felt anywhere near better but I had to get on with it.'*

PEOPLE TEND to forget that a caesarean is still a major operation, and it will probably be several days before you are really fit to care for your baby beyond feeding her. It is often assumed that mothers want to have their new babies with them all the time, but many caesarean mothers don't – not because they're selfish but because they want to sleep undisturbed for a few hours to help get the effects of a general anaesthetic out of their system, or because they want to take an hour to soak in the bath, not only to soak the dressing off as instructed, but also to come to terms with the scar on their stomachs.

Sushma felt awful too, but: *'When I did get together with some other mothers, they said, "Oh, everyone feels awful. It's just having babies that does it. Not you." And that made me feel much better.'*

NEVERTHELESS, there are some problems specific to caesarean mothers that will take some time to get over, and one of these is wind. The operation and anaesthetic disturb normal bowel activity. Sometimes the bowels then swell up with gas, and this fills the abdomen, often putting pressure on the diaphragm. It helps if you get up and move around as soon as you can – though this can often be the last thing you feel like doing. Moving around helps disperse and dispel the wind and gradually your system will return to normal. You may find that you are thirstier than normal anyway, and this is a good thing – fluid intake also helps. While it is a temporary and minor problem, wind can be very uncomfortable and can seriously undermine your morale if you just want to get over the operation as quickly as you can and get on with looking after your baby.

If you have had a caesarean and are feeling poorly, the following may be useful:

- A partner who takes over as much of the childcare as possible
- A single room – if you're not offered one in hospital, ask
- Straightforward, easily understood advice and instructions from the nursing staff as to the best ways of feeding, changing, and bathing without putting pressure on your scar
- Pain relief. Don't be frightened to ask for what you need – and pain-relieving medications are improving all the time, becoming more effective while not interfering with breast milk production.

STRESS AND ANGER

THERE ARE TIMES when even the most delighted parents find it difficult to cope with the exhaustion and stress that a new baby can bring. This in itself sometimes increases our stress and guilt levels, as Bridget admits: *'I wanted my baby. I wanted to have children very much. I still want her! But sometimes I want someone to take her away for a while. It's very claustrophobic and wearing. And as soon as I've thought that, I feel guilty, because I was the one that wanted her.'*

Tiredness can seem all-consuming, says John: *'I was so tired I thought I'd never get enough sleep in my life again. I was at my wits' end.'*

When people think you're the expert and in control, it can be frustrating says Daisy: *'I find it hard that people think I know what to do all the time. If she starts crying, they say to me, "Why is she crying?" and I say, "Well, how should I bloody know?"'*

Frustration and exhaustion can sometimes spill over into anger, and sometimes this anger can be directed towards your child. Everyone feels like this at times – and the occasional angry word or action is nothing unusual, as Jennifer explains: *'I was lucky, I had done some reading in psychology and I knew it was normal to feel a bit down and strange in those first days. I kept saying to myself, "This is an okay feeling, Jen, don't worry about it." If I didn't know it was normal to feel negative emotions, I might have been worried about it or upset, but I knew it was actually more usual to react like that than to skip round saying, "Life's wonderful and it's all a bed of roses and I'm so happy."'*

Recognising that you are angry with your baby – even if you feel guilty about that anger – can come as a shock to many parents as Hazel discovered: *'I was getting more and more wound up and tireder and tireder. He was in the bed with me, and every time he made a noise, I was up, breastfeeding him, and this had gone on for weeks, until it reached ridiculous levels like eight or nine times a night, and there came a point where I picked him up and screamed, "No! No! No! I'm not doing it any more." I put him in his cot in the other room and shut the door and that was it. I went back to bed saying to myself: "He will survive, he will still be alive in the morning. It's not going to kill him to be on his own the rest of the night." I would never, ever have believed I could do anything like that. I thought mothers who did things like that, leaving them to cry, were cruel. I wasn't being cruel by then, I was just doing something I had to do.'*

IT IS THIS shock, that a parent can find themselves doing what they never believed they would do, and the shock that their baby is turning out to be an ordinary baby and not the Dream Baby, that can be so confusing.

Fiona admits she had a very rosy view of motherhood: *'I know that now, and Joe's only two months old. Before he was born, when I was reading through the magazines, there'd be articles in there like "Ten Things to Try if Your Baby*

Cries" and I wouldn't read them. I'd turn the page, thinking, "Oh, my baby won't cry." I get very angry with myself, more than anything, because if I'd allowed myself to look at the reality, I wouldn't feel as stuck in it as I am now.'

IT IS OFTEN the difference between our vision of what life will be like with a baby and the reality of what life *is* like with our baby that leads new parents to feel a great sense of frustration. No wonder we get angry with ourselves, and with friends if we think they've maintained a conspiracy of silence about the realities of parenthood.

No wonder we get angry with the people we feel have misled us, says Lynn: *'I was cross with my antenatal teacher. I said, "Why didn't you tell me it would be like this?" And she said, "I did."'*

So it's no wonder we get angry with our baby, the cause of all these uncomfortable feelings.

IF YOU ARE beginning to feel angry, resentful or aggressive for most of the time, though, then you need extra help. It's not always easy to recognise or accept how angry you do feel – especially if you had a dream of parenthood that you feel you're somehow not living up to – but the safest thing to do is talk through with someone just how you feel before you feel any worse.

Hazel doesn't exactly feel angry, just resentful and she finds this hard to cope with: *'I really resent some things, like worrying about whether my scar is going to come open, and feeling like I'm hobbling around like an old crone. And I didn't realise how difficult it would be for me to sleep. Not just because of Ben being awake, but because I'm worrying about him all the time. Even when he's asleep, I worry about when he's going to wake up. When he's dropped off for the night and I'm tired and I want to go to sleep more than anything, I can't because I'm listening to him breathe. No matter what I'm doing or where I go, I'm listening, listening all the time, so I'm always on edge, always tense. I resent that, but I resent it in me, I don't know why I'm doing it to myself.'*

IF YOU ARE feeling overwhelmed by your emotions, especially if they are negative emotions that are making you unhappy, the best thing

Voluntary organisations are used to hearing about parents' problems with:

- Your feelings towards your baby
- Your relationship with your partner
- Worries over money
- Ways of parenting with a disability
- Your worries about your baby
- Experiences of racism or prejudice.

that you can do is talk over with someone how you feel. Organisations like Parentline offer a listening ear to any parent who needs help to cope.

All calls to voluntary 'helping' organisations are confidential; if you don't want to, you don't even have to give your name. If you call, you will find yourself talking to someone who is a parent also, so knows how hard it can be. If you require specific help with a particular problem, they can also point you in the right direction to a specialised agency.

So if you ever feel that your troubles are too trivial – or too terrible – to bother your doctor or health visitor with, and you'd rather not share them with friends and relatives, call someone who's ready for calls like yours.

The reverse is true, of course: you may just want to tell someone how wonderful everything is, as does Zoë: *'Oh, it is, it is lovely. It's everything I hoped it would be. When I'm feeding Oliver, it's the time I feel closest to him, and I think he has a special look when I feed him and it's lovely. I love it. I enjoy it. People say, "Oh, don't you find being at home boring?" But I've never felt like that, not at all.'*

FEELING DOWN

SOMETIMES, when the baby blues don't magically disappear, and you find that your low feelings are dragging on and dragging you down, you may wonder what's wrong. You may wonder if you have 'postnatal depression' – a subject which is being heard more about these days. Perhaps. It may simply be, however, that you have postnatal exhaustion. Many mothers will feel down, uncertain, vulnerable and permanently tired in the first weeks after birth. If you're tired but feeling generally okay in yourself, then you probably have exhaustion. If you're tired but irritable and aggressive *as well*, and not feeling right, or feeling that you've been treated badly, then you are probably depressed. Another difference is that if you're exhausted, your moods will vary, up and down, while a depression is characterised by a flat

tone, when day after day seems the same. Perhaps the main difference, however, is that while exhaustion will clear up with rest, a more deep-rooted depression will not.

Exhaustion

IF YOU THINK you've got postnatal exhaustion, don't go blaming yourself: in fact, don't go doing anything because you've been doing too much already. That's the message your body and mind is trying to give you. Remember: no one is going to come round and give you a silver star if you've redecorated the spare bedroom; the baby won't give a hoot if her bib isn't ironed.

It may be that all you need to do to alleviate exhaustion is rest. But this can be hard to admit to yourself, and even harder to do, as Judith found: *'I knew I was doing things which really didn't need doing, knew that it didn't matter if the kitchen floor wasn't washed every day, but I was still washing it. I was ironing sleepsuits and reading up about weaning foods – and this at a time when Nat was still totally breastfed, so I didn't need to do it at all, but I was doing it to make sure I got everything right when the time came. I knew about spinach, and how much iron there was in a portion of potato, and I'd put Nat in her babybouncer so I could get the breakfast dishes out of the way . . . and now I wonder why. Why didn't I play with Nat when she was bright and breezy in the morning and do the breakfast dishes later? Why didn't I ask Joel to bring home a take-away instead of peeling potatoes?'*

IF YOU CAN allow yourself to do the bare minimum, you'll probably end up with a much happier baby and a much happier self. Don't get yourself down by thinking you have to live up to unrealistic demands.

See those pictures in the baby magazines? The ones where shiny happy parents tend a shiny happy child in a broderie anglaise nursery? Yes, you wanted that to be you, but, really, it's not any of us. Look at those pictures again. Notice how many times the words 'posed by models' appear by the side of the photograph. Now look at the pictures of the real people in those magazines. Chances are they'll look as pale, washed-out and shell-shocked as you feel.

Realising this helped Judith: *'Once I began to look – at the adverts, the TV, the magazines – I saw how fake everything was. It was a dream. And we were real. There was no point trying to live my life like a photograph. I kept saying to myself: those people in the magazines, they could put up with what I'm putting up with for about a minute-and-a-half, tops.'*

Another way of beating exhaustion is to get out of the house: somewhere, anywhere; go to the park, the baby clinic, your friend's . . . Not only will you relax a bit more when the furniture polish is out of reach, you will find that mixing with other people, sharing and talking will help to lift the tiredness.

'Three of us from my antenatal class still get together and that's wonderful. We compare notes, and two of us went shopping together and bought all these toys, and then we spent half the day here and then half the day at her house, and it really shares the load. I felt awful the week before, but it really lightens the load if you're with someone. You can live with it, somehow.'

Depression

THERE ARE many reasons why women become depressed after they have had a baby: it could be due to changes in hormone levels, or social pressures, or unremitting tiredness, lack of support, or the gap between their expectations of what life would be like with a new baby and the reality they are experiencing. Whatever the reasons, postnatal depression is an illness, and as such is largely outside of any-one's conscious control.

'I never thought I could feel like this. I wanted a baby so much and now I'm absolutely miserable. I hate it. I don't hate her, but I hate all the rest of it. And I told Gordon so. If I hadn't I'd have hit them both. Or walked out. The temptation to walk out, well…'

Postnatal depression is more common than you may have thought: up to one in ten women can be classified as 'depressed' in the year fol-lowing childbirth, a fact which may be of help when you're convinced that you only feel so wretched because you're such a failure, and one of the reasons you feel such a failure is that you're so miserable at a time when everyone's telling you that you should be happy.

IF THE GAP between the dream of what life would be like with a new baby and the reality of the new family is one of the causes of postnatal depression, then it stands to reason that men can get it, too. And they do, as Brian found: *'Everything was very flat all the time. People expected me to be happy, to smile. And I had no interest in any of it, none whatsoever. All I kept thinking was: it was so much easier when Debby was just pregnant. We weren't woken up five times a night then.'*

More changes are generally required of the mother when a baby arrives in the family – she is more likely to have to give up work, change her expectations, learn to take on a new role and a different lifestyle at a time when she is most tired – but fathers need to under-go some adjustments, too.

'"This is the end," I kept thinking. "No more nights out. No more staying late or having a drink after work. Nothing but mortgages, mortgages, income

BEATING THE BLUES

- Remember that your needs are just as important as everyone else's and be good to yourself: allow yourself time to read a magazine while the baby sleeps, ask your partner to sort out the evening meal, forget ironing.

- Ask for help – get your parents/sister/long-lost cousin to call round and make the evening meal; take up your neighbour's offer of bringing back some shopping.

- Socialise, but only in situations where you feel comfortable: don't go to places where your confidence in your abilities may be undermined.

- Eat well: a nourishing intake for you needn't be time-consuming and an apple will make you feel better in the long-run than a packet of crisps.

- If you're bottle-feeding, get your partner to take on some of the night feeds.

- Remind yourself that everyone feels uncertain about motherhood at times: every single one of us has had a moment where we've wondered if we did the right thing in giving birth to this baby. Love is not a tap you can turn on and off; getting to know and love this baby may take time more time than you expected, that's all.

tax and decorating". No wonder I was so miserable.'

For parents on their own, without the safety valve of a partner to hand the baby over to or share feelings with, the pressures can be compounded.

'I was desperate to meet other mums, I'd talk to anyone as long as they had a baby. And the girl who lives in the basement flat, her baby's a bit older and she said come round to one of these NCT things and I thought, "Oh, I don't want to do that, it sounds like everyone sitting around eating butterfly cakes." But she persuaded me and I went with her . . . and it was horrendous. Everyone was sitting round and eating these flapjacks. I felt like a fish out of water and when I came home I felt even worse because I thought I'd never find anyone I could really share my feelings with.'

Postnatal depression can be mild, in which case a few good afternoons out or nights of unbroken sleep might get you on top of things; or severe, in which case you will probably need to see your GP and get more specialised help. Gentle anti–depressants may just tide you over this rocky patch so you can take up your role again with equanimity.

Most women feel better if they can talk through their anxieties. The problems really start when they bottle their emotions up and don't tell anyone just how awful they're feeling.

'I think it's really important to get out and see as many different people as you can, because you're not necessarily going to get on with the people nearby, and I found the people in my hospital class easier to get on with than the people in *my NCT class – there are certain people you click with and others who you don't. So my strategy is to go to as many things as possible and then, out of all the people you meet, you'll find one or two who have got a baby near the age of yours and who you get on with.'*

Postnatal depression is an illness that varies greatly from woman to woman, but the important thing to remember is that it is a *temporary* state. Many local contact groups and voluntary organisations will be able to put you in touch with someone to talk to about your depression, and one of the most reassuring things can be that the supporter herself has had postnatal depression and has successfully recovered. See the **Directory** for more information.

Men and depression

ALTHOUGH ONE of the main causes of postnatal depression is often the hormonal changes that occur after childbirth, there are other reasons as well why a woman can feel down – and these other reasons can just as equally affect men and bring them down, too.

> ### If you are supporting your partner through postnatal depression:
>
> - Let her talk – don't try to jump in with solutions straight away – let her get to the heart of her worries.
> - Be patient. This is an illness that your partner has – it is not just her being 'difficult'. With your help, she will recover.
> - Be reassuring where you can – postnatal depression may cause small problems to get blown up out of proportion.
> - Let her be silent when she needs to be and let her cry when she needs to. It will help if she does not feel under pressure, and it will help if she can express her emotions rather than hiding them inside.
> - Encourage her to see her GP – gentle, non-addictive anti-depressants may help.
> - Get in touch with organisations like CRY-SIS (see **Directory**) if you feel that your baby's crying is contributing to the problem.
> - You may feel helpless – but by being there and listening, you are already helping.
> - If you think the problem is becoming serious, get help from your doctor.

In many ways, it can be more difficult for men to recover from depression: they do not have access to the same support networks and social occasions that women take for granted (we still tend to call it the mother-and-baby clinic, after all). Some of the things women can do to help them through the bad times – talking, sharing, commiserating and supporting – aren't as easily available to men. This lack of understanding is something Alan vividly remembers: *'I didn't know who I could turn to, who I could talk to. There was a blank wall I'd come up against. Everyone was painting a picture of us as being a happy family, every-*

Most women with postnatal depression will:

- Have days when they feel much better and days when they feel much worse but, as the days go by, the bad days will decrease and the good days will increase
- Take some sort of medication to help them through it, most commonly anti-depressants, though you may need to try several kinds before you find one that helps you
- Want to know when they can get better, but no one can say this for certain: it may be a couple of weeks, it may be much longer before they feel complete-ly back to normal
- Benefit from talking to someone, whether it is a friend, relative, health professional or supporter from an NCT or MAMA group (see **Directory** for details of how to contact these).

Some women with postnatal depression will:

- Need to go into hospital for a short while to help them relax and recover
- Benefit from hormonal treatment with oestrogen or progesterone – ask your GP or consultant for details
- Benefit from alternative therapies: homoeopathy or acupuncture, under the guidance of a qualified therapist.

thing wonderful, and I just felt on the edge of despair all the time. I thought, "If this goes on another day, I'll get in that car tomorrow morn-ing, drive off, drive somewhere and never come back."'

Seeking further help

IF YOU are worried that you just seem to feel 'down' all the time and can't find any joy in life with your new baby, insist on an appointment with your GP where you can talk through how you feel and discuss what sources of help and support you need. It's always better to say how you feel and move on than to keep bottling it all up inside. And remember – depression is only ever temporary: you will come up again from being so down in the depths; it's only a matter of time.

BEING YOURSELF

IN MANY WAYS, parenthood is a 'divided' state. There are divisions between: your old self...your new self; the parent you are...the parent you would like to be; the parent you thought you would be...the parent you are; the parent who loves their children...the parent who resents their children.

YOU CAN be all of these things at the same time, though you may sometimes feel torn apart by the divisions within you. You may love your baby intensely, yet still resent the fact that he won't let you sleep; you may have wanted to give your baby unending love and attention yet still find yourself popping a dummy in his mouth and parking him in

Your new self

.... *113*

front of the TV at two weeks old because you want to get the dinner cooked in peace.

What you need to do is to relax into being the sort of parent you're comfortable with: one whose standards are ones you have imposed and are ones you can live with. Don't try to be a 'perfect' parent according to other people's rules.

Ingrid discovered this months later, but remembers how she used to be: *'In the early days, I kept the house spotless. People came round and I gave them cakes I'd baked myself. The health visitor called and I always had this shining baby to show her. What did I think was going to happen? That she was going to come round and give me marks out of ten for how well I'd shone the silverware?'*

Be prepared to bend and change your own rules if they patently don't suit your baby or you and your partner. As your baby grows older and you grow more used to him you may want to change certain routines or allow yourselves more flexibility. This happened to Beverley: *'I was the ultimate dummy snob. When I used to see kids wandering about with dummies in their mouths, I thought it looked awful. Actually, I still think it looks awful. And I said, "I shall never give my baby a dummy." And then, when Josh was going through a phase of being absolutely horrendous, he was crying for 18 hours a day – actually, I say that, but it certainly seemed like 18 hours a day – a friend of mine suggested a dummy and I went out to*

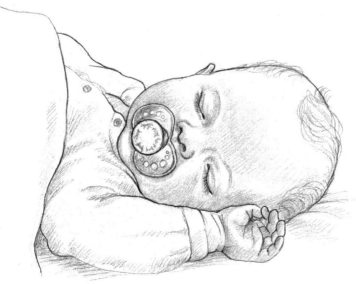

Boots and came back and popped the dummy in his mouth and off he went to sleep. I said, "God, I was at the point of strangling that baby." So which is better? I see other mothers look all sniffy at me now and I think, "You don't know, you just don't know."'

ONE WAY through might be to recognise and accept the complexity of parenthood. If it was simple, no one would ever need to read a book like this.

SELF-IMAGE

THE WAY you see yourself will have a great effect on how you adapt to parenthood. The trick is not to let other people's perceptions of you – however jaded or stereotyped – colour your view.

Frances has found motherhood a challenging experience: *'In some ways I'm a much more confident person now, and that's come because I'm taking total responsibility for my baby. I have no partner to depend on, not even many relatives near, so I do feel as if it's all up to me. I have to seem confident, to seem in control, as otherwise people would start criticising me for being irresponsible, or pointing the finger if I couldn't cope and saying, "We told you so." So because I've got to seem confident, I've started to be confident.'*

Rebecca on the other hand knows that she should try to be more confident: *'I've already noticed that people have started to consider me as "only" a housewife or "only" a mother, and I can feel myself starting to feel uncertain in situations because of that. I'm aware of the danger of retreating into myself and losing all the assertiveness I used to have.'*

IF YOU are beginning to feel you may have lost your self-image under a pile of nappies and baby wipes, it may help to put your current situation and role as a mother into a wider context – think beyond the day-to-day realities, as Olivia did: *'The way I got through it all was I read all these very political books, feminist books about mothering, and sociological books about childcare. They made me see a different side to motherhood, how it was undervalued by society, and that made a lot more sense to me. I began to see that my feelings and frustrations were shared and they weren't all my fault. I could relate much more to a book which talked about the politics of family life than to someone telling me not to worry if he ate his green beans with his ice cream.'*

Camille thinks she took some of the childcare books too much to heart: *'I think that's because I am a single parent and I thought, "Right, she hasn't got a father, I just have to be the best possible parent that I can." And somebody lent me this book which told me I should sleep with my baby and if I didn't, she'd grow up mentally disturbed, and how in the Western world we don't hold our children enough, we should carry them all the time, even when they're five because our arms will grow strong . . . So I was struggling along Church Road one day with Ella in my arms and I met someone who said, "Why don't you just push her in a buggy?" And I thought, "Why don't I? My arms are dropping off." Sometimes I think women set out to make life deliberately difficult for themselves. I certainly feel as if I did.'*

SLEEP

WHEN YOUR baby is adapting to new sleep patterns, you have to adapt right along with him. Your baby is likely to wake two or three times during the night, at least, and this will be very difficult at first. And then if your baby doesn't wake, that can be just as difficult, as Eileen relates: *'Michael's three weeks old now, and he generally comes into our bed at some point in the night. Once, we woke up at five and Mick had to jump out of bed to go and look at him because we couldn't believe he could still be in his Moses basket and still be alright.'*

HELP FROM BOTH SIDES

If your partner is very tired there are things that you can do to help them:

- Soothe the baby when the baby cries
- Bathe the baby
- Change nappies
- Take the baby for a walk in the pram
- Organise a take-away for the evening meal
- Do the shopping.

And if you have a partner who is trying to help you through your tiredness, there are things that you can do that will help:

- Let your partner get on with things in their own way
- Do not criticise
- Do not feel that you ought to do everything yourself
- Do not feel that you ought to be able to do everything yourself.

Cathy's baby hasn't learnt the difference between night and day yet: *'She will feed in the night but sometimes I'll be up and awake for over an hour, walking her about. You can see she's not hungry, because she won't take the rest of her feed. She just hasn't learned yet that the night is not for playing in. I hope the message sinks in soon, because it's in those early hours of the morning I get to the end of my tether, even though I try not to get angry or upset.'*

NUTRITION

AS MOTHERS, we spend a lot of time nourishing our children. We also have to nourish ourselves – sometimes spiritually and mentally with some soothing relaxation or meditation – but let's not forget the nitty-gritty: you won't feel on top of things if your idea of a well-balanced meal is three crackers and a packet of crisps that you've successfully managed to eat off a plate on your knee without the baby kicking it over.

You need a good diet as a new mother. No matter how much you want to 'get back into shape', you will need to keep up your nutritional levels if you want to avoid becoming run down, tired and depressed. Also, if you are breastfeeding, you may find you are hungrier than usual – and your baby will much prefer a happy breastfeeding mother to one worrying constantly about her diet.

Sushma finds it very difficult: *'I try, I do. But I'd much rather go out and get a pizza than get uptight about food. And if Alistair wants a proper dinner with potatoes and things, he can do it himself.'*

QUICK MEALS AND SNACKS

- Microwave baked potatoes with cheese
- Tuna sandwiches
- Yoghurt
- Bowl of soup with a wholemeal roll
- Baked beans on toast
- Scrambled eggs
- Banana
- Avocado.

FOR SOME new parents, the effort involved in preparing meals seems too much – but snacks can be just as filling and nutritious if you choose wisely. Have vegetable soup and a wholemeal roll rather than a packet of crisps. If you are breastfeeding and find that this stimulates your appetite, have an apple or a sandwich rather than a bar of chocolate.

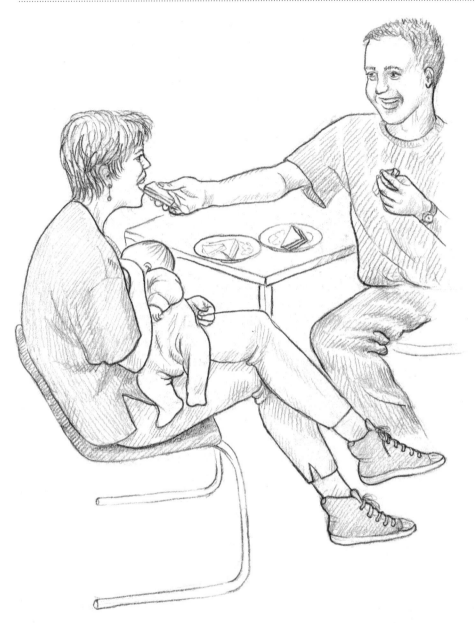

Teeth

PREGNANCY MAY have taken a toll on your teeth, especially if you couldn't keep much food down or if you found it hard to keep up good levels of nutrition and calcium intake. Breastfeeding will also demand adequate calcium intake, so if you keep up your milk-drinking and eat other dishes based on dairy products, like cauliflower cheese, baked potatoes with grated cheese, rice pudding, or foods which take their calcium from other sources, like salmon sandwiches, you will be doing your teeth and gums a favour. If either you or your baby are cow's milk intolerant, foods from other calcium-rich sources such as chick peas, tinned fish and eggs become doubly important now.

You can also, as a new mother, take advantage of the free dental treatment on offer until your baby's first birthday. To find a local NHS dentist, look in the phone book for the number of the Family Health Service Authority (FHSA) for your area and ask them for a list of dentists you could visit.

EXERCISE

TAKE IT EASY in the first weeks, and make sure the doctor signs you off as physically recovered at your six-week check, but then, if you can get yourself out of the house once or twice a week for exercise, you'll be doing yourself one of the greatest favours you can as a new mother. Not only will you feel better, you'll actually increase the amount of energy you have available for doing other things.

Exercise need not be a chore…

Gwen found the comments people made quite personal: *'People would say things like "Are you back to normal yet?" meaning my weight and shape. And I'd say, "Well, bits of me are back to normal." But I wouldn't say which bits.'*

NO MATTER how assiduously you have exercised and how carefully you have eaten during your pregnancy, the pregnancy itself and the labour will have altered your body shape. It will take some time to get back to the way you used to look – if, indeed, you want to get back to the way you used to look – and, as you will soon gather, it takes everyone a differing amount of time to achieve this.

For some, like Hilary, her new figure wasn't important: *'My antenatal class made me sick. There they all were about three weeks after their baby was born simpering around and saying, "Oh, I can just get back into my jeans now." I thought, "You should be enjoying your baby, for heaven's sake, not worrying about whether or not you can wear your jeans right now."'*

Virginia's description may sound familiar: *'I pushed my finger into my stomach and it was like pushing my finger into a sponge, so soft, with no resistance. And no strength.'*

Jess found it more difficult to organise time on her own: *'Whereas I could probably leave one with mum or dad, two is a different kettle of fish. I have tried it, and it's very hard – both for me because I'm worrying all the time I'm away how the other person's coping with the twins, and for the other person, because it is hard work looking after them! Eventually what I did was line them both up in their baby chairs in the sitting room and dance to the tape in front of them. I don't know what they think is going on but I don't care – it keeps me happy!'*

SOME WOMEN, though, find it easy to start, but not to keep going. The main reasons seem to be the difficulties not only of making time, but finding someone who will look after the baby if you want to take part in exercise like swimming, as Philippa reveals: *'I did go to a post-natal exercise class, which was a good start, and very easy because there was a supervised crèche, but as Sophie got older, she didn't like to be left, so that was one of the things that fell by the wayside. Looking back, I think I should have*

EXERCISE

Getting started with exercise

- Some pools have crèche facilities on certain mornings that allow new parents to swim in peace for a while; call your local pool for details

- Your local NCT branch, YWCA or Child Health Clinic may run postnatal exercise classes, where you can exercise and meet other new mothers; at NCT classes, time is given every week to discussion as well, so you can talk about your new role as well as work on your new body shape

- Try one of the videotapes specifically aimed at postnatal women if you'd rather exercise in private or have trouble getting out.

persevered. I'd have been happier, and stayed in the habit, and she would have got used to being looked after.'

The sooner you start to do some gentle exercise, the sooner you'll notice a difference but, as Lahli found out, there are many excuses: *'My stitches did take a long time to heal, so I used that as a wonderful excuse for a while. Then I noticed that my breasts were, well, shall we say, not quite what they were? When Sasha was about six months old, I stopped feeding her and confidently waited for my ample bosom to return to its former glory. Which it didn't. If anything, it just got floppier and floppier. I thought, "Right, start now, before this spreads to the thighs." '*

REMEMBER, NOW is not the time to aim for Olympic standards, but it will boost your self-confidence no end to swim a length or two once or twice a week. And it won't hurt your figure, either.

There are also some more specific physical legacies of pregnancy that merit you paying particular attention to them in the first year of your baby's life in order to assure your long-term health, such as strengthening your pelvic floor.

...but fun all round.

Pelvic floor

AS MANY as one in five women suffer from some form of stress incontinence during pregnancy and the postnatal period. This is a condition where their muscles have lost strength during the pregnancy, either because the pregnancy hormone relaxin has relaxed them into this state, or because the muscles have been stretched by the pregnancy and delivery. As a result, they leak small amounts of urine at times of stress – such as when sneezing, coughing or laughing. This can be very frustrating for those who had hoped to get back to normal the instant the baby emerged, and a great cause of worry and potential embarrassment.

Pelvic floor exercises

THESE ARE so important that they merit a little sub-section to themselves. The pelvic muscles are located across your pelvis like a hammock and around your vagina. If you want to know exactly where your pelvic floor muscles are, try stopping in mid-wee for a few seconds. The muscles you can feel contracting then are the ones in your pelvic floor. Do this only once or twice – just to find the muscles. Do not do this regularly as frequent retention of urine can cause infection.

Keeping your pelvic floor strong helps to avoid any problems with stress incontinence and can also reassure you that your vagina will return to more or less how it was before delivering your baby.

Separated pelvis

THE HORMONE relaxin, which softens the ligaments in your pelvis in preparation for birth, can sometimes make them so soft that the bones at the front of the pelvis separate, especially if you push too hard or for too long during labour. This condition, known as *diastasis symphysis pubis*, is being diagnosed more frequently these days and can be very painful. If you think you might be suffering from DSP, let your health visitor know and she will be able to put you in touch with an obstetric physiotherapist and a support group to share information.

THE PELVIC FLOOR EXERCISES

A simple pelvic floor exercise is to contract your pelvic floor muscles gradually and gently as far as you can. Many women find the image of their muscles as a 'lift' helpful, and can envisage this lift rising through several 'floors'. Hold the lift on the top floor for a count of three, then let the muscles relax and the lift fall again. As your muscles grow stronger, you will find that you can hold the lift at the top floor for longer, perhaps up to a count of five. As your muscles strengthen, you may also find that the 'top floor' gets higher. What's important, though, is to do your pelvic floor exercises frequently, whenever you remember.

Pelvic floor exercises can safely be started while you are still pregnant and contribute enormously to the strength of the muscles that control urination. For further details on different exercises, or if you want to check that you are doing them correctly, ask your midwife or health visitor. If you have developed stress incontinence and the problem is severe – some women find that they cannot leave the house for fear of leaks – ask for a referral to an obstetric physiotherapist. In addition to exercises, there are now many treatments available, including electrotherapy (a painless process in which the muscles are electrically stimulated), which have very high success rates. If stress incontinence is a problem for you, rest assured that it is a problem which is common: ask for help so that you can get on with your life again without this nagging worry. With help and exercise, stress incontinence can be overcome.

MAKING TIME TO REST

IF YOU have just given birth, your body has been through tremendous changes. You need to give your body time to recover, to adapt to your new regime, and to regain its strength. Rest, and not driving yourself to the limits of exhaustion, will be one of your main weapons in the battle to achieve this. Perhaps an attitude like Diana's is the right one: *'I'm lucky, I've never been houseproud. I can sit here with the house in an absolute state. I can sit here and read a book and think, "Sod it, I'm looking after myself."'*

THINK OF REST in these positive terms, and it may be easier to allow yourself to sleep when the baby sleeps, and to rest when you can.

MAKING TIME FOR YOUR NEEDS

IF MOST new parents feel guilty about allowing themselves to rest, then it's doubly so when it comes to making time for their own needs. It can be difficult to allow yourself to spend some time enjoying an activity that has nothing to do with the baby and many mothers find they spend a lot of any leisure time they do get simply coping with residual guilt, as Hazel found out: *'I can't bear to leave him when he's awake. Generally about nine o'clock in the morning, Ben will have a nap, and it's then that I'll get myself washed and dressed and get all the breakfast dishes done. It's always a challenge: can I get everything done that I want to before he wakes up again? Sometimes I'm just getting the bath run when I hear him begin to fret. Once I brought him into the bathroom with me, hoping that he'd just stay in his basket quietly while I had my*

GETTING ENOUGH REST
Do not:
● Spend every minute of the baby's nap time cleaning the house
● Iron bibs
● Iron cot sheets
● Iron almost anything
● Make yourself miserable trying to apply standards from pre-baby days that aren't important now (like dusting the skirting boards)
● Hover round the baby's basket waiting for the baby to wake up.

bath – and I didn't want to let him out of my sight – but it was hopeless because he howled and it echoed all around the bathroom and my nerves were on edge after 30 seconds. So now, I just go to him. It's unbearable for me to hear him cry. I just have to pick him up.'

BUT, ONCE the first flush of excitement has passed, it is time to rediscover what your needs are.

When you say good-bye, don't carry guilt away with you.

MAKING TIME FOR YOURSELF

SPENDING SOME time gloriously *alone* may be one of your needs, not just one of your luxuries. If it is something you feel you need to do, then this need should not be ignored. Yes, most of us would probably hesitate before saying, 'Look, I *need* a relaxing lavender bath, followed by half an hour in which I *need* to lie on the sofa, painting my toenails red and watching "EastEnders".'

It's far more likely that we'd hint, gently, that this is what we'd *like* to do, and get grumpy if our hint isn't taken up. Yes, you may not need a lavender bath, but you do need time to be yourself, to look after yourself, to re-establish yourself as a person in your own right.

A mother who is able to take some time for herself, without guilt, will be much less stressed and more able to cope with the demands that being a new parent will place upon her.

Many women cultivate an interest in activities like yoga or swimming before the baby arrives, but somehow don't manage to keep up with them afterwards, even though they would be the perfect postnatal stress-buster.

QUICK REFRESHERS

- Take a walk on your own. It doesn't matter if it's raining as you won't have to worry about the baby getting wet
- Have a nap if your relaxation techniques are effective enough to let you wind down and sleep in the middle of the day
- Sink into a warm bath, perhaps with some essential, refreshing oils
- Practise some yoga and let your worries go
- And, while you're doing all these things, unplug the telephone. Then you can't be interrupted.

The baby needs you to do this too – a more relaxed, stress-free mother will be better company and want to play more.

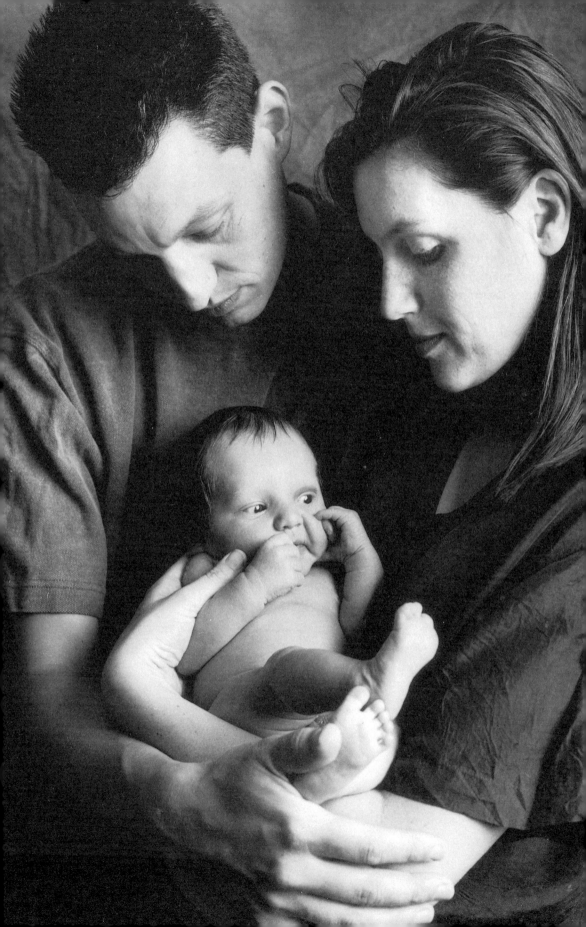

CHAPTER *four* You and your partner

A GREAT many thousands of words have been written about mother-hood, about society's image of the mother, about whether mothers should stay at home with their children or go back to work. Slightly less has been written about the role of the father.

Indeed, it is only in recent years that there have been more than isolated instances of men choosing to stay at home to fulfil the new role of 'house-husband'. If you look at the advertising aimed at young families, you will see that it is mainly aimed at mothers. If you visit groups where babies can play in company, you will see from their very name, 'mother-and-baby groups' that the organisers expect to see women turning up with their offspring, not men. The father who is the main care-giver is still relatively rare.

But this is as limiting for fathers as it is for mothers. In all of these practical arrangements there is a tacit assumption that the father will never be as closely bonded to his children as the mother is; that his responsibility is to go out and earn the cash, and there it stops unless he chooses to 'help' at home. Maternity leave stretches into weeks, paternity leave? Well, you're lucky if you get two days.

Having to conform to such stereotyped, narrow roles can cause tension between couples. In the excitement – and sometimes in the stress and upheaval – of the early days with your new baby, as you adjust to your new roles and responsibilities, it's easy to forget that all of this only happened at all because of the loving relationship between you and your partner.

It is that relationship on which the whole of your family life is based; if that relationship is not happy or turns sour, or the two of you come into conflict, family life may crack apart at the seams.

EXPECTATIONS

NO MATTER what you think family life is going to be like, you can't really guess. Sometimes it measures up to your expectations, for others – especially for an uncertain father – it's totally unlike anything you've ever been prepared for. Mick explains how he felt at the beginning: *'Before Michael arrived, I'd never really been close to a baby. Eileen and I were the eldest siblings in our families and the first to splash out into parenthood. We didn't even have any friends who'd had babies, so it was uncharted territory for everybody. And, quite naturally, we had no idea what we were letting ourselves in for. We managed to organise moving into our new home about a month before Michael arrived, but we were embarking on the middle-class dream of doing up an old house, near the city centre, so when he was born, we had no carpets, bare plaster walls drying from a damp-proof course and no water in the top part of the house. But we didn't think that would be a problem. We thought we'd get along fine because the baby would sleep most of the time and we'd have plenty of spare moments to carry on with the decorating.'*

John and Kate were determined to do everything together for the best well-being of their baby: *'We had it all worked out – sharing child-care, one of us might stay at home with this first baby, the other could stay at home with the second, and we'd split the feeding, too. Kate was going to breastfeed, that much we knew, because it was so much more natural than bottles. But she could have one night on, then one night off, and on the nights off I'd give bottles of expressed milk and that would give me an equal chance to bond with the baby . . . Why didn't anyone ever tell us we were living in Cloud Cuckoo Land?'*

AS WELL as causing a reassessment on the home front, the arrival of a baby will start to signal some changes at the place where the main breadwinner works. The arrival of a baby can sometimes necessitate major changes of attitude, as Paul makes clear: *'I now tell everyone that I'm going to be out of the office at quarter past five. If I don't get the 5.30pm train, I'm not home before Jessica goes to bed. At first this was met with absolute incomprehension by my boss. Why wouldn't I stay late to write a report? Why wouldn't I just do this or just do that? I made the boundaries clear very early, though.'*

IF YOU are able to make your new boundaries and new commitments clear at work, you are lucky. In these days of high unemployment, pressures on people to work extra hours – paid or not – are very strong, as Richard points out: *'I was at a meeting with someone from another company and as it was coming towards five, I hinted that I'd like to get away soon to see the twins before they went to sleep. "Oh, can't your wife do all that?" was the response. One answer, which I didn't say, was that she could, but I wanted to. Another answer is that I am their father, and no one else can do that, no.'*

While some men cherish their new responsibilities, others find it hard to work out just how much extra they might now be called upon to do in the way of support. Helen didn't realise that she'd have to explain to her husband what needed doing: *'We were very lucky – I thought we were very lucky. Chris had a week's paternity leave and I thought, "How wonderful, he's going to look after me." But when I came home from the hospital, all the laundry was still on the radiators where I had had to leave it when I got rushed in – only now it was curled up and stiff as cardboard. And there was no food in the fridge. And I was starving. I wasn't altogether surprised, but I had secretly hoped that having a daughter would somehow miraculously transform him into a household expert.'*

For some mothers nothing changes: *'Life was just going to be the same in a lot of ways. Either I'd nag him to do things, or I'd do them myself.'*

Paula sees things differently: *'I always felt I'd wanted a baby more than Neil, so once Abby was here, I felt she was more my responsibility than his. I felt if I pushed him to do too much, he might walk away, saying he'd never wanted children anyway.'*

Andrew explains his thoughts on being a father: *'I wasn't at all certain I wanted children. I knew Jan wanted children and when we knew a baby was on the way, she was over the moon. I wasn't. I was very apprehensive. I'm still apprehensive and that's now that Emily's here. If you really wanted me to be honest, I would say that I could have lived my life quite happily without being a father, without children. And that doesn't mean I don't love Emily, it means that I can look at my life as it might have been and I wouldn't have been unhappy about it.'*

For some men, parenthood comes as a pleasant surprise: *'I thought I'd hate being a father. And I don't. It's not as hard for me as it is for Caroline, but it's part of me. Being a father, taking on some of that responsibility, that's who I am.'*

For others, like Matt, parenthood comes too early: *'I still wish, much as I'm happy to have Lucy here, that Hilary and I had been able to spend more time together just the two of us. We'd only been together six months when we found out Lucy was on the way. And she wasn't planned. We'd gone on holiday and the change in time-zones had meant that Hilary's taking the pill wasn't as effective as it should have been. So she was about five months pregnant before we even realised. And then there was no option. I don't know if we'd have gone on to have children eventually, or even if we'd have stayed together, but now we are together, I wish I knew her better.'*

REALITIES

In the months leading up to the birth mothers-to-be may look at their partners and wonder what sort of father they'll make. Sometimes the realities can be a pleasant surprise.

Jennifer's husband Gordon, was very supportive when she was finding breastfeeding difficult: *'He never suggested I should stop because he* knew I wanted to breastfeed and he knew it was the best thing for the baby, so when everyone else was saying to me, "Oh give him a bottle for a while," Gordon kept me going, saying, "Oh, I'm sure you could carry on till three months like you wanted," and I'm really glad we did it.'

Fiona has also had a good start to parenthood: *'I've been amazed. I've been amazed just how loving and supportive Ian has been. If Joe wakes in the night, it's usually for a feed, but Ian gets up anyway and brings him from his basket over to the bed because I still find it very difficult to move with the pain from the scar. And I've found that the best way for me to feed Joe is to sit up and place him on a pillow and then, when I want to turn him round to feed from the other side, I just turn the pillow, and that way I don't have to lift the baby up. But if he's wet and he needs his nappy changing, Ian will do that.'*

Some mothers find that the father takes a while to adapt – often getting stuck over very minor details or tasks. Hilary's partner, Matt, baulks at one particular duty: *'I will not, not, not go out with the pram. Every time I walk down the street with Lucy in her pram, people look at me like I've abducted her.'*

Beverley is amazed at how fatherhood seems to have shortened her husband's memory and concentration span: *'The daily care of Josh is still very much my responsibility. If I've got to go into work early or something, I'll say to Alistair, "Can you give him breakfast?" and he'll say to me, "What does he have, then?" I find it incredible that he can't have noticed he's had a jar of baby breakfast every morning at eight o'clock for the last month and a half.'*

Agnes had an unhappy start which took great courage to overcome: *'I didn't enjoy things when we first came home. I was frightened by the baby, by looking after him, and worried about the breastfeeding all the time. And Paul was getting really upset about it. We were hardly speaking to each other and had terrible rows and we couldn't wait for Sam to go to sleep and then it would be, "Don't wake the baby! Don't wake the bloody baby!"'*

Adapting to the sharing of tasks sometimes has to be negotiated; it does not always happen easily or naturally, as Faith discovered: *'Ross wanders round holding Jordan and showing him off to his friends and his family, very much the proud father, beaming all over his face, but that doesn't mean he won't just hand him back to me when Jordan starts to cry.'*

Paula suggests that maybe men think differently to women anyway and parenthood just emphasises this difference: *'As a mother, you're always thinking about a million different things. You've always got food and the sleeps on your mind, whereas I don't think fathers have at all. So they leave it to you. And you do it because they don't. If I sat here and said, "I'm not going to do anything at all", Neil would probably get his act together. But it would be more stressful than it's worth, watching him do something like try to feed the baby. It's all: "How hot does it have to be?" and "Which teat should I use?" And then watching the actual feeding is a nightmare because the baby turns her head away and then she'll spit it out, and Neil will go, "Oh, my God! Oh, my God!" And I think, "Why don't I just do it myself?"'*

EVEN WHEN the responsibility goes the other way, there are still difficulties to be negotiated, as Mark points out: *'Where am I supposed to go when I'm out on my own with her and she needs her nappy changed? There's a mother-and-baby room at Asda. Not a parents' room. And if it was a parents' room, all those breastfeeding mothers would probably be up in arms saying that they used to have somewhere nice and quiet to feed without men walking in and now they don't any more. How about one room for feeding and one room for nappy changing?'*

With responsibilities come frustrations and resentments: that is what responsibility means. If there weren't demands you didn't want to fulfil, or tasks you didn't want to do, you wouldn't be human. There are bound to be times when one or both of you resents:

- The baby
- Your partner
- The world in general.

Melanie describes how she decided to make her partner get involved: *'Just when I was starting to get the hang of it all, when Hamish was about seven weeks old, he came down with a cold and it kept him awake almost every night for a week. He didn't want feeding, or changing, or anything, he just had this really runny nose and he was miserable. The first couple of nights Simon just slept right through it and I lay awake nursing this baby and seething with resentment. The third night, I woke Simon anyway and asked him to go down and make me a cup of chocolate. I wasn't desperate for a cup of chocolate, but I was fed up of suffering alone and didn't see why he should get away with it any more.'*

ROLE REVERSAL

THE GENERAL lack of recognition and feeling of exclusion from the baby world becomes even more apparent to those men who not only participate in the child-rearing, but adopt responsibility for the greater part of it.

Mick took on full-time responsibility for their son and found the coffee morning circles hard to crack: *'When Eileen became pregnant, it was obvious to us both that she would have to go back to her job after maternity leave. I am in the final year of my degree course and the chances of me landing a highly-paid job immediately are thin. So it was a matter of circumstances rather than deliberate choice, but we both felt it was the best thing to do, and why shouldn't it work? The main things I've found over the last six months, though, is that I've probably been much lonelier than Eileen ever would. People just don't think to include me in activities, or if they are having a get-together, it is clear they don't want me there while they are talking about breastfeeding or sex.'*

TIME

WHEN YOUR resources are stretched to the limit, one of the hardest things can be finding time for each of you as a person. Your baby comes first, your partner comes second . . . where does that leave you?

Cathy explains how she felt: *'There's a song, "You don't know what you've got till it's gone." I felt like that. I didn't know I had so much freedom until it was taken away from me.'*

Beverley confesses how she needed her own space now and again: *'In those first three months, I had such a lot of work on, finishing the university course, and I had these dissertations to do, and my friends were tremendously helpful. I'd say, "Can you just take Josh out for the afternoon because I've got all this reading to do?" And they'd take him. Of course, I did have work, but I could have done it when he was asleep. I just wanted him away from me for a while.'*

There will not only be pressures on your time now, but your time for the foreseeable future, as Matt describes: *'Up until now, I could have chucked it all in, gone off across the Sahara, sailed round the world. Now, I can't up and off so easily. So although you're tied down from your own choosing, you are still tied down.'*

Dawn, mother of triplets, recognises that it is not only a mother who feels the pressure: *'It's put a tremendous pressure on Peter although he's never directly said so. Everyone talks about all this pressure on women when they have to make the decision about whether to stay at work or stay at home, but nobody talks about the pressure on a man because it's taken for granted that he'll have to provide for his family. I hadn't realised just how great a burden that could be on a family until it happened to us. I know Peter worries about his work a lot more, always wants to do regular hours, because money is a big issue.'*

People talk about a conspiracy of silence that leaves them in the dark as to what life will really be like with a baby. Sometimes this conspiracy can be broken down, and it's often easier for women to do this especially if they know each other well enough and have the courage to be honest about the realities of their daily living. Where the conspiracy is less easily broken down, however, is on the matter of couples and their relationships. It seems to be okay to admit you're finding the baby difficult, but it's less easy for:

- Men to find someone to talk to about how they feel
- Men or women to admit the difficulties in their own relationship that the arrival of the baby has brought about.

Wendy agrees that most people hide their true feelings: *'When you get together with a group of mothers, a lot of the time it's all incredibly twee.*

Everything's lovely, and their husbands are wonderful, and this from people I know have had blazing rows the night before.'

TIME FOR YOU AS A COUPLE

IF YOU make sure you set aside some time for you to be together as a couple, whether this is at home once your baby is asleep, or by asking someone to babysit so that you can go out regularly, this will provide a valuable base on which you can keep your relationship alive and let it grow. You are important to each other in your own right, not just as the mother/father of this baby.

Tim's comments are typical of many parents: *'I just wasn't prepared for the total transformation a baby would make to our lives. I hardly saw Joyce in those early days, and whenever I did, we were both so tired we had nothing to say to one another. We didn't let ourselves enjoy it, I think.'*

Sometimes one partner clearly resents the baby's presence, as Kay explains: *'I love being a parent. I love being a mother to this little tiny baby. Geoff hates it. He finds it really difficult. He wakes up in the morning some-times and the baby's crying and he groans and says, "Oh, no." He wishes the baby was . . . well, if not there, not born yet. Or that there was someone else to look after him. He feels the baby gets between us and interferes.'*

Madeleine is finding it difficult to nurture her relationship with her partner: *'I am finding it hard, yes, but that's because I feel I've lost Ross, in a way. Even when he is here and Jack's asleep, we can't count on more than an hour in peace before Jack wakes up again – he has a very poor sleeping pat-tern – we're nothing but Jack's servants at the moment.'*

Some parents find that the baby can bring them closer, as Zoë explains: *'David gets a lot more from me now. And I've got a lot more time for him. Our leisure time, our time together, is much more positive and active now that we've got a baby. We do more things together instead of going off to do our own thing.'*

Ingrid is happy with how her relationship is growing: *'To be honest, I think he likes me being more dependent on him. The home is now the centre*

*of my life and I'm able to give John and our home much more than I did before
now, and I'm giving because of the baby.'*

Others find that they need to make a positive effort, however, to
maintain their previous closeness, but that effort is usually worth-
while, says Simon: *'We live in a small village and we have let it be known*

that we would like a babysitter every Wednesday evening at eight o'clock so Melanie and I can go out. We don't go anywhere fantastic, usually just drive to one of the neighbouring villages for a drink and a go at the crossword, and a chance to catch up on what's been happening without getting distracted into watching the television and not talking. So it's like magic, every Wednesday at eight o'clock one of the village teenagers arrives and out we go. Hamish knows them all by sight, we know them all and their families, so it's been a wonderful arrangement. We know that we're going to have a chance to talk about something at a definite time during the week, and that's really helped keep channels of communication open.'

Beverley is sure that it did help that they were both very verbal people: *'When I was feeling down, I'd tell Alistair I was feeling down. When he was feeling down, he'd tell me. So we both knew we were going through similar things. And the feelings were similar. Like, "God, this baby's really boring sometimes." That was when Josh was tiny, he's four months old now and very smiley, so he's made us more smiley.'*

CHANGES IN YOUR RELATIONSHIP

AS YOU move from being a childless couple to being a family, the relationship between the two of you as parents will certainly change. Sometimes these changes begin to be apparent before your baby is born.

Fiona describes how she and her partner actually see a lot more of each other now, but nearly always in a domestic setting, which could become stifling: *'Towards the end of the pregnancy, I didn't fancy going out much. Before that, we used to go out two or three nights a week, just to the pub for a drink, or round to see friends. Before you have a baby you can just spend money like that! But as the baby was getting nearer, I wanted to stay in, so Ian stayed in, too, and we've become much more home based, more home conscious. So although we can't get out as much now, we were already getting used to it. It had been a slow change. If it had been dramatic, like, "He's born so we can't go out to the pub any more", it would have been disastrous for our relationship.'*

SEX

FOR MOST women who have just given birth, sex is the last thing on their list of priorities. You may be having to cope with any or all of the following:

- A new baby
- Feeding
- Stitches
- A sore perineum
- A caesarean scar
- Changes in your body as a result of the pregnancy
- Changes in your body as a result of the delivery.

Given this, it is often a source of amazement to new parents in those first weeks how any couples ever manage to have more than one baby.

It can be a shock to see how your body has changed – nine months is a long time and you become used to your pregnant shape – there

may be a caesarean scar, stretch marks or just a flabby stomach. Laura describes her shock: *'I'll never forget lying there in the bath – you have to soak the bandages from the caesarean scar off in the bath by yourself, and I didn't want to do it – I was terrified of what I'd find underneath. And I was horrified when I did see. There was this enormous smile at the bottom of my stomach and it looked grotesque. I turned away from my own body then, and I still haven't accepted this new body as my own. I don't know when we'll start having sex again because if I can't look at myself without feeling sick, what will Paul think?'*

It can be a shock to your system to try to forget the birth and babies and remember your body also has a sexual function, as Deirdre discovered: *'It was a joke – Mark wanted to and I was just disbelieving. All I'd thought about in relation to my nether regions for the past few weeks was how to go to the loo and relieve my constipation without straining my stitches.'*

WHILE MANY books breezily suggest that 'somewhere around the six-week check' is the norm for resumption of sexual intercourse, nobody knows quite where they get this figure from. Some couples may feel up to it. Some certainly won't, feeling so tired, emotionally drained and overwhelmed – sex is the last thing on their minds. Common sense will tell you, for example, that if you have had an episiotomy, you would be wise to wait until the stitches have dissolved and you feel comfortable again.

In most cases, whatever feels right to both of you will occur naturally, happily and without problem – whether this is at six weeks, 16 or 62.

Unfortunately, for some couples, it is not so straightforward. A typical scenario is this:

- The new mother wants to feel loved and wanted and enjoys having her partner's supporting arms around her
- The partner feels that this physical contact is an invitation to resume sexual intercourse
- The new mother feels too fragile to cope with sex yet and pushes her partner away
- The partner feels angry and rejected
- The new mother feels angry and a failure.

LACK OF communication, a fear of being hurt, physically and emotionally, can make things worse for a couple experiencing this kind of stressful situation. What you need to do is talk about how you feel, but that may be one of the most difficult things in the world. If you are both unhappy with your situation, talking to a counsellor or someone from an organisation like Relate might help.

It will also help if you both remember that there are no time limits on this, although you may both feel under pressure to resume a 'normal' sex life.

Physical check-ups, even the most routine, raise the question of contraception, which may be way down on your list of concerns, as it was on Raisa's: *'First of all the nurse at the hospital asked me what sort of contraception we were planning to use and I just looked at her aghast. I'd only just had a baby. Did she think we were going to run home and leap into bed with gay abandon? I could barely walk.'*

IF YOU find it too early to be making more decisions, don't feel rushed, just bear it in mind for when the time is right – as Erica did: *'I know they have it listed on their forms so they have to ask about what you're*

*going to use, but the fact that we'd been asked about it before we left the hos-
pital, and then the doctor at the six-week check was saying, "Yes, there's no
reason why you shouldn't go ahead and have intercourse now," made me feel
as if everyone else in the world was only waiting for the go-ahead and we
were the odd ones out. But I just had no interest in it, none whatsoever.
Whenever I went to bed, I fell asleep the instant my head hit the pillow.'*

For some women, the desire to have sex with their partners may be
there, but it can get mixed up and confused with other worries which
hold you back.

Fiona says she was terrified: *'Quite honestly, that's the only way to put it.
I knew my body was different, but I wasn't sure how different it would seem
to Ian. Even when the stitches – and I didn't have that many – had healed,
and I knew I was as well as I was going to get, I didn't want to have sex. I
was worried that my vagina would have stretched – you hear such horrible stories – and that it would feel all loose and sagging, and that would have made
me feel so old and unattractive. If he had said anything, anything at all, that
first time, about it feeling different, I'd have never let him near me again, I
swear.'*

RECOVERING FROM the physical aftermath of labour does impact
upon your sexual relationship with your partner because it is here that
all physical and emotional barriers come down. We can only go on
hiding our worries for so long and then we have to face them. If you
have lingering doubts over the way your body feels to you and your
partner after labour, perhaps it will help to remember the following:

- Your vagina is made of flexible, elastic tissue
- Childbirth is a job for which your body has been designed
- Your body's powers of recovery are remarkable
- Having a baby adds a dimension to your relationship rather than
  taking one away.

THESE FACTS alone may give you the confidence to feel proud and
happy in what you and your partner have achieved together and to
enjoy the new dimension to your relationship that sex after children
can bring.

Parveen describes a very common feeling amongst new parents: '*It didn't appeal at first, and do you know why? Because I was frightened of being a grown-up. Sex before was play, now we knew just how serious it could be. It still has its playful element, but underneath that we're adults now — with adult responsibilities, and we have to be responsible to each other as adults. There's a commitment there that there wasn't before.*'

It can be especially difficult to distance yourself from anything to do with babies: '*I did not enjoy making love when I was still breastfeeding, I must say. It didn't bother John, if I'm honest, but it did me. As soon as I started feeling anything, I could feel the let down reflex begin and that was very disconcerting. It made me think of the baby and then worry about whether the baby would wake up and then my mind would have wandered so much I'd lost whatever impetus or desire I might have had in the first place.*'

BREASTFEEDING AND the fact that milk may be released during sex may be highly attractive to some men, more problematic for others.

Callum describes how he felt towards his partner: '*I really didn't have any sexual feelings towards Mandy when she was breastfeeding. If I did think about her in that way, I'd go all uncomfortable. I can remember my own mother feeding my baby brother, so the images of that were very strong and got in the way.*'

Other men, like Peter, do feel differently about other aspects of sex: '*I was frightened of hurting her, I was frightened of upsetting her, I felt guilty asking for sex as if by doing that I was asking her* not *to think about the baby for a while. Certainly in those early days it was baby baby baby all the time.*'

Some women are hesitant about having sex again because they can tell that their vagina is dryer than it used to be and are worried that they won't be able to enjoy intercourse because of this. However, there are solutions, one of which is recommended by Tina: '*For the first time in my life, I knew what KY jelly was for. It was like a revelation.*'

IN A SURVEY of its readers, *New Generation*, the quarterly journal of the National Childbirth Trust, found that the time when couples resumed sex after the birth of a baby varied a great deal:

How old the baby was	*Percentage*
Around a month old: an enthusiastic fifth	20%
Between one and three months old: a popular choice	45%
Between three and four months old: a few more by this time	18%
Around five to seven months: a sizeable minority	13%

Of these mothers, most felt that the timing was right for them, although some would have liked it to be later.

Those who felt that they would have preferred to wait mentioned a variety of problems that had an effect on this decision:

- Pain and discomfort
- Stitches
- Not feeling physically ready
- Loss of libido (i.e. not feeling like it!)
- Tiredness
- Not feeling emotionally ready
- Not feeling happy about their body.

SOME COUPLES would have liked to have started making love again much earlier than they did, but found that the things that stopped them were:

- It was too painful
- They were waiting for stitches to heal
- They were too tired
- They didn't feel like it.

There were also couples who had not yet resumed sexual intercourse at the time of the survey, and some of these couples had babies that were between one and two years old.

A PARENT AND A LOVER

SOME PEOPLE find their sexual identity and confidence is confirmed and enhanced through the birth of their baby. At last, all that their bodies have been designed to do, they have done. Nature has focused

all that sexual activity towards this one goal: the birth of the next generation. Suddenly sex becomes more meaningful in the context of
this fertility.

Other couples, often those for whom there was previously a split
between their sexual fulfilment and any thoughts of procreation, find
the merging of the two, their libido and their parental role (a merging that the arrival of a baby forces them to acknowledge) rather
harder to cope with.

If you and your partner are having difficulties – for example, if one
of you is ready to resume your sex life and the other is not – it might
be worth taking some time out and thinking through what your feelings really are:

- Are you saying you're tired all the time because you're worried
  that your partner won't find your new body attractive?
- Are you pretending you don't want to make love to her because
  you're worried that she will reject you?
- Are you frightened of hurting her?
- Are you frightened of being hurt?

Madeleine and her partner Ross worked things through together: *'I
thought it would take a couple of months, to be honest, for me to feel like having sex again, and I was about right. We started kissing and cuddling in bed
again and having some sort of sexual activity when Jack was about two
months old. It was around five months before I felt like trying intercourse
again, and we did it once and I didn't enjoy it so we went back to the things
we'd been doing before. But that was fine, we were having sex in a way, even
though it wasn't intercourse, but it kept us both happy enough so that it wasn't
a problem.'*

Hilary found a solution that suited her new family: *'One of the best
things that happened, ironically enough, was that I stopped trying to
breastfeed when Lucy was around five weeks old. Not only could I get more
sleep, which made me feel better, but Matt could do the night feeds and he
really quite enjoyed that! Cooing over her, he could take part where before
he'd been excluded. And that meant when he came back to bed, the bed
was ours. Before, sex had been non-existent because Matt had always felt
that I was "the baby's". He said to me last night, "I thought that your*

breasts were the baby's and not mine, or not ours." Lucy had definitely had first call.'

Vicky expresses a fear which many new mothers experience: *'I was very hesitant at first. I'd read about how some men didn't like their wives having children because it stretched the vagina and sex wasn't as good afterwards. I thought, "I know I've been stretched down there, Anthony's head was so enormous that it's bound to have had an effect on me, even with the episiotomy." So I kept putting it off and finding excuses. I just didn't want to face the possibility that my husband would go off me, that I wasn't going to be attractive any more.'*

IF YOUR problems don't seem to be solving themselves, and don't seem likely to go away of their own accord, then both of you may benefit from counselling to help you through this time. Counselling simply means talking to someone else. Sometimes just talking about your confusions and worries can help make your feelings clearer.

Asking for outside help does not mean that you are a bad parent or that you are a bad partner. It means that you are being a good enough parent and partner to know when you do need help.

DIFFICULTIES

WHEN YOU are both learning how to be parents, it is easy for one parent to assume that the other has come along with them on the learning curve.

Madeleine's story is amusing, but fortunately, most new parents end up learning very quickly after their first few mistakes: *'Last night, Ross got Jack ready for bed and he came through and the baby had dungarees on. And I said, "He can't sleep in that!" And Ross said, "Why not? It's all I could find." So you find yourself giving a lecture on strangling.'*

Laura says she and her husband began to argue because she was falling into traditional roles – which was something she hadn't really wanted to do: *'So Paul would go off to work every day and leave me alone in the house with this tiny baby, and because the house was then my domain, I felt people – and Paul – would criticise me if it wasn't absolutely perfect. And then if Paul did try to contribute, I'd get cross with him — about the housework or about the babycare: "Don't pull the nappy tapes too tight!" "Don't let the soap get in her eyes!" "Don't you know that I don't keep the soup tins in that cupboard!" And if he didn't take part, I'd shout at him for not taking part. "Why have you left these soup tins all over the floor?" "Why haven't you bathed her?" I wasn't much fun to live with those first few months. Mind you, it's easy to see that now. It wasn't then.'*

Madeleine offers some more home truths, but would be the first to admit that parenthood is easier for her because she's 'doing it' all the time, so has her routines: *'Jack's got to be calm before he'll go to sleep, so it's no good playing with him after his bath and getting him really excited, which is what Ross does, and then putting him in his basket and saying, "Go to sleep." I got very cross yesterday and Ross said, "Oh, I'm only playing," and I felt like Big Bad Mother.'*

SOMETIMES EITHER one of you will kick against the situation, perhaps finding the responsibility of a family too overwhelming, perhaps resenting the arguments that happen now in ways they never did before, perhaps starting an argument for reasons you can't quite put your finger on . . . perhaps having genuine disagreements over bringing up baby.

In the early weeks many of these disagreements are over minor points, but you may already be discussing childcare and finding your views differ, as did Ruth: *'We have very different views sometimes, on the way that children should be brought up. It's surprising, but it's not something you talk about beforehand. You just assume everyone thinks the same way as you.'*

Tina and her partner David had some bad evenings when Oliver was tiny: *'He would scream and scream and neither of us knew what to do, and David got it into his head — I think probably from his mum — that what we ought to do was give him gripe water. Well, I resisted that, because I was resisting everything people were telling me. And I was very impressed with a book I'd just read and I was very stubborn, and I would only do what the author said and she said that a baby only needs breast milk so I thought, "Right, he's not having any of this gripe water." So we listened to him scream every evening and it went on for five days. I tried everything to pacify him. Everything. And in the end I gave him gripe water. And I wish I'd given it to him before, actually, as it did seem to help.'*

TALK TO your partner. The more you talk, about how you feel, about how you want to feel, the easier it will be for you to be honest with each other and to make informed decisions as a couple about all aspects of your lives together. If you are reading this book before your baby arrives, then start talking now, in this precious time before you have a baby to distract you, about your beliefs and attitudes and hopes for parenting. If your baby is already here, make the effort to be together as a couple, however difficult that is to achieve.

SINGLE PARENTS

WITH SINGLE-PARENTING on the increase, the need for relevant support and information is ever more urgent. Single parents, whether male or female, need different, perhaps more proactive sources of support, available easily and at any time of the day or night. For a lone parent, trying to cope with a screaming baby all alone in the middle of the night, there isn't a sleeping partner in the next room to call: such complete isolation can be terrifying.

Given that most single parents were married or in a relationship when they became pregnant and it was during pregnancy or shortly after the birth that their partner left them, their own emotional strength and balance has already received a battering. Frances recollects the time her partner left her:

'I was eight months pregnant, feeling huge and ugly, with no interest in anything but what was going on inside my bump. Gary, my partner of ten years hadn't wanted a baby and had been becoming more and more distant from me. We never discussed names or whether it would be a boy or girl – it was as if the baby didn't exist. Then he left me – he went abroad for a couple of months. Funny thing is, I've seen him around town with another woman and guess what – she's pregnant!'

Jo felt very vulnerable to advice: *'I read in one book, I can't remember which, that if your baby was hot you should give her boiled water to drink, so*

I boiled this water and cooled it, and then she didn't want it, and I thought, "I'd have been better off not bothering about any of this and just feeding her as normal", but you've no one to stop you when you go off down this road of boiling water when you're on your own.'

SOME OF the strongest stresses occur at the point where you can't hand the baby over to a partner while you recover your energy . . . or your sanity, as Nicola describes: *'When she was very little and I was finding it hard going through the days on hardly any sleep, the health visitor said to me, "Wake her up and feed her before you go to bed, and then she might sleep through." And it was the worst thing I could have done. I went in at something like eleven o'clock, and she was asleep, and I woke her up and gave her a breastfeed and that was it, she was awake. At three o'clock in the morning I was still sitting there thinking, "Why did I do this? She was asleep. This was very, very stupid of me." I've never felt so lonely or unsupported as that night.'*

THOSE WHO arrive at single motherhood are sometimes 'older' mothers, those who have chosen to follow a career, or travel, before deciding to have children. They may either have chosen to be single, but much more frequently their partner has left them during their pregnancy. There can be positive advantages to being a more mature single mother as Susanne shows: *'I am a lot more patient and I have a lot more empathy with my daughter than I would have done ten years ago, which was the "normal" time, around the age of 30, to have children – when most of my friends were having children. I can appreciate her a lot more because it was such a deliberate choice to have her, and I never feel trapped by having a small baby, the way I know some mothers do, because I've "done" the travelling, I've "done" the world. Also, I'm reasonably financially secure, I have my own house, and I'm well-established in my work – I don't have to worry about getting on with my career because I'm already at a place I want to be in my career. Despite the tiredness, I've felt refreshed and renewed by Katy.'*

WITHOUT LOOKING at the latest exact figures for families who are being brought up by a lone parent, we all know from the intermittent government press releases that such families are increasing. At the time of writing, around 15% of children are being brought up by only one parent, and most of the lone parents are mothers; some by choice, some not.

'Doing it all myself, it got pretty manic. It got to the point where I would never leave the house without the Handiwipes.'

Sometimes, however, the circumstances are not what the mother herself would have chosen. For some women, the arrival of their much-wanted baby becomes a time tinged with sadness as they greet their baby alone, without the baby's father.

Beth, for example, whose partner left her when she was seven months pregnant, unwilling to participate in family life or take on the responsibility for a child, found the experience daunting: *'The absolute worst time was when I was in labour. Nothing can come close to that. Here was this moment that we'd both originally looked forward to so much, talked about, something I thought we* both *wanted and now here I was on my own. I sat here in the front room as the contractions got stronger and I wept and wept. All the time I was trying to centre in on the baby, make the time of the birth a joyful one, but I was struggling. There were people I could have called, friends who'd promised to be with me, but I could feel that the labour was slow, and I was mourning for the way things should have been. I think I'd been waiting for Alan to come back, and waiting for "real life" to begin again, and now, with these contractions, and the pain building up, I knew "real life" never would. This was real life now, this baby that was coming, and it was going to go on like this, and I felt very, very lonely.'*

Naomi's partner walked out too, although at first she hoped it was just an overreaction: *'I knew he was hesitant. I knew he had doubts but, to be honest, so did I. I think everyone does. You wouldn't be normal if you didn't wonder, "Have I done the right thing?" or "Is this really what I want?" But the thing is, you're supposed to work your way through that together. He had decided it wasn't for him after all. "Babies", he kept saying in this deep mournful voice, "babies." And shake his head. So off he went. What about me? I couldn't go. I was stuck. And, much as I love her, I'm still stuck.'*

THERE IS no evidence, despite people looking for it, to show that children brought up by lone parents are any less happy than children brought up by two parents. Yet research does show that single-parent families are more likely to be living in poor housing and on a limited income. The most common causes of stress for single parents seem to be:

- Money
- Loneliness
- Feeling under pressure
- Exhaustion
- Feeling that you're not coping
- Not having another adult to talk to
- Not wanting to ask for help.

WHEN YOU are a single parent, by choice or otherwise, your lot can seem doubly difficult as you take on parenting roles that are usually shared between two people. It can be difficult to ask for help: feelings of guilt or failure, or an idea that you should be able to manage on your own, get in the way. Yet some parents who *have* a partner have to ask for help: why shouldn't you?

Both Kathy and Liz explain how they often feel:

'It just sometimes seems easier for me to go out and get something done myself than to explain to someone else what I want done, or what I want from the shops, or anything like that. Soldiering on, they call it.'

'I seem to have less time than anyone else I know. They gather round and discuss things like: "Shall I go back to work?" I don't have the luxury of time and peace to think – I just had to get on and go back to work otherwise we'd have been out on the streets.'

BECOMING A family is a demanding business. Adjusting to the new way of life can be fraught with problems of routines, relationships, practical arrangements and emotional demands. Being a single parent can make that business of becoming a family a lonely task, even if it is what you have chosen, and often a sad task, too, if it is not what you have chosen. Either way, the responsibility involved can be devastating. But most single parents would not change the fact that they had their baby.

Terri admits that she gets lonely: *'I get overwhelmed, yes, but it was my choice and this is what I want to do. It's been much better lately as I'm now sharing my house with another single parent and that's given us such freedom in the evenings to go out and do things, we're not used to it. We never had so many social invitations before!'*

Indra's baby Rascha is six months old: *'When I look at her I feel a tremendous sense of achievement. I mean, look at her: she's fine, she's thriving, she smiles, and we have each other to love.'*

Lucy can also see the positive side: *'One thing that has happened, that I don't think would have happened in quite this way if Steve hadn't just walked out, is that Christopher has a very strong, very caring extended family. My parents see him a lot, even Steve's parents see him a lot, have him over for afternoons, soon for nights away, I think, which is right, as they're his grandparents too. So Christopher's growing up with a wide network of relatives to turn to should he ever need to, which I think is something very positive for him.'*

THERE ARE many associations and organisations that try to make life easier for single parents and you will find that they have much to offer in the way of a listening ear and smart advice. But no matter how much practical help you receive, for many single parents, the truth, as Beth explains it, is like this: *'I have lots of people who help, who sympathise, who share, who understand, who talk, but none of them, not one of them can ever feel the same about Rose as I do because none of them are her parent. I can never talk to anyone about "our" daughter. Rose has one other parent, and he's not here. How am I going to explain that to her in any way that seems fair?'*

IF YOU are a single parent and share some of these feelings, it may help to remember that you don't have to carry the burden alone all the time – there are other single parents out there who feel just like you do, and getting together to share your frustrations and resentments can be refreshing enough to allow you to focus on the positive things in life again.

CHAPTER *five* You and the world

THE WORLD can suddenly seem very different when we've had a baby. For the first weeks we may make a safe little nest for ourselves, but then we must not only come out into the world again but also find our new place within it.

People in the street will turn and smile, and you may feel that the sun is shining on you and your new baby.

On other days it may feel like you've become public property, that every passing stranger has a comment or a criticism: *'I wouldn't bring him out without a hat, dear'*; *'If I were you, I'd take that dummy away from her.'*

Your view of the world will depend on your mood, the weather, if your baby slept last night . . . so will your view of the people in the world: your mother who has suddenly become a grandmother; your partner's parents now have their own new grandchild, too; your father will now be your child's grandfather. Friends will look on you differently now you're a mother or a father. Everything shifts and adjusts.

For some, those adjustments bring nothing but joy, as they revel in their role of new parent. For others, the changes are harder to accept.

Either way, your baby is at the centre of it, at the heart of your new world.

BACK HOME

AFTER YOU'VE given birth, it's common for parents to see things differently, not only on a global level, with more concern for the future of the planet, the environment and the victims of wars and disasters, but also on a small, localised level. Even the house and your own street can look different. That's because you're different.

At home

NAOMI DESCRIBES how different her house appeared when viewed with the eyes of a concerned parent: *'Everything was potentially danger-ous. Houseplants. Handbags. Table corners. The kitchen was a complete no-go area. I felt nervous doing the ironing in case he pulled on the cord and tipped everything over and the house burned down, and my mother had to remind me that he was seven weeks old, asleep in his basket and about ten feet away from the ironing board.'*

The outside world

MEG WAS amazed at how strange and new her local chemist's appeared to her – after only two days in hospital following the birth: *'I asked James to stop the car outside the chemist's on the way home from the hospital and I popped in to get some Panadol. I found myself looking at the people and the shelves in a strange way, as if I'd been gone years and I expect-ed them all to be different. Everything seemed very brightly coloured and unfamiliar.'*

The first outing with your baby will be exciting, thoroughly planned and, if you're on your own as Rose was, it may be quite an ordeal: *'The first time I took Thomas out for a walk in his pram – we wanted to go to the park, well, we got there alright, he slept most of the way and I was pleased to think all this fresh air was doing him some good. But then on the way home he was crying and wanted a feed and I couldn't pick him up and push the pram at the same time, and the traffic seemed very noisy and very dangerous, and I could hear a dog barking which panicked me, and by the time I got home I was a bag of nerves.'*

IF YOU take your baby for her first outing and come home roaring with rage, you won't be the only one. Expect to meet, in the course of your baby's first year:

- Children's shops where the door is too narrow for a pram to go through
- Pubs that allow dogs in but not babies
- Restaurants that ask you not to breastfeed in public

- Hundreds of shops or shopping complexes where the place you want to go to is not on the ground floor, there's no lift, and certainly no one to help you up the stairs with the buggy.

Hilary describes one of the experiences she had with her daughter, Lucy: *'The world as I had known it was suddenly changed beyond recognition. I took Lucy up on the train to Victoria, which was fine, but then getting her across London on the Underground was a nightmare. So many places where there are only escalators and no lifts. And there's all these signs telling you to fold your pushchair on the escalator and carry it. Well, that's fine, but how am I supposed to carry the pushchair and Lucy and the two bags? Then I suppose I'd have to get to the bottom, put the pushchair up again, put her in it, push her a hundred yards and then repeat the whole process again for the next escalator down. And then all the way back up at the other end. So you throw safety and caution to the winds and you balance your way down this escalator, teetering on the edge of the step and everyone's giving you such hostile looks you go bright red. And then coming home we got to Victoria early and I thought we'd go and have a cup of coffee. Well, all the main restaurants and coffee shops are up a flight of stairs and then an escalator. No lifts. I asked. Who designs these places? How can they get away with it so that mothers and children are so completely excluded?'*

Rose finds her view of facilities provided for wheelchairs and pushchairs has changed too: *'Since I had Tom I've been much more in sympathy with the needs of disabled people. I'd always looked on things like "wheelchair access" as a bit of a luxury before, and now my heart leaps if I see one of those signs because I know I'll be able to get in with the buggy.'*

GETTING ABOUT

THERE ARE many ways of getting your baby from A to B: slings, prams, buggies, aeroplanes and supermarket trolleys can all transport babies.

There won't be many of us who don't take our baby somewhere in a car, however, during the first year, and very many of us bring our baby home from the hospital in one.

Car safety

IF YOU take your baby in a car, there are some basic rules to remember and observe religiously:

- Never put a seat belt around yourself and the baby. In a crash, the weight of your body would move forward until the seat belt stopped you. At 30mph, if you're of average size, you would squash your baby between you and the seat belt and exert a force on your baby's body so strong your baby might be crushed to death

- A babyseat is safer than a carrycot, although some doctors may recommend the use of a carrycot in exceptional circumstances; for example, if your baby is premature and very small

- Do not use rear-facing babyseats in the front of a car fitted with a passenger airbag. This is because the seat is so close to the dashboard that the expanding airbag itself is likely to cause serious injury in the event of a crash

- Rear-facing babyseats provide very high levels of protection. They are generally much safer than forward-facing babyseats

- Even rear-facing babyseats are safer if you strap them in on the rear seat rather than on the front passenger seat. Your baby is then even more protected from impact

- Strap your baby in

- – every single time.

Beth describes an incident that was nearly a tragedy: *'Car safety is about the only topic I get on my soapbox about. I hear people say things like, "We'll drive carefully", as they whizz off with the baby sitting on their knee, or "We'll go slowly", as if that made a difference. I want to scream at them, "It doesn't matter what you do. It's the other idiots on the road you have to watch out for". When Carla was three months old, we were hit by a lorry. Out of the blue. Not our fault. She was thrown about a great deal as we spun off the road, and she was covered in cuts and scratches from the broken glass from all the car windows. We even picked pieces of glass out of her nappy. The car was a wreck. But she was alive. But if we hadn't strapped her in, she wouldn't be.'*

LEGAL RESTRAINTS			
Who?	Where?		Who's responsible?
	Front seat	Back seat	
Baby/child under three years of age	Appropriate child restraint must be used	Appropriate child restraint must be worn	Driver
Child aged between three and eleven years and under 1.5 metres in height	Appropriate child restraint must be worn if available; if not, an adult seat belt must be worn if available	Appropriate child restraint must be worn	Driver
Child aged twelve or thirteen, or younger child if he or she is more than 1.5 metres in height	Adult seat belt must be worn if available	Adult seat belt must be worn if available	Driver

WHEN CHOOSING a car seat for your baby, bear the following points in mind:

- Infant carriers are used rearward facing, in either the front or the back
- The infant carriers that most shops stock are suitable for your baby from newborn to six or nine months of age and then you will need to invest in something more suitable for an older baby. The exact age will depend on the weight of your baby – some small babies may stay in a carrier until they are more than nine months old
- Many infant carriers have fabric or solid carrying handles. These are a great bonus as they mean you can lift the baby in and out of the car without waking her
- Make sure the seat has a harness that will hold your baby securely in place and is easily adjustable
- If the cover cannot be removed for washing, it will soon get dirty and messy. A removable cover is a sensible investment

- A head support may be another useful addition: it will stop your baby's head rolling uncomfortably around as you negotiate corners
- Not all seats fit all cars. It's worth checking that the one you've got your eye on will fit safely in your car. Most shops will let you take the seat to your car, and with the help of an assistant double-check the fit before buying.

> **Remember:** Beware of buying a child's car seat second-hand. If it has been involved in an accident, there may be no visible marks but the protective structure will have been weakened. It may be the worst bargain you ever bought.

Hands-free transport

THE MOST obvious advantage of a baby sling is that you can carry your baby about and still miraculously have your hands free to do other things.

There are:

● Front carriers

These are usually suitable for newborns onwards, and are very reassuring as the baby is carried close to you. The model you buy may need additional head support for a newborn. Some can be adapted into alternative positions as your baby grows. Some straps are too short to fit around men's chests, so double-check the fit before buying.

● Backpacks

These look a bit like putting your baby in a rucksack. They are usually sturdy and safe without weighing three tons. Only suitable once your baby can sit unsupported.

● Slings

These are a modern version of tying your baby to you with a blanket. They allow your baby to be carried in a variety of positions, usually off to the side.

There's no point describing in a book the virtues of a wide variety of models of baby carriers and slings: the essential thing is to find one which suits you and your baby.

Sylvia was enthusiastic: *'I couldn't understand why more people didn't use carriers. So much easier than trawling a buggy about. And you can't take a buggy on a walk through the woods.'*

It's not always so straightforward though. Raisa describes her experience with a sling: *'I was really looking forward to carrying Jody about in the baby carrier. I'd seen other mothers with their babies strapped to their chests like that and they always looked so safe and warm. I thought, "What a brilliant invention! Keeps the baby safe and lets the mum go out and about, too". So I got one. I used it once. I couldn't do the straps up properly by myself so I was really uncomfortable. Jody hated it and screamed all the time and wriggled about and, as this was happening right under my chin, I couldn't ignore it. Everyone in the shop turned to look at us and they could see this red-faced baby screaming away and squirming to try and get out of this contraption. I never tried it again as I was made so unhappy by the whole episode and sold it at the nearly-new sale.'*

NEW MODELS and new designs come on the market every season, so you need to have a good look around at what's currently available before buying.

TRANSPORTATION

- Make sure you buy any device for transporting your baby from a reliable manufacturer and from a reputable stockist
- Make sure you can fasten all the straps or press together all the fasteners unaided. It'll be pretty useless if you need someone to lift the baby into it, for example, and you're on your own most of the time
- Make sure it's comfortable, for you and the baby. Straps that suit most people may just mould themselves around your particular self at precisely the wrong point.

Buggies

THESE SEEM to be the universal mode of transport. Choose from the sort that fold flat – often sturdier but requiring two hands for the manoeuvre; or the 'umbrella fold' which, with one foot and a bit of practice, can be folded into a long thin shape for getting on to buses, single-handed.

Or there are 3-in-1 buggies which start off as a pram and convert to a pushchair for an older baby. There are even types that take a carrycot or a car seat – the variety is endless.

Apart from considering which of these types would suit you best, your main priorities will be:

Safety

- Manufacturers don't have to fit the five-point integral harness that is safest. If the buggy you choose doesn't have one, you can attach your own harness to the D-rings that most buggies come with, and that should stop your baby wriggling out
- When your baby is tiny, an upright buggy isn't safe or suitable. You will need one that reclines to a horizontal position.
- Make sure the model you choose conforms to British Safety Standards
- Before you leave the shop, make sure you know how to fold, collapse and reassemble the buggy with all straps, bars and harnesses in the right position.

Ease of use

- Buggies with fixed wheels are cheaper but some parents find the ones with swivel wheels more manoeuvrable
- Make sure the buggy will fold down with its raincover on (Imagine the alternative!)
- If you want to use your buggy a lot, you will not want it to weigh an oppressive amount. However, you don't want one so flimsy that it is neither robust nor safe. Compromise on the side of safety
- Do not buy if the handle height will give you backache.

Hazel describes her initial experiences going out and about with her baby: '*The first time I took him out in his little pram, I wheeled it really carefully to avoid all the bumps in the pavement, but then Ben would just stay awake and stare at the sky and the minute we got inside a shop and he was awake, he'd howl. I can understand that, though. If you go into a shop and you tilt your head back and look up at the ceiling, there's all these bright fluorescent lights, and it must be really blinding for a baby who can't turn his head away. But we've since found that the best thing is just not to be so precious with the pram – Ben actually likes the bumpy bits the best.*'

Prams

PRAMS CAN be great value second-hand, protect your baby from the weather very effectively, and provide a smooth, comfortable ride. You will need a pram tray to put shopping in, though, because it is more difficult to hook shopping bags over the handle (which you shouldn't do, anyway).

Agnes was able to afford both a pram and a buggy, for the ultimate in flexibility: *'I loved being out with my pram. I loved sailing down the street like Mary Poppins with this old-fashioned grey boat. Bump, bump, bump, and it was so well-upholstered and well-sprung that the baby didn't feel a thing. Trouble was, it wasn't very manoeuvrable down shop aisles or in the supermarket. I felt like we were refugees from a lost, more gracious age. So if I knew I was going to the supermarket, I'd put Sam in the buggy. For a more leisurely stroll in the park, the pram.'*

BALANCING THE BUDGET

SPEND TOO long reading the baby magazines, and you will begin to get the impression that every new baby requires a new nursery, completely outfitted by designers so that the up-to-the-minute changing unit matches the cunning little balloon stencils on the freshly emulsioned wall. Do not be deceived. If you have the time, the inclination, the space and the money, fine…it can be a real joy to plan and prepare a nursery in those last couple of months of pregnancy. But if your budget does not stretch to co-ordinated curtains, do not fret. Your baby will not mind if her cot is not new. To your baby, a second-hand cot is perfectly acceptable if she can sleep in it comfortably. Besides, after six months of wear, tear, bouncing about and using the top rail as a teething aid, most parents would be hard pressed to distinguish the new from the second-hand cot anyway. If you buy a second-hand item, check it meets current safety standards, can be easily cleaned and that any worn parts (like teething rails) can be easily replaced.

Adopting such a common-sense attitude can save you hundreds of pounds. Babies are expensive enough, why add to your problems? Do you think your baby will hesitate before possetting over that dry-clean-only lambswool sleepsuit? She will not. When, therefore, your friend with a toddler arrives with a basket of used baby clothes, do not sniff at them. Will they keep your baby warm? Comfortable? Then fine. Take up your sister's offer of the loan of a baby bath, your

SECOND-HAND SENSE

- Search through the classified ads to find the items you want
- Check all items carefully from a safety point of view
- Take advantage of offers to lend items
- Babies do not know – or care – if the outfit they are wearing is this season's or last. Wait for the sales
- Try to buy neutral colours that would suit any baby, boy or girl.

neighbour's offer to lend you a Moses basket. These things are used for such a short time, they can easily do service for several babies.

This can be more difficult if you have twins or more, like Dawn, but even so, make the most of any offer – you don't have to have three matching sets of everything:

'We've got triplets and one of the main differences between our children and others is that ours don't get many hand-me-downs. We also have to buy specialised equipment, like the pushchair that will take all three of them, which is much more expensive than either a double or a single buggy. And child benefit doesn't take that into account.'

THE ONLY thing that you must try to avoid buying second-hand is a car seat. Car seats may have been involved in accidents that have weakened their structure, without leaving any visible marks, and, in a second crash, may not protect your own baby.

Lihla's comments are not unusual: *'We don't have my salary now and that's made a terrific difference. As well as having to come to terms with not working, I'm having to come to terms with how expensive everything is. You always think you've just paid out for something, like nappies, and then you're paying out for them again. You buy a big item, like a buggy, and then you find you need a rain cover. And no sooner is the rain cover fitted than you need a parasol because there's a heat-wave on.'*

FRIENDS

'THE DAYS can be very monotonous, there's no getting away from that. Much as I love him, there's a limit to how many times I can push that train along the wooden track without screaming with boredom. I just have to go out.'

MANY WOMEN find that their friendships undergo a seismic shift once they have children. If friends from your 'previous life' don't have children, it may become more difficult to mix with them, and this at a time when you most need friendship.

Laura says: *'Our old social life has just disappeared. We used to go out to football matches with friends, go out to the pub on a Saturday night. Well, I think our friends still do, but we don't . . . we stay in and wait to see if we've won the National Lottery. Paul always says that if we win, the first thing he'll do is splash out on a babysitter so we can go out and celebrate.'*

KEEPING UP with old friends can take a bit more organising than it used to: you probably can't just pop in during the day because they're at work, and you can't get round there easily at night because your child doesn't go to sleep without a final breastfeed from you about 9 o'clock. And if you do go round at a weekend – having organised enough nappies, wipes, beakers, drinks and bottles – you find that your friends aren't set up for a toddler and you spend the whole time worrying about what your child will do first: pull the ornaments off the shelf or be sick on the new sofa. But if you do make the effort, you will not regret it.

Lynn has come to the conclusion that all friendships take a bit of effort: *'Whether you've had children or not, friendship is about doing things together and having things in common, and if you've had things in common before the baby, you'll still have them in common afterwards, even though you may not have babies in common, if you see what I mean. When my friend Ruth had a baby, I didn't see that it would stop us seeing each other – but that's because I knew so little about babies, actually. I thought if you put them down to sleep from Day One, they just slept. All through the night. So I'd make arrangements with her to go out for a drink as normal. Now that I've got a baby myself, I'm amazed she did it. But I remembered her example when I had Adam and, when I thought my world was getting too tiny, out to the pub I'd go.'*

Sometimes friends are for the short term: *'I became friends with this woman from my antenatal class for one reason and one reason alone. We had nothing in common, didn't like any of the same things, didn't go to any of the same places...but one thing we did do together, and that was give birth. That was it. We were on the postnatal ward for a couple of days together and after*

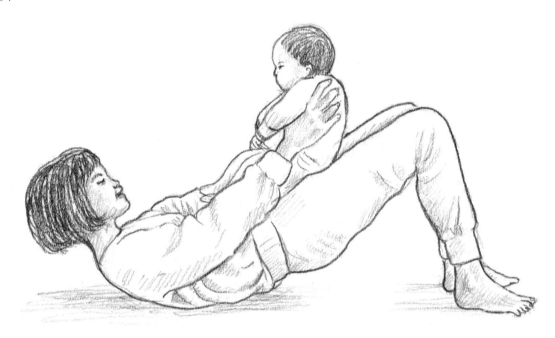

that we were never off the phone. Commiserating, comparing notes, saying, "Hurrah, one day nearer the day when they go off to school." For a couple of years, Fiona was my closest friend. And if it hadn't been for that coincidence, I'd never have spoken to her again and never thought twice about it.'

THERE ARE many advantages to getting together with other parents who have children of a similar age to your own. You can share common problems and suggest some hitherto undreamt-of solutions. You can share information about baby clinics, the health visitor to be aware of and the 'Babies Need Books' morning at the local library.

But there are some disadvantages to watch out for. In particular, beware the dreaded comparisons. You may have thought that comparisons could not possibly begin until the baby was old enough to do something remarkable, but one of the first lessons new mothers learn is that this is not the case. If you let it, the comparing game can begin on the postnatal ward. It quite often begins with a labour debriefing: *'Oh, I had a 58-hour labour, 27 stitches, three episiotomies, four forceps and twins…'* and moves swiftly on into the realms of newborns: *'Of course, my Jack weighed nine pounds at birth.'*

Novice players of this game will invariably make the wrong reply. If you say, *'Oh dear, how awful for you'*, you'll be told: *'Better to have* them big, though. *Healthier than the small ones. Now* yours *looks a bit on the small side...'* If you say, *'Oh, nine pounds! How lovely! How proud you must be',* you'll get a three–hour lecture on the trouble they're going to have keeping him fed, while you'll find your six-pound bundle a dream.

What is it about babies that brings out the worst in us?

Minor variations in achievements are what life is all about. They add interest. Beyond that, they are generally meaningless. Do you think the world will ultimately care whether Jessica ate sprouts first in her baby group?

On the move...

ANOTHER ASTONISHING fact about women and children is just how many women move house when their children are small. When this happens, you need to:

- Make contact with women in your new area who also have young children
- Keep up friendships from your old life.

Although the second may seem the only thing you can do at first, the first option is undoubtedly easier, if you know where to look. This is where national organisations really come into their own, as Maureen explains: *'I came here with a ten-day-old baby, knowing no one and having nowhere permanent to live. The NCT was a lifeline to us, as it is, no doubt, to many people across the country who move frequently with their jobs. I was a bit daunted going to the open houses at first, and wish they'd had the bumps-and-babies mornings the branch has now, but as you got to see the same faces, met people with children round the same age, and experienced the same tears and trials together, friendships soon developed, both for us and our children.'*

BOREDOM

SOME NEW parents sail through the first year saying, *'How come we never knew how much was on TV in the daytime?'* and enjoying every minute of their time at home. Being at home with your new baby can be quite restrictive, but you do have a great deal of autonomy: Shall I go shopping today or tomorrow? Shall I go to the clinic to get her weighed this week, or not bother? Shall I stay in bed with the baby until ten o'clock?

Other, more energetic, parents may ask themselves, *'What activities can I do with my baby?'* The isolated may simply say, *'What other ways are there to assuage loneliness?'*

Of course, the boredom factor can be alleviated by expeditions to the outside world, and these do depend on the seasons of the year.

Roisin admits: *'I found that winter very difficult. It would be dark by about half past four and we'd sit in and I'd think, "Oh, well, only eighteen hours till tomorrow."'*

Naomi found it very hard adjusting to being a mother at home: *'Although I loved Karen, and although I liked being at home on a day-to-day basis, I could see that it wouldn't suit me for the longer term. I was losing all my interests and everything that was "me". Then someone I met at the clinic told me about the National Women's Register, who had a local branch. Well, it didn't sound very me, but I thought I'd give it a go. And I really had a good time! We talk about everything, often with a guest speaker — and it made such a change from nappies and fishfingers. I feel very refreshed when I come home, with my mind recharged and full of energy.'*

RELATIVES

UNLESS WESTERN civilisation has undergone a remarkable revolution by the time this book hits the streets, I feel on fairly safe ground stating that your ideas about the best way to bring up children will probably differ from your own parents'; and your ideas will invariably differ from those of your partner's parents.

When it's your own family dispensing guidance, you can feel free to ignore it or state your objections to it. When it's your in-laws dishing out instructions to give the baby a bottle, or telling you, *'Just let her cry, she'll soon learn who's boss,'* it's much more difficult to tell them to stop interfering. And not very conducive to good family relationships, either.

If you're fighting the older-generation battle, either because you feel your decisions are being undermined or because your way of bringing up your baby is being interfered with, support from your partner can be vital. Make it clear that you have chosen together the best ways to bring up your baby and don't back down. If necessary, make it clear that you are going to pay some attention to medical progress over the last 30 years or so.

FOR MANY new parents, however, the arrival of a new baby is a time when old family relationships are rediscovered and re-cemented.

Olivia never had much to do with her mum before: *'I do now! Suddenly I have a much better understanding of what life was like for her when she was bringing us up, and I feel she understands what I'm going through.'*

IN MANY cultures, the closeness of the extended family is taken for granted.

Top ten from 30 years ago

Be prepared to explain to relatives the good reasons why all the following have fallen out of fashion:

- Four-hourly feeding
- Gripe water
- Overwrapping (there is all the difference between securely swaddling your newborn in a muslin and wrapping him in so many blankets he turns as red as a tomato)
- Rinsing dummies under the tap before popping them back in the baby's mouth
- Adding cereal to the bottle
- Leaving the baby to cry. ('Don't spoil him, dear')
- Fresh air – even if it involves prams, mittens and snow
- Ironing the vests and bibs
- Plastic pants. (I know one grandmother who battled valiantly to get them on over a disposable)
- Matinee jackets – sometimes alternated with bootees and sailor suits.

Jeanne enjoys the security and support it brings: *'My mum would have been mortified if I'd tried to get a childminder or a babysitter for Chantelle. I'm the youngest of her children, and the last one to have a baby, so she calls Chantelle "my baby's baby". And if I sent the "baby's baby" somewhere else to be looked after, she would be devastated. So I see my mum every morning and every night when I drop Chantelle off and pick her up again, and she always gives Chantelle her meals, and has something hot waiting for me if I'm going to be too late to cook dinner at home. I don't know what life would be like if our family wasn't close. I think I'd hate it.'*

IN OUR culture, children are often living a long way from their parents when they have children themselves, and this hard-won independence can suddenly seem like a hard-won extra burden.

Meg regrets not living closer: *'I'd love it if my mum was living round the corner. I'd absolutely love it. I'd love to pop in and see her in the afternoons, and get her shopping from the supermarket, and make her cups of tea. And I'd love it if she could pop in here and chat and play with Henry. People sometimes say, "Oh, you're lucky she's not here to interfere", and maybe if she was here all the time and interfering, I would feel like that. but I notice nobody complains about having their mum nearby when they've got to leave the baby with her while they pop to the hairdresser, or when they need her to babysit. I worry Henry's going to grow up not knowing his grandparents – you can't just pop to Dundee, given the cost, it's a twice-a-year expedition at the most – and I think that's a real loss in his life.'*

Lauren also misses the company of her family: *'I feel very sad that Rachel won't be as close to her grandparents as I wanted her to be – they live too far away. She hardly remembers them from visit to visit yet, and I think they feel a bit disappointed by that, as well. It's no good reminding myself* they'll love her just as much as my grandparents loved me – of course they will, but it won't be that day-to-day loving.'

AT AROUND the age of eight or nine months, many babies develop a fear or distrust of strangers, and if this coincides with a visit from grandparents your baby does not remember, she may well treat them with the same indifference she treats most strangers, which can be upsetting, or will actively protest if they try to gather her up in their arms. She's not a stranger to them, so it may be hard for them to realise that they are strangers to her.

Gwen describes one such event: *'My brother sort of swooped down on her and picked her up and Ellen just howled. And howled. It made the visit a disaster. He was very upset by it, I was embarrassed by it and Ellen was distraught by it.'*

GRANDPARENTS AND other relatives often get a great deal of pleasure buying or making gifts for your baby. They may not always be to your taste, but the baby doesn't care.

Isabel decided there was only one thing to do: *'I dressed her up in these pink knitted clothes and sat her on a pink cushion and took her picture. She never wore them again, but I sent the picture off to her grandma who made them, and to this day that picture has pride of place on Eve's sideboard. It made her very happy.'*

EVEN IF you don't get on so well with the older generation, your children will grow up to see them very differently – as loving grandparents – and that is a relationship to cherish.

EXPERTS

Help and support

CLINICS, HEALTH VISITORS, midwives, GPs, family, other mothers, NCT, support groups. There are many different people who will become involved at one time or another in giving help and support to you and your family.

A community midwife has a statutory responsibility to care for you for the first 28 days following delivery. In practice, this often means that they will visit you at home several times, reassure themselves that you're managing okay, give you a number to call if you're worried about something or if you think there's a problem and leave you to get on with building your family in your own way.

Helen had a bad experience at one of the home visits: *'I went right off my midwife when Gilly was a week old and she wanted to take blood from her heel for that test that they do. It took so long that I couldn't stand it. First of all Gilly was too cold with her sleepsuit off so the blood wouldn't flow, so the midwife bathed her heel in some warm water and tried again, and again…It took about ten minutes to get these few drops of blood out and she was holding Gilly and pressing her leg, and Gilly was being so tolerant the whole time but giving these little whimpers. It's the worst thing that's happened.'*

Fiona feels quite differently about her midwife: *'I'll really miss my midwife. I met her before we went in to hospital, she came through the birth with me, and has watched Joe grow. This morning she said, "Oh, he doesn't look like a newborn any more", and she's right. His hair is fluffing up and he's lost that "just got here" look. But she's only able to notice that because she saw him born. I feel quite jealous that she's going to go on to other mothers and babies and give them her attention now.'*

As THE midwife's responsibility ends, you will be introduced to your health visitor.

A health visitor is a qualified nurse who has undertaken further training to qualify as a health visitor. She has a brief to promote health in the community. Most of us associate health visitors with children partly because, for a health authority, focusing on and maintaining children's good health is a useful way of preventing major problems developing in the adult population. All pre-school children have a health visitor, usually the one attached to their GP's practice.

As a rough guide, you will first meet your health visitor when your baby is around ten days or two weeks old, when she will come to visit you at home, picking up where the community midwife left off. There are no rigid rules for how often or for how long the health visitor will 'visit'. It varies according to individual need. You can always contact her or visit her at the clinic if there is something that you are concerned about – wind and sleep are the top two topics according to my health visitor – and she will want to keep an eye on your baby's progress and growth before his first developmental check at six to eight weeks, which is carried out by a doctor.

Amy describes her health visitor as: '*A National Treasure. She's stood in my front room and done my ironing at times when I've been so desperate with the twins I wanted to stand on the street and give them away. "Let's get this sorted", she says, and she does.*'

Eileen feels if you have too many different people to call on, you could end up with too many different pieces of advice: '*They have some good advice, I think – I've seen one or two health visitors now in the clinic and they're always willing to talk. But one said to try a musical mobile in the evenings when it's difficult to get Michael to drop off, so of course the next day I went out and got one. And it's very nice and everything, keeps him amused, but it also keeps him wide awake watching these things go round and round and he's no nearer sleep than he ever was. So the next week I mentioned it to another one and she said, "No, music's the wrong thing. Babies need peace".*'

THE CHILD Health Clinic will become your main opportunity for talking to your health visitor. It is here that you can have regular weighing done if you would like to monitor your baby's growth in that way (as the charts may measure average rates of growth in bottle-fed babies, they may not reassure breastfeeding mothers), you can ask questions, and often you get an opportunity to meet other parents who live nearby.

Helen enjoys going to her clinic, but is not totally convinced by the advice she is given: '*Sometimes I find myself sitting in front of the health visitor at the clinic and she's giving me pieces of advice and I'm sitting there and smiling and I know I'll never pay any attention to them. Like last week I said that Gilly seemed to get choked by the first few gulps of a feed, as if the milk was coming out just too quickly, and she said, "Express some before a feed so the pressure isn't so great", and I smiled and said thank you. But I can't see myself doing that as I never know when she's going to want to feed –*

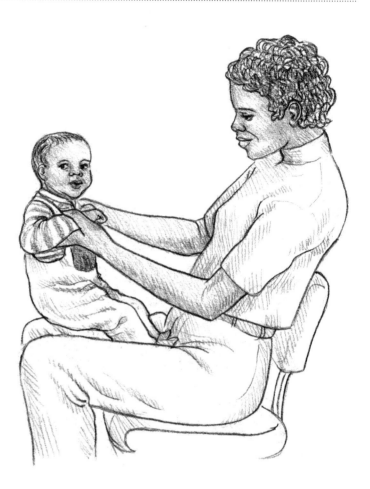

there's no pattern to it yet at all. I only know she wants feeding when she cries and, quite honestly, if she's lying there howling, there's no way I'm going to be able to leave her while I express some milk. I tried it once and it took me half an hour to get three or four drops out and I can't see that making much difference. So I'll just go on and hope Gilly settles down. You always ask, though, in case they've got this magic formula up their sleeve.'

Parveen thinks it's an opportunity to reassure yourself once a week that you're doing okay: *'Sometimes I think I ask questions even though I know the health visitors won't have any definite answers, like about the wind or about her sleeping, but you ask just for reassurance. I do. I want to be told more than anything that I'm not the only one in the world with this problem and that I'm really not so terrible after all.'*

Developmental assessments

THESE ARE checks that are offered to all pre-school children so that progress can be monitored and any potential problems spotted and dealt with before they become more serious. Your child will not be asked to recite poetry, count backwards from 100 or perform the *pas de deux* from *Swan Lake*, although the way some parents behave, you'd think this was the case.

Vaccinations

YOU WILL be offered the chance to have your child immunised against a range of childhood diseases when he is still very young. A baby's immune system needs to become strong, to fight off all the germs and diseases he will naturally come into contact with throughout his life, and for most illnesses your baby will benefit from being left to do this on his own. Immunisation primes the baby's immune system so that when they meet the real illness their own body will already have the necessary antibodies to fight it off quickly and efficiently. The vaccines currently on offer in this country will protect your child against:

Schedule of Assessments

The exact timings of the developmental checks will vary according to your area. They are all carried out by your health visitor except the first 'six-week check', and often the pre-school check around five years is carried out by a doctor.
A typical schedule would read:

- 6 weeks
- 8 months
- 18 months
- 3 years
- 5 years.

Never wait for the next developmental assessment check if there is a problem bothering you. For example, if you think your child is developing a squint, if you think your baby may have hearing problems, then call your health visitor for an appointment straight away.

- Diphtheria
- Pertussis (whooping cough)
- Tetanus

} These three are given together as the DPT 'triple' injection.

- Polio

} This is given by mouth.

- Measles
- Mumps
- Rubella

} These three are often given together as the MMR injection.

- Hib (Haemophilus meningitis B).

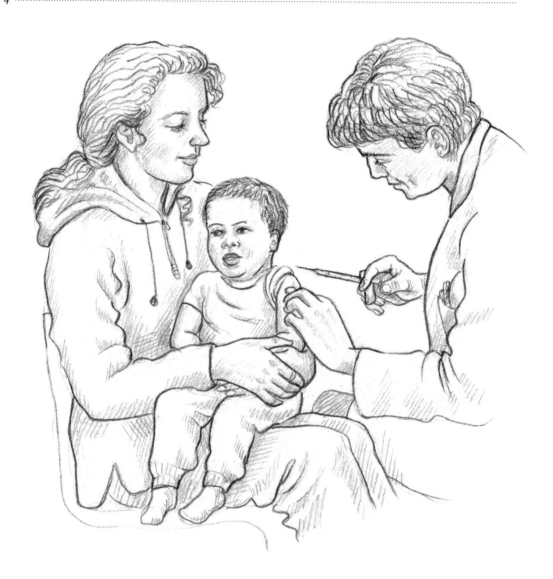

THAT IS the reasoning behind the immunisation programme in the UK. Yet, for some parents, whether to accept these immunisations or not is the first major decision they need to make regarding their baby's long-term welfare, and it is a choice that some find hard to make.

Almost all parents have worries when the time comes for their baby to be immunised – after all, here is your perfect healthy baby and someone wants to come along and inject him with a cocktail of chemicals. Callum's fears are commonplace:

'I don't want to take him for his shots, I really don't. I know it's in his best interests and everything, and I know logically that I want him to be immunised, but the thought of deliberately taking him along and holding his arm so that someone can stick a needle in it horrifies me.'

SOMETIMES, however, parents reach a definite decision *not* to have their baby immunised. The main reasons for this are:

- A strong belief in homoeopathic alternatives
- Medical reasons: for example, no MMR (measles, mumps and rubella) injection in a child who has proved to be allergic to eggs (because some forms of the injection are cultivated on eggs)
- A religious belief that leads parents to prefer not to immunise
- Personal reasons, for example: an unwillingness to risk their child's health with the whooping cough vaccine.

From time to time, the extremely rare possibility of brain-damage as a side-effect of the pertussis (whooping cough) part of the triple vaccine gains publicity and causes many parents to agonise over whether to have their child immunised.

Whooping cough is a potentially lethal illness: every year it kills around seven children. The chance of brain damage from the vaccination is tiny: it is less than the risk you run every single time you take your child out in a car. Nevertheless, some parents decide that any risk at all is not worth taking. Felicity explains her feelings:

'Why should I run the risk of damaging my child when the chances of her catching whooping cough are minimal? I have brought her up on breast milk, good food, clean air, and I do not believe that science is right on this one. I believe we fight off illnesses best with a strong immune system, not by dosing ourselves with poisons.'

Mishal felt differently: *'I do believe in vaccines. I am a firm believer in protecting children from diseases they don't need to catch or suffer from. Yet while I took Kavita along to the clinic for her jabs with no question, I did impose my own limitations. For example, I felt that at two months she was really too small to have a major shock to her system. She was still indoors with just me most of the time and I felt I would be doing her a disservice not to let her simply grow a bit more. So I put the timings of all the triples back just by putting them off for a month each time.'*

Kate let her son have most of the immunisations: *'He'd had the DPT, and then the MMR, and then they offered me the Hib vaccine and I said no. I just felt he'd had enough and he'd reached the limit, as if his immune system would just go into overload if they put any more into him. I read up about the protection it was offering and decided, on balance, not to go ahead. I expected a real battle from my health visitor over this, but she was surprisingly supportive. I think this was because she could see that I had thought about it carefully and wasn't just doing it on a whim.'*

IMMUNISATIONS ARE not compulsory, so, whatever your decision, it must be yours and yours alone. But make sure you do decide. Don't let your baby catch whooping cough just because you forgot to take her for the triple.

There are circumstances in which you should not have your baby routinely vaccinated:

- If she has an acute illness
- If she has had a severe reaction to another vaccine
- If she has suffered from brain damage or convulsions
- If a close relative has epilepsy
- If your baby is developmentally delayed.

A few babies need BCG (which protects against tuberculosis) if they're considered at risk; a few need Hepatitis B – check with your doctor.

IN ALL of these cases, ask for a discussion with your doctor before going ahead. You may wish to put it off until you feel able to make an informed decision.

You can have your baby's vaccinations done at the Child Health Clinic or at your doctor's surgery, but you can always ask your health visitor for extra information about them before you make up your mind, and she should be happy to take the time to discuss with you any worries or concerns you may have.

IMMUNISATION SCHEDULE		
What	**How**	**Recommended age**
DPT (Diphtheria, tetanus and whooping cough)	Injection (together in one injection)	2, 3 and 4 months
Hib (Haemophilus meningitis B)	Injection	Variable
Polio	By mouth (and very bitter!)	2, 3 and 4 months
MMR (Measles, mumps and rubella)	Injection	Between 12 and 15 months
Diphtheria and tetanus	Injection (both together)	Booster at school-entry age
Polio	By mouth (still bitter!)	Booster at school-entry age

CHAPTER **_six_** *You and the future*

IT SOMETIMES seems as if having a baby throws our sense of time out of joint for ever. When we are looking forward to the baby's arrival, the time slows down, it seems as if the anticipated date will never arrive.

Then, when our baby arrives, time speeds up – we cannot ever get done in a day all the things that we wanted to achieve; or it slows down completely – the days take for ever to pass; or in some cases the time just goes awry and we find ourselves falling asleep in the middle of the afternoon or still wearing our dressing gown as we prepare the baby's lunch.

Even stranger things happen to time as our baby grows. This is not something new. This is something our parents told us: make the most of it, it all goes so quickly; they grow up so fast.

And they do: before we know it, we are into the future.

Before the future takes you by surprise, therefore, it is worth spending some time considering just what it is that you want, for yourself, for your partner, for your baby and for you all as a family.

YOU ARE NOW A PARENT

ADJUSTING TO parenthood can be a slow process. It is a process that begins in pregnancy and can end when we are ready to accept and acknowledge ourselves as parents. That may not happen overnight, and it may not happen for a long time. It may take even longer for us to be happy in the role we have undertaken.

Tina explains how she felt: *'I'd spent all this time preparing for the birth. But that was it – for the birth. Not what came afterwards. I hardly gave that a second thought except how lovely it would be when my baby was finally here. So life was a bit of a shock, I can tell you.'*

Joanna was pleasantly surprised by motherhood: '*Having a baby has been better than I thought it would be. Before Tyler was born I thought he'd scream all the time, howl, need his nappy changed constantly and I'd wander round in my dressing gown going, "Never mind, never mind." I think this was partly to do with the fact that Chris left me during the pregnancy and I knew we weren't going to get back together again, so I was prepared for life to be dreadful. But Tyler was actually very good fun. Entertaining, and I enjoyed being with him – but it was hard to think of myself as "a parent". I'd see things about single parents and I wouldn't feel that they applied to me. "Single parents in school fuss," that sort of thing. Nothing to do with me. I was just me, me and Tyler.*'

Sometimes parents just want some space to be parents as John did: '*I want to get on and do things my way. People say to me, "Oh, don't worry about this," or "Don't worry about that," and I think, "Of course I'll bloody worry, she's my baby!"*'

Milestones

THE TERM 'milestones' – especially if applied to a baby's development – can feel very misleading. It seems to imply that your baby should have acquired a particular skill or achieved a particular feat by a given age. Before our baby arrives, we look forward to his first steps, her first word. Only when we are in the reality of it do we realise that things aren't quite so clear cut as that: before your baby walks, he will have stood, and before he stands, he will have crawled; before your baby says, 'Mama', she will have said 'mmmm' and 'maaaaa'. It can be difficult sometimes to decide exactly when something happens for the first time – it is all part of a process, a gradual unfolding of change and development.

Parenthood is exactly the same. We are all different sorts of parents at different times and, after that initial bombshell when the dream baby of your pregnancy turns into the real baby of your life, the change from one stage to the next is gradual.

That is why we as parents may find the future so hard to think about: what sort of parent will we be, or want to be in a few years' time?

And how would you like to think of yourself in the future?

May gives her view: *'If you had told me a year ago that I would have a child who had learning disabilities, who would be utterly dependent on me for the foreseeable future, I'd have walked away. I'd have said words like "No", and "Not me", and "Never". It just wasn't on the agenda. And look at me now. This is where I am and where I want to be.'*

MANY PARENTS find that what they want from parenthood changes, too. When your baby is born, she is a helpless creature, utterly dependent on you and the care you give her. In just one year she is transformed – in ways that will never happen so fast or furiously again: into a mobile chatterbox (even if much of it doesn't make sense) who can pit her will against yours if push comes to shove . . . and will often win.

> **How do you think of your-self most of the time?**
>
> ● A parent
> ● A mother
> ● A father
> ● A partner
> ● A husband
> ● A wife
> ● A daughter
> ● A son
> ● An individual

Olivia demonstrates how many pre-parents think: *'Whenever I thought of myself as a parent, it was always with a baby. First this tiny baby that I'd be wheeling about in a pram, and then there was a jump – I could see myself with a school-age child, or one about eight or nine, going on trips to museums and things. I don't think I acknowledged that I'd completely missed out the whole toddler stage, or pre-school stage. Probably because I knew I wouldn't enjoy it.'*

IF YOU wanted to stay at home with your child in those early months or years, you may find that the need to re-establish yourself as an individual becomes stronger as the years pass.

Wendy has reached this point: *'I've done enough. Jamie is three and Patrick is five. I've done my stint of staying home wiping bottoms and runny noses and now I need to change – to get out from this place.'*

OTHER PARENTS find, on the contrary, they are quite happy for their baby to be looked after in a crèche or nursery when she is very tiny, so that they can take a break from work later, when their child is old enough to participate in more activities and to enjoy more family days out.

WORKING

WHAT YOU do about work will depend on:

- You
- Your baby
- Your circumstances – financial and personal
- Your job
- Your childcare.

WHAT IT will *not* depend on is your expectations. How you feel when your baby arrives can be vastly different from how you expected to feel.

When Terri was pregnant she worried all the time about how she was going to go back to work: *'I was working in a large branch of a department store and wanted to stay on the career ladder, eventually managing a whole store myself one day. I couldn't imagine myself being a mother at home. In the end, I stayed home with Juliet for a year and a half. Colleagues at work kept saying, "How could you do it?" The answer is, "I enjoyed it!"'*

MANY PARENTS find that the decisions they make while they are pregnant change once their baby is born. You can't decide how you will feel when your baby is here, although you may well make a decision and stick with it. You need to do what feels right, although sometimes juggling the maternity leave, the price of buggies and the cost of redecorating the spare room into a nursery can take its toll.

Amy explains why she went back to work: *'By the time I've finished paying the childminder, there's hardly any money left over, so I'm not doing it for that. Why I'm doing it is because I was getting in a vicious circle: the twins wake early, breakfast, lunch, cleaning; on it goes until the evening when I fall into bed absolutely exhausted. It would just go on like that every day if I let it. I had no time to myself, none. But at work, I have. I'm working, but I can just get on and do it, let my mind slide, relax a bit . . . It's the change that helps. It keeps me from going mad.'*

Raisa says that she went back to work to regain her self: *'When I'm going to work, people call me by my proper name. They don't say, "Oh, Mrs Smith, we're ready for you now", or, "Is Jody's mum here?"'*

PARTLY BECAUSE of the way our society is constructed, and the fact that the physical care of children is not demonstrably valued with large financial rewards, full-time parenting has a low status.

We define ourselves so often by our paid work, and if being 'just a mother' is not what you want, sharing the tasks of parenthood will be at the back of your mind from the start, and you will be planning how to accomplish the combination of work and children without letting either side down.

There are several options you can look at or combine:

- Working at home – either employed or self-employed
- Working part time
- Working full time
- Job-sharing
- Full-time parenting
- Postponing all decisions until some later date.

Working at home

THIS CAN have advantages: you can set your own hours, work when the baby sleeps and not worry if you leak milk over your jumper. But it can have its frustrations, too, as Roisin describes: *'Life's more frustrating than I expected it to be, in that I had this rosy idea that, because I work from home, I'd just be able to carry straight on. Everyone said, "Oh, how lovely, the best of both worlds." Do you know what I say to that? Ha! I tried it once when he was asleep, but he was just too distracting.'*

Laura found more success through dividing her work time and care time into definite areas: *'Before I actually had Jessica, I had visions in which I worked serenely in my office at the top of the house while a nanny downstairs tended lovingly to her daily needs. I was within reach for breastfeeds, on hand for emergencies . . . and the sun always shone, naturally. These dreams fell to bits, not on arrival of Jessica, strangely enough, but on first contact with the nanny agencies in the vicinity. Most thought it would be practically impossible to get a nanny to work with me on the premises. In the end, I went for a day nursery. I had to work, there was no option, and this way we both knew where we stood. When Jessica was at home, I played with her and looked after her. When she wasn't, someone else did. It got over that hurdle which I've seen other women come up against, of, "Get out of this room! I'm working!"'*

WORKING FROM home can also often mean enlisting the support of a partner when emergencies mean the work spills over into 'care' time.

Madeleine works from home and describes what happens whenever she is up against deadlines: *'I had a couple of weekends when I had to work, when Jack was really small, like six weeks old, and Ross said he'd cope fine. Well, I didn't say anything the first time, but when the second one came round I had to say to him, "Looking after him does not mean letting him cry in the living room while you read the paper." And I had enough guilt before I said it.'*

Working part time

THIS IS, according to who you talk to, and according to what sort of day they have just had, the best of both worlds or the worst of both worlds.

Gwen is quite adamant about her decision: '*I am definitely, definitely, definitely a happier mother because I go out to work two days a week. I am very lucky, because I can leave Ellen with my mum, and it's somehow much more reassuring to be leaving her with her grandmother than a nursery, but I know that if I had not gone back to work, I would have gone bananas.*'

Ruth knows that when things go badly at work it's not the end of the world: '*I do get the best of both worlds. Of course there are times when I think I get the worst of both worlds, but that's after I've had a bad day with either Freddie or the office. But having a baby puts everything in perspective. I don't think it's the end of the world now, if something goes wrong at work. I don't get in such a flap over things, I can have more of a long-term view of things, so all in all it's made me much happier.*'

Naomi has also made it work for her and her daughter, Karen: '*I think it's fine. Three mornings and two afternoons a week, Karen gets professional, highly-qualified nursery staff looking after her. It's their job. They have nothing else to do but look after my baby for the time that she is there. I have a million other things to do when she's at home with me. She's much, much better off. And we started her so young, she'll always have been going there as far as she knows. It'll never be strange to her, or a wrench. She has me, and she has the nursery, I think it's two positive influences.*'

ONCE YOUR baby starts at a crèche or nursery, or with a childminder, expect a sudden increase in sniffles – not because of separation, but because of the common cold. Children who haven't any older brothers or sisters will have developed less immunity to germs and viruses. Now, as they encounter them for the first time, colds increase. The good news is that by the time your child goes to school, his immune system will have developed greater resistance and he is less likely to catch endless colds than the children who haven't been in day-care.

Choices in childcare will depend on your preferences and what is actually available in your local area, and what you can afford. But a word of warning from Mishal: '*Whatever childcare you get, you're made to feel as if you should be eternally grateful for it. Even if you have a childminder that you really like, you're at their beck and call, and you have to be really thankful all the time that they're so* good. *We should expect good childcare, think of it as our right, not grovel for it.*'

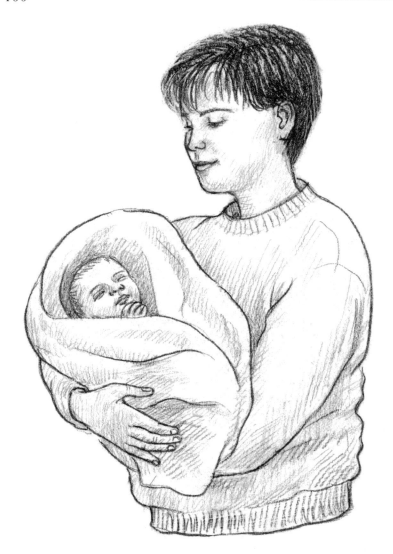

PART-TIME WORK is perhaps more vulnerable to pressures than a full-time commitment either way. People can expect you to be able to accomplish more than you feel you can while your baby is so young, as Bridget found: *'People keep asking me whether I've gone back to work yet and I don't know what to say. So I feel, yes, well, I should be able to have a job and look after the baby,* and *I should do my freelance work,* and *I should be happy and we should be happy* and *I should cook the supper. Now, although I know logically that that's not right, all those feelings are there, and a terrible burden.'*

Working full time

WE OFTEN think of this as the most difficult option of all. But that need not be the case, as Ursula makes clear: *'Well, I had thought I would go back to work. Of course. I'm an accountant – I do people's books. What else was I going to do? And then we had Andrew and everything was wiped away. In that moment, when he was born and we could see that there was something not quite right, everything changed. Other parents, no matter how much they don't want to admit it to themselves, make plans for their children from the moment they're born. Even before they're born. We did, in a general way. We wanted a child who would be bright and happy, who would do well in life, have lots of friends – who doesn't want that for their children? And then, when we knew Andrew had Down's, that was it. Accounts came second. Of course in the end I did go back to work. Part of me did not want to treat Andrew any differently, and that decision included going back to work. If he hadn't been Down's I'd have gone back. So I did. But, you know, work just didn't matter so much any more. And when I was at work, the Down's didn't matter so much any more. It balanced out. I'm glad I went back because it was better for all of us.'*

Some women positively welcome the return to work – it brings them a freedom they could not hope to achieve at home, as it did for Zoë: *'One more day at home, and I'd have sent him off to an orphanage. I was so glad to be back where people didn't whinge if I didn't give them their lunch on time, or spit their breakfasts at me.'*

SOME WOMEN go back to work secure in the knowledge that their baby's midday nutritional needs will be amply catered for by the bottle of expressed milk they have left. Some women express quickly and easily by hand. (See the NCT book *Breastfeeding Your Baby* in this series for step-by-step guidance on this.) Other women find a breast pump useful, especially if they're away working for a few days and want to keep up their supply.

Virginia could not bear to use a breast pump: *'While I think most women manage quite happily with the breast pump, there will always be a few like me who cannot stand the sight of their nipple being sucked down a perspex tube and squeezed out of all recognition while jets of milk squirt relentlessly into the attached bottle. I expressed once. Then I saw some definite advantages to formula.'*

THE MORAL of this story is that if you are going back to work full time, you need to be prepared to be adaptable. Your let down reflex may not work well away from your baby; your baby may not take to having his familiar milk from a bottle; you may find the hum of the electric pump too disconcerting.

So it is with all aspects of returning to work: what you think will work well on a theoretical basis may turn out to be a disaster. On the other hand, solutions that you had hitherto considered unsuitable – leaving him with your mother-in-law, for example – may turn out to be lifesavers.

Agnes warns against being undermined by books that present your decision to go back to work in a negative light: *'I read loads and loads of books when I knew I was going to go back to work to find out the best ways of doing it, and how you could ease the transition, and I found them very undermining. Most of them are written like, "If you really have to go back to work, then beware, because your baby might get close to the childminder and that's not very good, is it?" They really lay on the guilt. My view has always been that parenting should be shared anyway, I've always tried to involve my friends with Sam, and I never felt the need to keep him all to myself, not by any means. So these books, the ones that talk about the mother-and-baby as this self-sufficient unit, attached by your invisible umbilical cord . . . it's just a load of rubbish.'*

Beverley firmly believes that the world is not yet ready for women who work full time: *'It says it is, but it isn't. I took Josh to the clinic for his hearing test, which they only do on Monday afternoons so I had to take time off work, and when he failed it, they said, "Oh, come back in a couple of weeks, he might have a cold, and we'll try again then." And when he failed it a second time, they said, "Oh, come back . . ." and I said, "No way. I am working, and I can't be at your beck and call like this. I have to lose an after-noon's work, I have to pay for the crèche session whether he's there or not, and I have to pay £1.20 bus fare there and back." And they said, "Oh, we can do a domiciliary visit if we have to", and I said, "You will have to if you want to do another hearing test." But they made me feel bad, like I was neglecting his health, that I was being deliberately difficult for not being at home all the time. No wonder some employers are hesitant about taking on women with babies: every five minutes they've got to take time off for a hearing test or a developmental test. It's a pain in the neck. And no one ever, ever, ever expects the father to do it.'*

Full-time parenting

FULL-TIME PARENTING can change your view of the world, says Gillian: *'I used to get very frenetic at work. I must find work, I must line up work for next week, I must make a living, I must be successful . . . and now I find that Greta is my work.'*

If you're going to stay at home with your baby, then you have to adapt to a different set of priorities and a different time-scale, as Sheila found: *'At work, I used to go through the days ticking items off on a list: done that, done that, done that . . . If I tried the same thing getting through the days with Annabel, I'd soon come a cropper. Breakfast – disaster. Nappy – all over the carpet.'*

Postponing all decisions

FOR MANY women, the decision can't be postponed indefinitely, but it can at least be put off until the maternity leave agreements have to be honoured. Sometimes the very period of indecision can be stressful in itself, admits Vicky: *'I've got another three weeks before I have to make up my mind about going back. And at the moment I can definitely say that I* don't *want to go back. People say you do change, your feelings can alter, but I don't think mine are going to alter in three weeks. I don't know how I'm going to decide.'*

Jennifer has postponed the decision indefinitely: *'I will go back to work some day, I know. But I've made no plans for it, and probably won't think about it now until we've had another baby because we know we definitely want two. Barney is the most important person in my life. I want to be the most important person in his. And how could I be that if I spent one hour a day with him and a childminder spent ten?'*

The priorities for you in the way of what you want from a job may now change radically too, as they did for Hilary and Mandy:

'I look at jobs completely differently now. I scan down the newspaper columns and think, "Oh, so-and-so's got a workplace nursery, let's see what sort of jobs they've got."'

'I want somewhere that's really committed to an equal opportunities policy. If I went to an interview and someone said, "What kind of childcare arrangements have you got planned?" I wouldn't be interested in that job.'

IF YOU'D LIKE to know more about the decisions parents have made when it comes to the point of going back to work, see Teresa Wilson's book *Work and Home* in this NCT series.

BROADENING HORIZONS

SOMETIMES, HOWEVER, the changes brought about by motherhood are far more wide-ranging. Being a parent is not only about battening down and getting used to reduced expectations, parenthood is also a time when we increase our skills, find new talents and try things we might not otherwise have thought of doing.

With our increased confidence and assertiveness, we may find that we can set our sights higher, cast our net wider.

Before her son was born, Fiona was really worried about work: *'I kept thinking about money and worrying and went round saying to Ian, "We're not going to cope! I've got to get this for the baby, I've got to get that for the baby too. . ." And after I had Joe, I lost that straight away. Now I don't mind about work. Yes, I do want to start again, and sometimes I find it frustrating when I see other people getting commissions that I know I'd have got. But I just think now, "Well, we'll have to cope." I'll go back to work one day, but I'm not going to rush out tomorrow and take on some piffling little design job because I need the cash, which I'd have done in the past. I just feel confident that when I am ready to go back, there'll be something.'*

Erica feels that taking time out to have a baby has been a really good opportunity for her: *'It means I can now think about retraining, or taking a different job, because I don't want to go back to teaching. People say it fits in well with school holidays, but it's so draining. It used to take up all my time and I'm not prepared to give that much of myself to my work any more.'*

Lynn doesn't know if she'll ever go back to her old job: *'I've changed since having a baby. I'm more confident in myself now, more sure . . . and more inclined to voice my opinion! I think I'm going to look into the possibility of retraining, find something that's better suited not only to the circumstances I'm in now, but the sort of person I am now.'*

PICKING UP WHERE WE LEFT OFF

FOR MANY women, the world of babyhood, however rewarding and fulfilling it may be to see their baby thrive and flourish, can be very claustrophobic.

Maureen regrets one particular invitation: *'I invited another mother round that I'd met in the baby clinic and she kept saying, "Charlie's doing ever so well, Charlie's ever so bright . . . I'm sure he's very advanced for his age . . ." and this Charlie was five weeks old. I thought, "If she goes on much more, I'll sling her out."'*

Raisa is going back to work and: *'One thing I'm looking forward to about going back to my old job is talking about all the things I used to be interested in instead of about babies all the time. I've been having chats with colleagues about things that I'll be picking up when I do go back, and we talk for ages and then right at the end she'll say, "How's Jody?" and I'll say, "Oh, fine, how's Ella?" which is her little girl, and that's it. I much prefer that to "What's Jody doing now? What's she eating? How many teeth has she got?" I don't mind talking about things like that, but with my health visitor or my mum, not everyone in the world.'*

Beverley has reached the end of her patience at home: *'I do want to go back to work. I've found being at home very claustrophobic, and very competitive. People are always saying to me, "Is Josh sleeping through the night yet? Is he crawling yet?" And if I say no, they go on about how their baby is doing this and doing that and how they like stewed-up carrots. I do not want to spend my time talking about whether our babies like stewed-up carrots.'*

WHATEVER OUR experience of parenting, whether we enjoy it or whether we chafe against its restrictions all the time, it will change us. We will be different people because of it.

Philippa answers one of the most commonly asked questions: *'Has having Sophie changed me? Well, before she was born, Frank and I promised ourselves she would just fit in with our lives, that she would adapt and join in with us right from the start. If I was breastfeeding, then she could easily come out to dinner with us in the evening. If we went on a long walk, we could just pop her in the baby carrier. Why didn't anyone put me straight? I would be too tired to go out to dinner. I would be too tired to go for a short stroll, never mind a trek through a forest. I was not prepared for this and found it very hard because I was the one having to do the adapting, not Sophie. So yes, mother-hood has changed me. I'm a better person now – more tolerant, more realistic, more even-tempered. But I've got to that point only because I've been through the frustrations and boredoms of being a mother.'*

Mark's actions may seem drastic, but at least they gave him time to think things through: *'I couldn't handle it at all, not at first. Everything was too difficult, too hard. All Anne talked about or thought about was the baby. I couldn't tell her anything that had happened in my day, or what I was worried about. And she just couldn't understand why I wasn't finding this baby interesting. As far as I could see all Max ever did was sleep and feed, and she'd say, "Ah, look at him now, look at him now." Finally, when Max was about five months old, I'd had enough. I went down to the airline ticket shop and bought myself a ticket to Washington State – I'd been there picking apples when I was a student – and spent about a month travelling on my own. Then I came back. And I came back because I wanted them back, Anne and Max. It took that time away to make me see it, but it also meant that I'd become one of those fathers who just walks out on his family. And that didn't make me happy with myself.'*

PROTECTING YOUR CHILD

AS A PARENT it is natural to worry about your child: are you doing the right things for her? Is she making the right friends? Should we encourage him to be sporty, or scientific, or does it all come natural-ly? This catalogue of worry can translate into over-protectiveness. Remember that most children just need guidance and parents who listen – very often it may be better to give information than instruc-tions or advice – that way your child learns to make decisions. However, you are bound to worry more if your child has been born with a disability. You may find that your view of the future is coloured by a worry as to how your child will cope with the days ahead.

Deirdre found that sometimes advice runs out: *'My GP didn't know anything either. All the time I was saying to him, "Well, the consultant says* this . . . or the consultant says that . . ." So I kept thinking there must be someone else we ought to see, someone else who would know more . . . but all it came down to was that I kept hoping there would be someone else I could go to see who would make her better. And deep down I knew there wasn't. I was clutching at straws. But even now, I haven't stopped. I still read about new "breakthroughs" at every turn. I can't stop myself. If there isn't that glimmer of hope, I'm condemning Alice to no hope, too.'

It can be difficult for parents to come to terms with their child's disability: 'People can get very rude, they ask questions they wouldn't dream of asking other parents. They say, "What's wrong with her eyes?" They say, "Can she see me?" And they're waving their hands in front of her face, they're staring down at her to see if she can see them. I want to walk down the street with no one looking at us. With no one asking horrible questions. That's what I want.'

IF YOU find yourself getting caught in the trap of being defensive about your baby, it may help if you try to break the ice first. Explain what's attracted attention: *'Oh, you're wondering about Sophie's glasses. She has to wear glasses because her eyes aren't focusing properly, but we hope her eyes will improve as she gets older.'* Or: *'Paul has a port wine stain birthmark but he will be having treatment for it as he grows.'*

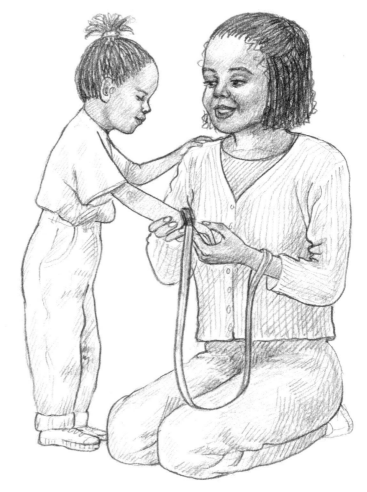

How much you tell people, if you tell people anything, is entirely up to you. It's not easy to be on the receiving end of so much curiosity all the time, and there may be times when you choose to turn your back, to turn away – and that is your right. You have the right to decide how much to tell people. They do not have the right to demand.

Deirdre wishes she didn't have to explain anything, but fears for the future as her daughter comes into contact with the world: *'I know as she gets older and she moves more out of the family circle, away from people who know what is the matter with her, then things will get more and more difficult. While she's at nursery and just at home with us . . . Don't you ever wish you could just stop time, stop the clock, and not let them go any further?'*

LOOKING FORWARD

WHILE PARENTHOOD can be a worrying time, it can also bring great excitement and fulfilment. You may find that although on a practical level you live from day to day, there will always be a tendency to look forward: to when she can sit up; to crawling; the first steps, until you realise that time passes so quickly anyway, it's enough to just enjoy each new moment.

Louise says: *'Do you know what I'm most looking forward to? When I can talk to him and know that he understands what I'm saying. I sing away and murmur all these comforting things, but of course he can't speak the language yet so it's all going in and nothing's coming back at me. I'm looking forward to when the words start coming back.'*

Jane believes the future is the time for herself and she feels a need to start planning: *'I'm enjoying having him being a baby at the moment. But when I look in my studio, I think, I'm going to have to get back to work sometime, and I'm just drowning myself in babies. He's going to be 16 and leaving home and I'll have nothing, nothing . . . Six weeks old and he's left home already!'*

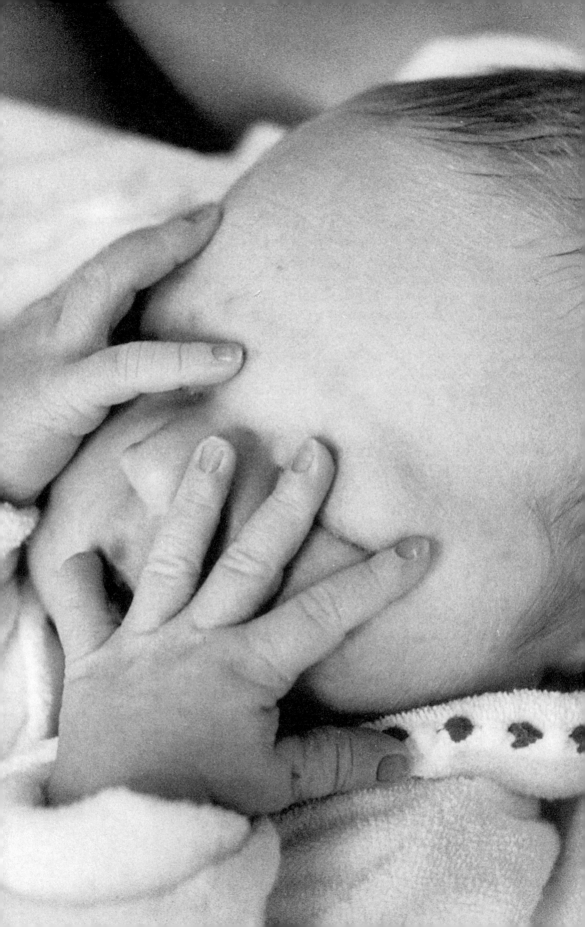

CHAPTER *seven* Becoming a family

THERE COMES a point when we stop being surprised by the fact that we have a baby, when we take life in our new family unit for granted.

Your baby may have arrived unexpectedly, may have even been unplanned; or you may have known the date of your child's arrival well in advance, if your baby was going to be induced, or you had a planned caesarean; or you may have adopted a child, in which case you may have been able to anticipate his arrival for rather less time than most parents.

Depending on the circumstances of our baby's arrival, and depending on how much parenthood measures up to how we thought it was going to be, we take more or less time to get used to him. But get used to him we do. Different families will have different ways to mark this point; in our family I knew we were used to Ben's presence when Peter let a whole day go by without taking a photograph of him.

Once we are used to our baby, we have stopped becoming a family, we *are* a family.

CEREMONIES

MANY PARENTS choose to mark the occasion of their child's birth with a formal ceremony, often involving naming, or christening. Catholic families usually arrange the baptism in the community church when the baby is a few weeks old. Orthodox Jewish families celebrate the circumcision of their boy babies when the child is about eight days old. Hindu families have a traditional ceremony where the baby is given her name and there is much joy and welcome in the family and around.

With a name comes an identity, and with that identity comes a place in society. For many parents, although these ceremonies are religious, they have wider overtones, of their child taking his or her

rightful place in the world, of being welcomed into a community. The key elements are friends and family together, celebrating and giving thanks for the baby's birth.

Lynn describes her son's christening: *'I felt wonderful – all the family were there to welcome him, and he wore The Family Gown for the ceremony. Granted, I couldn't take in much of the words of the christening as I was mainly concentrating on keeping him quiet and jiggling him up and down, but I liked being part of us all there together.'*

Ingrid had a less happy experience: *'We argued about being there in the first place. It had never been something I'd thought about beforehand simply because I didn't know how strongly I'd feel about it myself. We hadn't been married in a church and that hadn't particularly bothered me – I'd been quite glad to escape all that tat of white dresses and your second cousin's little girl having to be bridesmaid – but now it* did *matter that we all came together and had this baby christened. And the simplest thing was to have it done in our local Anglican church where the vicar was very supportive and welcoming and where John's family had been in the congregation so he knew us. You'd have thought, though, from my side of the family, that we were subjecting this child to a DIY christening from Woolworth's, definitely second-best. I sometimes think that nothing less than the Pope himself popping over from Rome would have done. And they made this very clear. So the day was frayed tempers all round. It should have been happy – I was happy, actually, but that's because I ignored all of the wounded looks from my relatives.'*

NOT EVERY family finds the ceremony something to agree about; for some couples this can be one of the first and deepest divisions in their new family life – especially if the dilemma is one they hadn't discussed in advance.

Jess managed to persuade her husband to have the ceremony she wanted: *'Richard is an atheist. Simple as that. He didn't want to be married in a church, he doesn't want to have a church funeral. Yet I still felt it was important enough to me to have the babies baptised that I should ask, and explain, and go on asking and explaining, until he could see how important it was. It was weeks before he agreed. Weeks and weeks of me asking how, if he didn't believe in anything, it would hurt to have a little water on their heads. Of course it wasn't as simple as that, and we both knew it, but he knew what I meant. And in the end, it was a measure of how much we felt a commitment towards our family that he did hold one of the twins and I held the other and we participated together, and if he didn't believe in it, that didn't matter. It was for me, to give thanks for the safe arrival of my babies.'*

NATURALLY, WHEN two families meet to celebrate such an event, such a happy, joyful event, the quarrels can be deafening.

Jane and John felt let down by both their families: *'We had a party when Lyle was about six weeks old, on a Sunday afternoon. We were in a basement flat then and it was usually dark, but it was summer and the flowers were out and the light was lovely and even Lyle managed to smile, and I'd been up late the night before cooking these little snacks and vol-au-vents . . . and all my family stayed on one side of the room and all John's family stayed over that side of the room and it was awful.'*

EVEN IF there is no formal ceremony, the arrival of a baby is an event that can trigger the worst of competitive instincts, as Erica discovered: *'Don's parents bought him a mobile, so the next day my parents were round with a squeaky book, which was topped by a rattle with a lovely bell sound, which was beaten by an activity centre, which kept me awake.'*

YET, WHETHER we have a formal naming ceremony or not, the ritual celebrations that we remember from our own childhood take on a new significance now that our baby is here.

Fiona and Ian took their son, Joe, up to Derbyshire to spend the holiday with her family: *'We spent the whole of that dark, wet and slow journey fantasising about and planning Joe's Christmases. We talked of the things we had loved as children and how we wanted Joe to have the same sense of mystery and joy surrounding the whole celebration as we had had. It really brought us close . . . as did the realisation of the added bonus of being able to relive Christmas without the cynicism and boredom that comes from having lived through 34 of them. We had no christening for Joe, because we're not churchgoers, but that winter holiday in the Dales, when all my family came to see him for the first time, was as perfect and happy a welcoming as anyone could have ever wanted. I felt he was taking his place in our family, and that was where he belonged.'*

Alan wanted his baby to start right at the begining: *'We bought an Advent calendar. He couldn't focus his eyes properly, but I wanted him to have an Advent calendar. I wanted him to be part of everything.'*

CARRIED AWAY by the thrill of it all, new parents should beware of promising to provide Christmas lunch for every living relative within a radius of 50 miles, tempting though this might initially seem.

Kay was almost tempted: *'I had my mum and dad coming because they wanted to be there for the baby's first Christmas, and then we had Geoff's mum and dad coming because they wanted to be there for the baby's first Christmas. All the baby magazines were full of 'Fifty Steps to the Perfect Christmas Dinner' but they all involved puréeing fresh chestnuts or putting seaweed in filo pastry (only five hours' work with three saucepans and a bain-marie required). I just wanted an article called 'How to Produce a Christmas Dinner that Everyone will Eat and Still Have Time to Enjoy Yourself' and a method that didn't involve getting up at 3am to pre-heat the oven.'*

WHETHER YOU are celebrating Diwali, Christmas, Chanukah or Eid, the emotions are the same: for the first time your baby is here to share it, and the festival becomes more precious through that simple fact alone.

ASSISTED REPRODUCTION

THE WORLD'S first 'test-tube baby' is now a teenager. Parents whose children have been born through IVF and other methods of assisted reproduction are becoming more and more numerous as techniques improve and become more widely available, yet they often have less well-publicised and specific problems to deal with when adjusting to the realities of parenthood – problems that other parents do not have to face.

Daisy feels she needs to be with her daughter all the time: *'I've waited so long for Becky, gone through times when I thought we would never be lucky, and now that she is here, it is hard just to accept that. I spend all the time worrying if I ever let her out of my sight . . . in fact, I find it difficult to let her out of my sight to start with. I would strap her to me, if I could.'*

When Rebecca had Edward, he became the focus of her life: *'He is very precious. We are very aware that Edward could be our only child.'*

This intense concern is common, and can be positive, as Daisy affirms: *'I think having your children through IVF can only make you a better parent. You reaffirm, time after time, that yes, you do want children. Other IVF mothers I know are also possibly a bit more anxious, a bit more protective than most, but they are also very attentive. Their children are in no doubt how loved and special they are.'*

YET EVEN 'miracle babies' cry, stay awake at night, bring up their feeds and have temper tantrums. This is only a problem if the parents have not been prepared for this, or have not allowed themselves to envisage such a scenario. Problems arise for parents when:

- They have convinced themselves that they are going to be the perfect parents because they want this child so much
- They find it hard, because everyone knows that they have actively chosen parenthood, to admit that they sometimes find it difficult, even depressing.

Jess thought people would laugh if she asked for help: *'When I was finding the twins difficult, I thought people would say, "You should have thought of all this beforehand, shouldn't you?"'*

ONE OF the reasons these difficulties are not always publicised is that the parents themselves are so loath to reveal them; after all, if you have spent years and possibly a small fortune trying to conceive, you want to revel in your achievement and make the most of parenthood, not dwell on its down-side. Yet there is, as with all aspects of parenting, a down-side, and to pretend this doesn't exist can be very harmful.

After all, even parents of IVF babies have a right to feel low, as any other parent does, but Rowena didn't see it this way: *'I just felt guilty all the time because I didn't feel I was coping, or not coping in the way I wanted to. There was a great feeling, both for me and Nick, that we'd made our bed and now we had to lie in it. We didn't have the right to complain. So I didn't complain but I went on getting more and more miserable.'*

Moira continues: *'People would say, "How are you?" and I'd say, "Fine", when I was nothing of the sort. But I couldn't bring myself to admit that things weren't fine.'*

THERE CAN also be enormous practical and financial problems facing families who have had their children through assisted reproduction. Often, families plan for the mother to return to work fairly soon after the birth, so that they can pay off debts or loans incurred to have their fertility treatment. Yet if they have twins or triplets (which is fairly

likely with this method), this can prove impossible, at a time when the financial demands upon the family are at their highest.

If you have had your children through assisted reproduction, you will find the understanding and friendship offered through specialised networks very supportive. This is especially the case if you are one of those families who do not feel able to tell friends or relatives that they had treatment in the first place. Yet fertility treatment does bring its own stresses, and possibly only other IVF parents will be able to understand them: seek them out.

ADOPTING

WHILE INFORMAL adoption has taken place since time immemorial, often between friends, sisters and other family members, it was only in the 1920s that it became legally recognised in Britain. Since then, nearly one million people have been adopted. Since the 1960s and 70s, however, with changing social attitudes and the easier availability of contraception, fewer and fewer babies have become available for adoption. The focus these days is often on finding families for older children and those with special needs. Policies also tend to encourage contact between the two sets of parents, though this can lead to its own stresses.

Abigail felt this stress for the first six months: *'Lily came into our family when she was just a few weeks old, but we had to love her and care for her knowing that her birth mother could change her mind and have Lily back at any time until she was six months old.'*

IF YOU are lucky enough to adopt a child, you need to make sure that you ask for and receive as much help and support as you need. This is especially the case if you adopt two or three siblings together: it may be difficult to find the chance to get used to the children one at a time.

It is essential to be firm with the authorities when you're adopting, says Diana: *'Even before the children arrived, we didn't feel that we were getting the level of support we needed from our social worker. Looking back, we should have insisted more firmly that there were things we needed to know and things we were not prepared to put up with.'*

Any parent adopting a child these days does so in the knowledge that the child will have the right, when they reach the age of 18, to find out about their birth parents. And the repercussions of adoption can reverberate over the generations, as they did for Caroline: *'When I gave birth to Luke, I was overwhelmed. This was the first person I had ever seen who was actually related to me. He had my eyes, my colouring. To me, that was astonishing. I couldn't have wished for a better family than the people who brought me up – and I have never wanted or needed to try to find out more about my own mother – but I grew up amongst people who did not look like me, and here, now, with Luke, I was making a family of my own, in which we all belonged.'*

No matter how happy the outcome of adoption, it brings with it questions and concerns that need never trouble birth parents. To make it a success, therefore, get help and support at every step of the way.

When it is a success, however, knowing that you have given happiness and a home to a child who needed it, can bring a satisfaction that birth parents can never feel.

Abigail describes this unique feeling and the bond it creates: *'I don't want to think about what might have happened to Lily before she came to us. I don't want to worry about what scars there might be. What I do want is to give her the love and happiness we had overflowing, that might have had nowhere else to go.'*

STEP-PARENTING

For some parents, families happen differently. They get 'ready-made' children when their partner has children from a previous relationship. Some days it can feel like you're walking through a mine-field. Whatever you do, it's going to upset someone, or you'll put a foot wrong and there'll be an explosion – just because there are so many people in the equation.

Amanda explains one aspect of step-parenting: *'If you have a tendency to feel guilty, then step-parenting gives you a great opportunity: you feel guilty that you don't love them enough; you feel guilty that you might be favouring your own children over the stepchildren; you feel guilty that you're making decisions that the natural parents might not agree with; you feel guilty that when they go through phases of being absolute shits, it's all your fault.'*

Penny married a man with children of his own already: *'I didn't just take on the man, I took on his children, and it's not like they're here all the time for me to get to know them, it's like having visitors every other weekend. I mean, who would you like to come and visit you every other weekend? To me, they're guests. I have to cook meals for these guests, entertain them when they're here and clean up after them when they're gone. As far as Brian's concerned, they're not an intrusion — your own children aren't an intrusion — but his children are an intrusion to me. And in the end they're kids, they get mixed up and confused, so you're not allowed to be cross with them, I don't want to be cross with them, they're good kids. Everyone tells me they're good kids, and I know they're good kids. But I don't want them visiting me every other weekend.'*

Clare tries not to feel resentful: *'The thing that gets me most is someone else making decisions about them when we're not consulted and we just have to go along because their mum knows best, she has them most of the time, and when you least expect it or haven't planned it, there's money got to go somewhere. Amy needs to go to summer camp, Michael needs a new pair of shoes, so you're just expected to cough up. And you're really made to feel like a wicked stepmother if you try to say, "Well I was hoping to put some money by this month for a holiday of our own . . ." So we contribute 50% of the resources with zero per cent of the decision-making.'*

Vivienne feels sad at other people's attitudes: *'Being a step-parent . . . the hardest thing about it that I've found is that it's very isolating. No one's interested if you say you've got problems. They say, "Well, you knew what you were taking on before you got into it", and to some extent that's true, you know that the children are part of the equation. But you don't know what it will feel like, especially when you have a child of your own and you're aware that you've put their noses out of joint still more. And if you ever complain, just once, you're being petty, because everybody knows they have a hard enough time of it as it is. People say, "Sasha, she's lucky, she's got both her parents all the time." So Tom and Elizabeth are already at a disadvantage in their eyes. How can I complain when I'm up against that?'*

BUT, AT the end of the day, as responsible step-parents, you can't take
the blame for things that are not down to you. Amanda tries to
remind herself that it isn't always her fault: *'I am not responsible for his
destiny and there's nothing I could have done about his parents' splitting up,
Mark's had a tough time – he was an only child until he was nine, then his*

natural mother had two children, then we had two children. Of course it is hard for him to accept that, but neither he nor I can change those things.'

Taking on responsibility for a child that is not your own can demand endless reserves of patience and respect – and that's just on the part of the step-parent. Perhaps the safest way forward is not to expect anything of the child.

Amanda continues: *'I care for Mark but I get little back – which I think is down to both of us. I hope that one day when he is older he will realise that I tried my best, and I think in many ways he does know that. But it is difficult to live in a house with someone who is not blood-family and that you can't love in the same way. Mark loves his mother unquestioningly and, although I know that is as it should be, there is a niggle, yes, that I have mothered him now for ten years and didn't get anything back.'*

THE NEXT CHILD

FOR SOME parents, there comes a point at which they want another child to add to their family – they often talk of the sense in which they feel they are 'two parents and a child' and want their child to have a sibling, and *then* they'll be a family.

Hazel was surprised how strong the urge to have a second baby was: *'When I was pregnant with Ben, I couldn't believe that we'd ever want or need more than one child. I felt so happy, so complete. So it was quite a shock when I felt the same old urge, the same instinct reasserting itself: it's like my subconscious was saying to me: "Have another baby" even though my conscious mind was saying: "Why? Why?" It was a very strong feeling, which, wouldn't go away. It started when Ben was around a year old. I was completely unprepared for it – I thought once you'd satisfied the urge to reproduce, the urge would go away. And here it was, back. I feel I ought to point out, though, that after we'd had James, the sense that two children were right for us was far stronger than any lingering urge to go for three!'*

ONCE YOU have decided that you would like a second child, the other major consideration is how big the gap should be between children. Most of us are lucky to have the choice, but sometimes it seems like the arguments as to whether a small or a large gap is best are equally valid: certainly, you will find people willing to argue the case either way.

Jackie and her husband had planned to wait a couple of years before their next baby, but things happened more quickly: *'I have a very small gap between mine – eleven months – and when the girls were small I heard a lot of people muttering about how I would just have to wait and see and how it wasn't going to be roses all the way. Well, they're both now five and I have to say it was one of the best decisions we ever made. Of course it wasn't roses all the way, it never is, but it was roses damn near most of the way. They play together, sometimes one coming up with ideas, sometimes the other. They have these conspiracies that shut out the grown-ups. Most five-year-olds, they have a sibling two or three years younger, not ready to play with them as an equal, but Cory and Christy don't have that. There were difficult times, when one was one and one was two. They were both getting around a lot and wanting to explore, and it seemed like I couldn't keep my eyes on both of them and when they weren't running about they were at the "It's mine" phase, but when I was pregnant that second time, I had a baby that still slept for an hour in the morning and an hour in the afternoon, and when Christy was just born, Cory was coming up to one, demanding, but not at that* very *demanding phase that they go through – the terrible "terrible twos". There is one big disadvantage – it's all going past too quickly. If I could, I'd have another two tomorrow.'*

Camilla's story is quite the opposite in terms of age gap: *'I really did start all over again: my older ones were ten and twelve. I didn't plan to have such a large gap – in fact, I didn't plan to have another child. It was because I'd got married again when I was 37, and Julian had no children of his own, and it didn't seem fair when I already had two, so . . . People would say to me that the only reason I could contemplate it at all was that it had been so long since I'd had a baby that I had forgotten what it was actually like.*

Nathaniel was born at home, and his older brother and sister saw him within seconds of the birth, and from that moment they were very tender and caring towards him. Of course some days it all gets on top of me: Susie and Daniel are of that age where I seem to be no more than a taxi service taking them to their various social events, and Nat gets fed up being in his baby seat

THE AGE GAP

LARGE GAP

Advantages	**Disadvantages**
● Spreads the hard work out into manageable chunks	● Children may grow up distant from each other
● Gives you time to recover your energies	● A long time at home as an active parent can make returning to the job market more difficult
● Gives you time to enjoy each child as an individual	
● Gives each child the chance to have a lot of your attention in the early years	● It may mean the older child having his freedom curtailed in ways he is more aware of as he gets older.
● Spreads the costs over a longer time.	

SMALL GAP

Advantages	**Disadvantages**
● Gets the hard work over with all at once	● All the expenses come closer together
● Means that you work hard – but for less time!	● Children may be more prone to squabbling as their interests often overlap
● Gives you time to enjoy your own life after 'parenting' sooner	● Things can be more difficult to manage practically: for example, the first may not yet be potty-trained when the second comes along.
● Lets the children grow up close and form a strong relationship.	

as we dash along the highways. And it is very hard to consider GCSE options for Susie when I am more worried about teething and Nat's grizzles. Puberty and toddlerhood happening in the same household isn't an easy option, but there is one thing I'm looking forward to, when Julian and I have the energy to go out in the evenings on our own again: built-in babysitters!'

EVEN WHEN parents have chosen the spacing that they thought would suit them best, there is no getting away from the fact of the demands and extra work that a second child involves: and this time there isn't even the novelty factor to tide you through those first sleepless weeks.

Clive, father of four, is more reticent about the most recent addition to their family: *'After Annabel was born, I felt less like a good parent than I ever had before. Alison had everything organised down to the last minute: there was one being fed, one being bathed; there was one going in the pram, there was one getting his shoes on. And whatever I did to help, it was wrong. All Alison talked about was the children, and whereas before I'd begun to see how we might come out of it and get our life back, now we were back to square one.'*

Most parents worry about the effect on their existing child or children, whatever the age gap they opt for.

Jean and her husband were glad to be able to enjoy their first son for a little while longer, but still felt guilty about how the next child might affect his life: *'Georgette was born by planned caesarean so we knew the night before that this would be Peter's last night with us as our only child. I felt quite tearful as I kissed him goodnight. It felt very definitely as if one important phase of our lives was ending, that we were moving on. I felt tremendously guilty in a way, that we both knew what we were in for but Peter didn't – that the world was going to come crashing down around his head. All that guilt, but all that love as well – and never any question that what we were doing was right, but terrified because we knew we'd love our second baby just as much as we already loved him and he'd take a long time coming to terms with that.'*

IF YOU have just one child, you will never have to tell him that he needs to wait while you take care of the other child's demands first. You will never have to tell him to share his toys with his sister. He will never have to miss tea with his friends because the new baby's come down with chicken-pox.

But if you have just one child, that child will never have the joy of sharing a game with his sibling, of having ready-made company on even the most tedious and wettest of school holidays, will never have anyone they can complain to about the awful injustices of their parents – someone who will understand exactly because those parents are their parents, too.

Maria tries to give all three of her children the time they need, though it is hard: *'If we'd had the knowledge or the choice, we certainly wouldn't have gone about things this way – one boy and then twin girls. First Jay got all the attention, then they did, and their needs are always so much greater than his simply because there's two of them and everything takes twice as long. But I try to say, "Right, the girls have had half an hour of me, so Jay can have half an hour." It doesn't always work but we all understand the principle.'*

FOR SOME parents, however, the decision over how big the gap should be is taken out of their hands. Some couples find it difficult, perhaps impossible to conceive a second child.

Patty and her partner Brian had their first child when Patty was still at university, unplanned, but much wanted. They decided to get married when Tommy was old enough to join in the celebrations. After five years of marriage and actively trying to conceive another baby they feel about ready to be content with their one and only child: *'Patty has found it hard to come to terms with the possibility of no more children. It seems so strange that Tommy was conceived so easily but now we have actually planned a pregnancy nothing happens! I'd support Patty all the way if she wanted to try infertility treatment, but she wants to conceive without technology or not at all.'*

Other couples actively choose to 'stop at one'. Simon and Linda are one of those couples and Simon explains their decision: *'Yes, I know people do go on to have two, but they're mad. Everyone assumes that because we've got one, we're going to go on and have another. Why? Jen's coming up to two now and we're beginning to get some of the old routines back, everything's on more of an even keel. I would never want to go back to those days where you never knew from one minute to the next what life was going to throw at you – what the baby was going to throw at you. We're past nappies. She sleeps through the night. She's at playgroup. Linda's back at work. And that's another thing – how could we afford it? We need Linda's money.'*

FOR SOME parents, this decision to limit their family is a painful one, and one not easily reached, as Delia describes: *'I'm not saying that Guy is worse than any other child, or that other parents don't have children who are such hard work, but Guy's worn us down until we have nothing left to give. And we still have to face as many years as it will take of him being like this. We can't risk having a second one like Guy. And say we didn't. Say our second child was naturally calm, loveable and endearing. Where would that leave Guy? He would become second-best, even to us, and I can't risk doing that to him.'*

THIS DECISION can be particularly painful when it is taken out of your hands and lies in the control of 'genetics'.

With an illness like cystic fibrosis (CF) which is caused by a defective gene, part of the problem is the insidious nature of the disease's transmission. You can be a carrier of CF without knowing it. CF 'carriers' are completely healthy and most are unaware that they are carrying a defective gene. Thus, the gene can pass undetected from generation to generation and only come to light when two carriers have a child. If that child inherits the defective gene from both parents, he or she will develop CF. Parents whose first child has been born with CF or a similarly genetically transmitted illness thus have to face a heartbreaking dilemma: should they have antenatal screening or not, to find out if their next child will also develop the disease?

Dora and her husband know only too well how tough tests and results can make your life: *'Catherine, our first daughter, has cystic fibrosis. When I was expecting again I had all sorts of tests when I was nine weeks' pregnant. It was another girl, and this time she was a carrier of CF. I cannot tell you how glad I was. There was no way I could have put another child through what I've seen Cathy go through.'*

If you have had one child with an inherited illness or disability, talk through carefully the implications of screening. Developments mean that testing methods are changing all the time; you need up-to-date information and advice before you can make any decision or choice.

BEING A FAMILY

THERE COMES for all of us a point when we stop *becoming* a family and simply start *being* a family. We never stop learning new skills, we never know what surprises our children may have in store for us, but there will come a point when we are over the shock of the new, when we don't have to remind ourselves that we are now parents – we just get on with it.

Sarah learnt that time flies during the early years: *'I thought my baby was the only baby in the world. Well, objectively I knew she wasn't, but . . . She was the newest, the youngest, the smallest and the best. And then suddenly, when she was about six months old, I started seeing newer babies. Smaller. How could this be? I thought the world had stopped when my baby was born. And then things got worse: my itsy-bitsy baby was actually getting quite big. Solid foods. Ready Brek. And the next minute, she was turning round and saying, "Hey, mum, where's my breakfast?" It was astonishing. If babyhood seems endless, rest assured — one day you'll look back and realise it was over in a twinkling.'*

It's easy to play the part of the 'experienced' mother to other, new mothers, as Alice describes: *'When Matthew was little I really used to resent older people telling me what to do, "Oh, give him a bottle", things like that. And now that he's getting a bit older — he's nearly one — I have to restrain myself from telling other people what to do with their babies.'*

Deirdre believes it is the simple things in life that children and a family enjoy: *'One of the nicest things about being a family that I have found is the way you get to have all your childhood favourites over again — Christmas, bonfires, Hallowe'en, pumpkins with candles in them . . . sometimes it's better than when you were a child yourself because you can see how beautiful it all is.'*

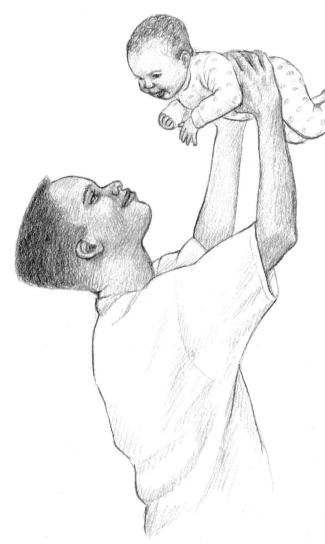

BEING A FAMILY is exhilarating, frustrating, rewarding, and unlike anything else you'll ever do.

It isn't a job that will be accomplished in a day, a week, or even a couple of years. Just as your baby took his place in your family, so, one day, he will have a family of his own.

Now that you know what having children does to your sense of time, it might feel like tomorrow.

Naomi makes the final comment: *'There's a line in* The Prophet *which says: "You are the bows from which your children as living arrows are sent forth." When you have children, you don't get time to be very mystical or spiritual, but sometimes, especially when she's gone to sleep for the night, and she's so peaceful and I look at her, I think, "Yes, you really are a living arrow. You'll go forward into a future that I will never see." And my aim must be to make her as straight and true as I possibly can.'*

Directory

THE SOURCES of help listed here are not intended to be exhaustive. There are many other voluntary organisations in existence which may be able to offer you specific information and advice, and others that will be able to offer you more appropriate support as your baby grows into childhood. In particular, there are many small organisations based on giving support for a rare disorder or a specific syndrome which will be able to offer the help you need. Your health visitor or social services department will be able to point you in the right direction or provide you with a directory of services available in your local area.

The work that some of these organisations do is multi-faceted and varied. We have not listed here all aspects of an organisation's remit, only those that are most likely to be immediately relevant to parents. For example, many organisations carry out research programmes, or help to raise funds for specialised equipment but, when parents first turn to them, it is usually for help and support, so it is these services we highlight.

When writing to any organisation, please include an SAE if you want a reply, as many of these organisations rely on voluntary donations.

The NCT runs a National Experiences Register which can be an invaluable source of information and support for new parents who aren't sure where else to turn. Parents from all over the country who have been through particular difficulties or situations, and are willing to share their experiences with others going through something similar, volunteer to put their names on the Register, which is then held by a national co-ordinator. The Register covers a myriad of topics, ranging from allergies, amniocentesis and asthma, to ventouse, water births and working, with everything in between. Very often, the co-ordinator will be able to put you in touch with someone nearby who will be able to share and to offer a listening ear. If you'd like to talk to someone, call the NCT on 0181 992 8637 and ask to be put in touch with the National Experiences Register.

Premature babies

BLISS/NIPPERS
(National Information for Parents of Prematures: Education, Resources, Support)
17-21 Emerald Street
London WC1N 3QL
Telephone: 0171 831 9393

IF YOUR baby needs to be looked after in a special care unit after birth, try reading *Breastfeeding if Your Baby Needs Special Care*. It gives information on the best ways of breastfeeding your baby, including a section on how to express milk. Available from NCT Maternity Sales Ltd, Burnfield Avenue, Glasgow G46 7TL. Telephone: 0141 633 5552.

Egnell electric pumps to help women breastfeeding sick or premature infants can also be hired through local NCT branches. Look in the phone book for your local contact number, or call the National office on 0181 992 8637.

Special needs

Association for Spina Bifida and Hydrocephalus
(ASBAH)
42 Park Road
Peterborough PE1 2UQ
Telephone: 01733 555988
ASBAH has a network of supporters who pro-
vide care and help to families.

British Institute for Brain-Injured Children
(BIBIC)
Knowle Hall
Knowle
Bridgwater
Somerset TA7 8PJ
Telephone: 01278 684060
Prescribes treatment programmes which can be
carried out at home by parents and volunteer
helpers.

Cerebral Palsy Helpline
Telephone: 0800 626216
Open: Monday–Friday 11am–9pm; Saturday
and Sunday 2pm–6pm.

Cleft Lip and Palate Association (CLAPA)
134 Buckingham Palace Road
London SW1 9SA
Telephone: 0171 824 8110
Supports parents of newborn babies affected by
this condition.

Contact-a-Family
170 Tottenham Court Road
London W1P 0HA
Telephone: 0171 383 3555
Contact-a-Family provides help and advice for
families caring for children with disabilities,
linking families both locally and nationally
round specific conditions and informing them
of appropriate support networks.

Cystic Fibrosis Trust
Alexandra House
5 Blyth Road
Bromley
Kent BR1 3RS
Telephone: 0181 464 7211
Helps and advises parents caring for children
with this inherited condition.

Down's Syndrome Association
155 Mitcham Road
London SW17 9PG
Telephone: 0181 682 4001
A parents' self-help group which promotes the
care, nurture and education of Down's children.

Birthmarks

YOU NEED to be referred by your GP to get
laser treatment for your baby's birthmark.
However, some GPs are not aware of the
recent developments in laser treatment, so you
may like to ask to see a specialist for a more
specific prognosis.

Naevus Support Group
58 Necton Road
Wheathampstead
St Albans
Herts AL4 8AU
Telephone: 01582 832853
Provides up-to-date information and puts par-
ents of children who have birthmarks in touch
with each other.

Bereavement

The Stillbirth and Neonatal Death Society
(SANDS)
28 Portland Place
London W1N 4DE
Telephone: 0171 436 5881
Offers telephone counselling and befriending to
anyone who has lost a baby.

Chapter One – You and Your Newborn

Caesareans

Many NCT groups can offer local contacts for women who want to share and discuss their experiences of caesarean birth.

Twins

Twins and Multiple Births Association (TAMBA)
PO Box 30
Little Sutton
South Wirral L66 1TH
Telephone: 0151 348 0020

TAMBA provides a listening and information service (TAMBA Twinline) on 01732 868000: Monday–Friday 6pm–11pm; Saturday and Sunday 10am–11pm. The service is confidential, can give up-to-date information on a range of issues and your call will be answered by someone who is a parent of twins or more themselves.

Additional services include a one-parent families group, a special needs group, a bereavement support group, a group for families with triplets, quads and so on, and a group for parents who have had twins (or more) following fertility treatment. They also provide some useful leaflets on *Twins*, *Breastfeeding Twins* and *Bottle-feeding Twins*.

When things aren't as you expected

Prematurity/Special care
Blisslink/Nippers
17-21 Emerald Street
London WC1N 3QL
Telephone: 0171 831 9393

Chapter Two – Learning New Skills

Holding

The NSPCC produces a useful leaflet called *Handle With Care* that contains some helpful advice on safe and positive ways of holding and caring for your baby.

Send an SAE to:
NSPCC (Publications)
42 Curtain Road
London EC2A 3NH

Feeding

You can contact your local NCT branch and they will put you in touch with a breastfeeding counsellor in your local area. The services of a breastfeeding counsellor are free. You do not have to be an NCT member to use them. If you are considering or have already given up breastfeeding you may find it helpful to talk to a breastfeeding counsellor. The counsellor is a mother who has breastfed her own children, undergone the NCT's own training and will offer support and information.

Association of Breastfeeding Mothers
26 Holmeshaw Close
London SE26 4TH
Telephone: 0181 778 4769
Gives information and support to breastfeeding mothers.

La Leche League
BM 3424 London WC1N 3XX
Telephone: 0171 242 1278
Information and support to encourage breastfeeding.

Crying

CRY-SIS
BM CRY-SIS
London WC1N 3XX
Telephone: 0171 404 5011
Provides emotional support and practical advice to parents whose babies cry incessantly or have sleep problems.

Home Start-UK
2 Salisbury Road
Leicester LE1 7QR
Telephone: 0116 233 9955
Offers parents support in their own homes.

There are many local **Parentlines**. You may see these advertised in Child Health Clinics, in your GP's surgery, or at mother-and-toddler groups. They offer confidential counselling to help combat stress.

Cranial osteopathy

For information on this technique, contact:
The Osteopathic Centre for Children
4 Harcourt House
19a Cavendish Square
London W1M 9AD
Telephone: 0171 495 1231

For the names of fully qualified osteopaths, contact:
The General Council and Register of Osteopaths
Telephone: 01734 576585

Growing

Child Growth Foundation
2 Mayfield Avenue
London W4 1PW
Telephone: 0181 995 0257
Information and advice for any parent concerned about their child's growth.

Nursing

Action for Sick Children
Argyle House
29–31 Euston Road
London NW1 2SD
Telephone: 0171 833 2041
Offers a library and information service for parents who are caring for sick children either at hospital or at home.

Bereavement

Compassionate Friends
53 North Street
Bristol BS3 1EN
Telephone: 0117 966 5202
Helpline: Monday–Friday 9.30am–5pm:
0117 953 9639
Offers friendship to newly bereaved and grieving parents who have lost a child of any age.

The Cot Death Society
1 Browning Close
Thatcham
Newbury
Berkshire RG18 3EF
Telephone/Fax: 01635 861771
Loans respiration monitors for infants who do not qualify under the Care of Next Infant (CONI) scheme. Advice and resuscitation videos are available. Not a bereavement counselling service.

Foundation for the Study of Infant Deaths
No. 14 Halkin Street
London SW1X 7DP
Telephone: 0171 235 0965 (General Enquiries)
Telephone: 0171 235 1721 (24-hour Helpline)
Provides information and offers personal support to bereaved parents.

Alternative Therapies

EACH THERAPY has its own official organisations.

For a list of addresses or more information send an SAE plus two loose 1st or 2nd class stamps to:
The Institute for Complementary Medicine
PO Box 194
London SE16 1QZ
Telephone: 0171 237 5165

Acupuncture is the use of an ancient Chinese system which involves the placing of needles into the body at highly specific points to focus and channel the body's natural energies. Many GPs accept the efficacy of acupuncture especially when dealing with problems like allergies and low spirits.
For the name of a local, registered acupuncturist, contact:
The British Acupuncture Association and Register
Telephone: 0171 834 1012.

Aromatherapy is the use of oils from particular plants which are either inhaled or absorbed through the skin. Consult a trained aromatherapist as the essential oils used are very strong and need to be diluted in specific ways before use. The main organisations are:
The International Society of Practising Aromatherapists (ISPA) and The International Federation of Aromatherapists (IFA).

Chiropractic is the manipulation of the spine to alleviate problems, usually those associated with the neck and the back. Releasing pressure on the nerves in the spine can help with problems in other parts of the body, too. Some chiropractors recommend the technique as a way of alleviating infant colic.

Herbal remedies make use of plant extracts and are usually gentle, with fewer side-effects than mainstream drugs.
Contact:
The General Council and Register of Consultant Herbalists
18 Sussex Square, Brighton
East Sussex BN2 5AA

Homoeopathy is a therapy that has gained credibility with the medical establishment over recent years. Perhaps this is because, despite the fact that the remedy contains a tiny quantity of whatever it is that would make the symptoms worse if given in large amounts, and despite the fact that the quantities involved are so minute that they shouldn't work at all, people do respond to homoeopathic treatments. Conditions like eczema and sleeplessness are particularly helped by this therapy.
   There are now many GPs who practise homoeopathy alongside conventional medicine. There are also several NHS hospitals where you can get homoeopathic treatment; for example, in Glasgow, Bristol, London and Liverpool.
For more information, send an SAE to:
The Society of Homoeopaths
2 Artizan Road
Northampton NN1 4HU
Telephone: 01604 21400

OR

The British Homoeopathic Association
27a Devonshire Street
London W1N 1RJ
Telephone: 0171 935 2163

On the whole, it is best to consult an expert when it comes to homoeopathic treatment, but, for simple conditions, you can treat yourself.

Illnesses

Asthma
National Asthma Campaign
Providence House
Providence Place
London N1 0NT
Telephone: 0171 226 2260
Helpline: Monday–Friday 9am–9pm: 0345 010203

Eczema
National Eczema Society
163 Eversholt Street
London NW1 1BU
Telephone: 0171 388 4097
Local groups and information advising on the general management of eczema.

Developmental Disabilities
In Touch
10 Norman Road
Sale
Cheshire M33 3DF
Telephone: 0161 9052440
Helps to make informal contacts between parents of children with learning disabilities and rare disorders for mutual support.

National Portage Association
127 Monks Dale
Yeovil
Somerset BA21 3JE
Telephone: 01935 71641
Portage is a home-visiting educational service which offers support to parents in the care and development of babies and children with a disability.

Eyes
Getting Started is a guide for parents whose children have been diagnosed with eye conditions such as squints, blindness or restricted vision. It is available free with an SAE from:
RNIB Information Service
224 Great Portland Street
London W1N 6AA
Telephone: 0171 388 1266

LOOK: National Office
Queen Alexandra College
49 Court Oak Road
Harborne
Birmingham B17 9TG
Telephone: 0121 428 5038
Provides practical help, support and advice to families with visually impaired children.

Sense
11-13 Clifton Terrace
Finsbury Park
London N4 3SR
Telephone: 0171 272 7774
Sense was formed by a group of parents whose children were born deaf/blind as a result of rubella. Provides advice and support for families of deaf/blind children and has a regional network of self-help groups.

Ears
British Deaf Association
38 Victoria Place
Carlisle CA1 1HU
Telephone: 01228 48844 (Voice/Text)
Offers information for all deaf children and parents.

National Deaf Children's Society
15 Dufferin Street
London EC1Y 8PD
Telephone: 0171 250 0123
Offers free advice, counselling and information on all aspects of childhood deafness.

Chapter Three – Your New Self

ParentAbility
NCT
Alexandra House
Oldham Terrace, Acton
London W3 6NH
Telephone: 0181 992 8637
Offers support and local contacts for parents
with disabilities.

Stress Incontinence

For a free leaflet on incontinence, send a
large sae to:
Continence Foundation
2 Doughty Street
London WC1N 2PH
The Continence Foundation also has a helpline
on: 0191 213 0050 from 9am–6pm Mondays–
Fridays.
They can put you in touch with local advisers.

Depression and Stress

Association for Postnatal Illness
25 Jerdan Place, Fulham
London SW6 1BE
Telephone: 0171 386 0868
Send an SAE for information.

Meet-a-Mum Association (MAMA)
14 Willis Road
Croydon
Surrey
CR20 2XX
Telephone: 0181 665 0357
Fax: 0181 665 1972
Helpline 3pm–11pm 0181 656 7318
Practical mother-to-mother support for those
who are isolated, lonely or depressed.

Exploring Parenthood
4 Ivory Place
20a Treadgold Street
London W11 4BP
Telephone: 0171 221 4471
Fax: 0171 221 5501
Parents' Advice Line 0171 221 6681
Offers a parents' advice line, group counselling
and discussion with the aim of preventing stress
and breakdown in family life – open to all parents, natural or adoptive.

National Childbirth Trust
Alexandra House
Oldham Terrace, Acton
London W3 6NH
Telephone: 0181 992 8637
Many local groups have postnatal depression
support groups or local contacts to whom those
with PND can talk on a mother-to-mother
support basis.

NSPCC Child Protection Helpline
Telephone: 0800 800500
This is a free, 24-hour helpline for anyone worried about a baby or child who may be in danger. It can begin an investigation if you are
worried that a child is being hurt, and also offers
advice and counselling.

Parentline (Organisations for Parents under
Stress)
Endway House
The Endway
Benfleet
Essex SS7 2AN
Telephone: 01702 559900
Runs a network of telephone helplines for parents
under stress.
Admin line: 01702 554782
Fax: 01702 554911

The Parent Network
44–46 Caversham Road
London NW5 2DS
Telephone: 0171 485 8535
Provides 'Parent-Link' support and education groups in local communities, offering parents a listening ear, and with the emphasis on encouraging parents to feel good about their own lives, with a chance to share ideas and experiences on ways of dealing with difficult situations at home.

CHAPTER FOUR – YOU AND YOUR PARTNER

Difficulties

Asian Family Counselling Service
74 The Avenue
London W13 8LB
Telephone: 0181 997 5749
An established national charity which assists Asian families with marital problems, offering professional counselling in a number of Asian languages.

British Association for Counselling
1 Regent Place
Rugby
Warwickshire CV21 2PJ
Can provide you with details of counsellors working in your area.

Relate: Marriage Guidance
Herbert Gray College
Little Church Street
Rugby CV21 3AP
Telephone: 01788 573241
Confidential counselling for relationship problems of any kind through local branches. Look in the phone book or contact the national address above for a local contact.

Single Parents

Association for One Parent Families
16-17 Clerkenwell Close
London EC1R 0AA
Telephone: 0171 336 8183
Provides support and information for single parents and their children, with practical help through co-operative effort.

HOP (Holidays for One Parent families)
51 Hampshire Road
Droylsden
Manchester M43 7PH
Telephone: 0161 370 0337
A voluntary organisation that arranges holidays for one-parent families, and outings of various kinds. For further information, call, or send an SAE with two first-class stamps.

National Council for One Parent Families
255 Kentish Town Road
London NW5 2LX
Telephone: 0171 267 1361
Runs an information service and provides support to lone parents.

CHAPTER FIVE – YOU AND THE WORLD
Safety

FOR A FREE copy of the booklet *Keep Your Baby Safe*, which provides much useful advice and guidance on all aspects of safety for your baby in his environment, send an A5-sized SAE to:
The Child Accident Prevention Trust
Clerks Court
18–20 Farringdon Lane
London EC1R 3AU

Friends

THE NCT, ALONG with its antenatal classes and breastfeeding support, can put you in contact with other parents in your local area who have babies of a smiliar age to your own. Every local branch is different, so the activities on offer will be different, but you will often find 'open house' meetings, where people get together in one another's homes to chat and catch up; and many branches have 'bumps and babies' events, where those in the last few months of pregnancy can get together with mothers who have only recently made the leap across the chasm into parenthood and have a baby of less than six months old. If you have a newborn, you may find these events quite reassuring and more peaceful without boisterous toddlers carousing about.

Your local NCT branch may also offer support groups for working parents, a fathers' group, a single parents' group, an evening social group – all very valuable when your baby is tiny and you want to share information and stories with other parents as much as possible.

To get in touch with your local branch, first try looking in the telephone book under NCT to see if the branch membership secretary is listed (you don't have to be a member to participate in social events, only if you want to take a more active role in the organisation of the NCT, but the membership secretary will still be your first point of contact). She will be able to tell you what's going on locally and how you can join in.

If you can't find a contact name in the telephone book, call 0181 992 8637.

Socialising

National Women's Register
3A Vulcan House
Vulcan Road North
Norwich NR6 6AQ
Telephone: 01603 406767
Offers women the opportunity to meet in each other's homes and take part in lively discussion. All welcome.

Boredom

Letterbox Library
Unit 2D
Leroy House
436 Essex Road
London N1 3QP
Telephone: 0171 226 1633
Produces a quarterly catalogue of books that encourage self-esteem by providing positive images for children. Also a quarterly newsletter for members.

Play Matters
(National Toy Libraries Association)
68 Churchway
London NW1 1LT
Telephone: 0171 387 9592
Maintains links between toy libraries – can give details of the libraries in your area.

Experts

Family Rights Group
The Print House
18 Ashwin Street
London E8 3DL
Telephone: 0171 923 2628
Advises families of children in public care, involved in child protection procedures, or receiving family support services.

Chapter Six – You and the Future

Working

Day Care Trust
4 Wild Court
London WC2B 4AU
Telephone: 0171 405 5617
Provides information for parents about child-care issues and promotes the development of high-quality childcare services.

Maternity Alliance
45 Beech Street
Barbican
London EC2Y 8AD
Telephone: 0171 588 8582
Information and advice on benefits and maternity rights at work.

Parents at Work
5th Floor
45 Beech Street
Barbican
London EC2Y 8AD
Telephone: 0171 628 3578
Provides information and advice about child-care provision and offers informal support through a network of local groups.

Widening Horizons

The Open University
Walton Hall
Milton Keynes MK7 6AA
Telephone: 01908 274066
The Community Education Office produces a number of home-study packs and videos which individuals can use to learn more about the baby, child development and family life. You can also ask about courses that interest you with a view to retraining or gaining an additional qualification.

Chapter Seven – Becoming a Family

Stepfamilies

Stepfamily – The National Stepfamily Association
Chapel House
18 Hatton Place
London EC1N 8RU
Telephone: 0171 209 2460 (General Enquiries)
Telephone: 0171 209 2464 (Counselling)
Provides support to all members of stepfamilies. More than half of all stepfamilies also have one new 'joint' child. The National Stepfamily Association has produced a booklet *A Baby of Our Own: A New Baby in the Family* for those parents who are thinking of having a new baby, and for those who already have a new baby and are looking for help on coping with some of the issues that may have arisen. It is available from the Book Sales Department of the National Stepfamily Association.

Assisted reproduction

FOR ADVICE on finding an infertility clinic, and on counselling, contact:

CHILD
Charter House
43 St Leonard's Road
Bexhill on Sea
East Sussex TN40 1JA
Telephone: 01424 732361
Provides counselling and information for people suffering from infertility.

ISSUE – The National Fertility Association
509 Aldridge Road
Great Barr
Birmingham B44 8NA
Telephone: 0121 344 4414
Offers advice, support and information to people with infertility problems.

Miscarriage Association

Local groups throughout the country offer
information and support for women and their
families during and after miscarriage.
The Association can be contacted at:
c/o Clayton Hospital
Northgate
Wakefield
West Yorkshire WF1 3JS
Telephone: 01924 200799

Adoption

For further information, contact:
British Agencies for Adoption and Fostering
Skyline House
200 Union Street
London SE1 0LX
Telephone: 0171 593 2000
Among the agencies' aims is the objective of
extending the opportunity for family life for
children with special needs.

Further Reading

NEW BOOKS are being published all the time and a browse through your local bookshop will unearth many which will appeal. The titles listed below might point you in the right direction if you need more information on a particular subject, and will give you an idea of the range of topics and authors available. Don't feel you have to buy them all, and remember that you will be able to borrow many of them from the library. Don't forget that your child can have his or her own library ticket from birth too!

Each author will have different opinions and ideas – sometimes they will violently contradict each other. Remember, that not all of these books are included because we agree or approve of what they say, but because they will all give you more information than is possible to include in one book, and will help you make up your *own* mind on a topic.

CHAPTER ONE – YOU AND YOUR NEWBORN

Baby Basics

Julia Berryman, Karen Thorpe and Kate Windridge 1995: *Older Mothers: Conception, Pregnancy and Birth after 35*. Pandora.

Wendy Blumfield 1992: *Life After Birth*. Element.

Dr John Cobb 1980: *Babyshock: A Mother's First Five Years*. Hutchinson

A Eisenberg, H E Murkoff and S E Hathaway 1993: *What to Expect in the First Year*. Simon & Schuster.

Dr Christopher Green 1989: *Babies! A Parent's Guide to Surviving (And Enjoying) Baby's First Year*. Simon & Schuster.

Annette Karmiloff-Smith 1995: *Baby, It's You*. Ebury Press.

Sheila Kitzinger 1994: *The Year After Childbirth*. Oxford University Press.

Maggie Jones 1994: *Mothercare: First Year Week by Week*. Conran Octopus. A diary for you to fill in.

Penelope Leach 1974: *Babyhood*. Pelican – the research behind much of her practical advice in: *Baby And Child*. Penguin.

NCT Publications Booklet: *Resource List for Parents with Disabilities*. Available from NCT Maternity Sales Ltd, Burnfield Avenue, Glasgow G46 7TL. Telephone: 0141 633 5552.

Dr Francis Peck 1993: *Handbook for Young Mothers*. Rainer Publications.

Libby Purves 1987: *How Not to be a Perfect Mother*. Fontana.

Miriam Stoppard 1995: *Complete Baby and Child Care*. Dorling Kindersley.

Miriam Stoppard 1989: *The First Weeks of Life*. Dorling Kindersley.

Lisa Miller 1992: *Understanding Your Baby*. The Tavistock Clinic.

Gill Thorn 1995: *Practical Parenting Pregnancy and Birth Book*. Hamlyn.

Fathers

Rob Parsons 1995: *The Sixty Minute Father*. Hodder & Stoughton Ltd. A practical parenthood guide for dads by a dad.

NCT Publications Leaflet: *Becoming A Father*. Available from NCT Maternity Sales Ltd, Burnsfield Avenue, Glasgow G46 7TL. Telephone: 0141 633 5552.

Caesareans

Sarah Clement 1991: *The Caesarean Experience*. Pandora.

Dr Colin Francome, Professor Wendy Savage, Helen Churchill and Helen Lewison 1993: *Caesarean Birth in Britain*. Middlesex University Press in association with the National Childbirth Trust.

Twins and more

Elizabeth Bryan 1992: *Twins, Triplets and More*. Penguin.

Elizabeth Bryan 1992: *Twins and Higher Multiple Births: A guide to their nature and nurture*. Edward Arnold.

David Harvey and Elizabeth Bryan (Eds.) 1991: *The Stress of Multiple Births*. Multiple Births Foundation.

J Lasker and S Borg 1989: *In Search of Parenthood*. Pandora.

Prematurity/Special care

Anne McFadyen 1994: *Special Care Babies and their Developing Relationships*. Routledge.

BLISS (Babylife Support Systems) has produced two booklets for the parents of premature babies: *The Bliss Guide to Neonatal Equipment* shows colour photographs and gives short explanations of the equipment that is found in Special Care Baby Units, and *Going Home: Taking your Special Care Baby Home* covers topics such as weaning, feeding, clothing and development. Each is available free of charge if you send an SAE to:
Blisslink/Nippers,
17–21 Emerald Street
London WC1N 3QL.

If your baby needs to be looked after in a special care unit after birth, try reading *Breastfeeding if Your Baby Needs Special Care*. It gives information on the best ways of breastfeeding your baby, including a section on how to express milk. Available from NCT Maternity Sales Ltd, Burnfield Avenue, Glasgow G46 7TL. Telephone: 0141 633 5552.

Special needs

Christine Eiser 1993: *Growing up with a Chronic Disease.* Jessica Kingsley.

Patricia Gilbert 1993: *A–Z Reference Book of Syndromes and Inherited Disorders.* Chapman & Hall.

M Stanton 1992: *Living with Cerebral Palsy.* Little, Brown and Company (UK) Ltd.

Dr R Newton 1992: *Down's Syndrome.* Little, Brown and Company (UK) Ltd.

Royal National Institute for the Blind: *Getting Started: A Guide to understanding your child's eye condition.* Available from:
RNIB Information Service
224 Great Portland Street
London W1N 6AA

Chapter Two – Learning New Skills

Holding

The NSPCC produces a useful leaflet called *Handle With Care* that contains some helpful advice on safe and positive ways of holding and caring for your new baby.
Send an SAE to:
NSPCC (Publications)
42 Curtain Road
London EC2A 3NH

Baby Massage

Peter Walker: *DIY Step-by-Step Guide to Baby Massage.*
A video available from NCT Maternity Sales Ltd, Burnfield Avenue, Glasgow G46 7TL.
Telephone: 0141 633 5552.

Feeding

Rose Elliott 1984: *Vegetarian Mother and Baby Book.* Fontana.

Annabel Karmel 1994: *Small Helpings.* BBC Books.

Jane Moody, Jane Britten, Karen Hogg 1996: *Breastfeeding Your Baby.* NCT Publishing Ltd.

Mary Smale 1992: *The NCT Book of Breastfeeding.* Vermilion.

Penny and Andrew Stanway 1978: *Breast is Best.* Pan.

Heather Welford 1994: *Feeding Your Child from Birth to Three.* Health Education Authority.

Sleeping

Dilys Daws 1989: *Through the Night.* Free Association Books, London.

Jo Douglas and Naomi Richman 1989: *My Child Won't Sleep.* Penguin.

Dr Richard Ferber 1985: *Solve Your Child's Sleep Problems.* Dorling Kindersley.

Deborah Jackson 1989: *Three in a Bed.* Bloomsbury.

Tine Thevenin 1987: *The Family Bed.* Avery, New Jersey.

Heather Welford 1994: *How to Get a Good Night's Sleep.* Thorsons.

Bereavement

Michael and Elaine Counsell 1992: *When Your Child Dies*. Mowbray Press, London and Oxford.

Jacquelynn Luben 1990: *Cot Deaths*. Bedford Square Press.

SANDS (Stillbirth and Neonatal Death Society) 1994: *Saying Goodbye to Your Baby*. SANDS. Available from NCT Maternity Sales Ltd, Burnfield Avenue, Glasgow G46 7TL. Telephone: 0141 633 5552

Juliet Swindells 1992: *Before You Say Goodbye*. Miscarriage Association.

Alternative Therapies

Miranda Castro 1992: *Homeopathy for Mother and Baby*. Macmillan.

Alison England 1993: *Aromatherapy for Mother and Baby*. Vermilion.

Anne McIntyre 1992: *The Herbal for Mother and Child*. Element.

Stephen Sandler 1994: *Osteopathy*. Optima.

Illnesses

Jane Houlton 1993: *Allergy Survival Guide*. Vermilion.

Developmental Disabilities

A D Kelsall 1993: *Children With Disabilities*. Disability Information Trust, Oxford.

CHAPTER THREE – YOUR NEW SELF

Your New Self

Jay Belsky and John Kelly 1994: *The Transition to Parenthood*. Vermilion.

Katherine Gieve 1990: *Balancing Acts: On Being a Mother*. Fontana.

Anne Lamott 1994: *Operating Instructions*. Bloomsbury.

Ann Oakley 1979: *From Here to Maternity*. Penguin.

Libby Purves 1987: *How Not to Be a Perfect Mother*. Penguin.

ParentAbility

Mukti Jain Campion 1990: *The Baby Challenge: A Handbook on Pregnancy for Women with a Physical Disability*. Routledge.

Mukti Jain Campion: *Video: Isobel's Baby*. Available from NCT Maternity Sales Ltd, Burnfield Avenue, Glasgow G46 7TL. Telephone: 0141 633 5552.

Lois Keith 1994: *Mustn't Grumble*. The Women's Press.

Veronica Lewis 1991: *A Good Sign Goes a Long Way: The Experience of Deaf Mothers*. RNID.

Exercise

Jane Ashton and Rosemary Conley 1992: *BBC Ante and Postnatal Exercise Video*. BBC.

Margie Polden and Barbara Whiteford 1992: *The Postnatal Exercise Book*. Frances Lincoln.

NCT/Gillian Fletcher 1991: *Get Into Shape After Childbirth*. Available from NCT Maternity Sales Ltd, Burnfield Avenue, Glasgow G46 7TL. Telephone: 0141 633 5552.

Depression and Stress

A free leaflet, *Help is at Hand*, is available from the Royal College of Psychiatrists, produced as part of its Defeat Depression campaign. It gives clear information on symptoms and different types of treatment, shows you how to seek help and how you can help yourself. For a copy, send an SAE to:
Help is at Hand
17 Belgrave Square
London SW1X 8PG

Dr Katarina Dalton 1989: *Depression After Childbirth*. Oxford Press.

Fiona Marshall 1993: *Coping with Postnatal Depression*. Sheldon Press.

Kate Mosse 1993: *Becoming A Mother*. Virago.

CHAPTER FOUR: YOU AND YOUR PARTNER

Difficulties

Robin Skynner and John Cleese 1988: *Families and How to Survive Them*. Fontana.

Single Parents

Jan Morris 1992: *Alone Together*. The Women's Press.

The Divorced Woman's Survival Kit: A Financial Guide. Send £2.95 (inc. p&p) to: Fiona Price & Partners Ltd, 33 Great Queen Street, London WC2B 5AA.

CHAPTER FIVE – YOU AND THE WORLD

Safety

For a free copy of the booklets *Keep Your Baby Safe*, which provides much useful advice and guidance on all aspects of safety for your baby in his home environment, and *Out and About With Babies and Young Children*, send an A5-sized SAE to:
The Child Accident Prevention Trust,
Clerks Court,
18–20 Farringdon Lane,
London EC1R 3AU.

For a free copy of the booklet *First Steps to Safety*, send an SAE to:
The Royal Society for the Prevention of Accidents
Cannon House
The Priory
Queensway
Birmingham B64 6BS

St John Ambulance Brigade 1994: *Fast Guide to First Aid for Babies and Toddlers*. Hascombe Enterprises.

Relatives

Rachel Billington 1994: *The Great Umbilical*. Hutchinson. (An exploration of the mother/daughter relationship.)

Joanna Goldsworthy 1995: *Mothers by Daughters*. Virago.

CHAPTER SIX – YOU AND THE FUTURE

Working

Amanda Cuthbert and Angela Holford 1992: *The Briefcase and the Baby: A Nanny and Mother's Handbook*. Mandarin.

Adrienne Katz 1992: *The Juggling Act*. Bloomsbury.

NCT Publications: *Breastfeeding: Returning to Work*. Available from NCT Maternity Sales Ltd, Burnfield Avenue, Glasgow G46 7TL. Telephone: 0141 633 5552.

P O'Brien 1992: *Managing Two Careers*. Sheldon.

Parents at Work 1994: *Balancing Work and Home*. Parents at Work.

Sandra Scarr and Judy Dunn 1987: *Mothercare/Othercare*. Pelican.

Teresa Wilson 1996: *Work and Home: Finding the Balance*. NCT Publishing Ltd.

Sue Woodford and Anne De Zoysa 1993: *Good Nursery Guide*. Vermilion.

Widening Horizons

Deborah Jackson 1993: *Do Not Disturb: The Benefits of Relaxed Parenting for You and Your Child*. Bloomsbury.

CHAPTER SEVEN: BECOMING A FAMILY

Stepfamilies

Erica De'Ath 1993: *A Baby of Our Own: A New Baby in the Family*. National Stepfamily Association.

Margaret Robinson and Donna Smith 1993: *Step by Step: Focus on Stepfamilies*. Harvester/Wheatsheaf.

Donna Smith 1990: *Stepmothering*. Harvester/Wheatsheaf.

The Future

The Cystic Fibrosis Trust 1993: *Genetics, carrier tests and tests during pregnancy*.

Patricia Hewitt and Wendy Rose-Neil 1990: *The Second Child*. Fontana.

Index

Being Pregnant Giving Birth

A NATIONAL CHILDBIRTH TRUST GUIDE

What are my choices for the birth?
What do we need to know about antenatal tests?
What does labour really feel like?
How can we best prepare ourselves for our baby?

- Through its antenatal classes, the National Childbirth Trust has helped thousands of parents to understand the process of pregnancy and birth, and to explore their own feelings, hopes and fears about becoming parents.

- Now in *BEING PREGNANT, GIVING BIRTH* parents share their experiences of the subject. They reveal how they coped with antenatal tests, being in labour, choosing pain relief, the birth of their baby, having a caesarean birth, and their first few days as a parent.

- *BEING PREGNANT, GIVING BIRTH* is a book for parents of the nineties: informative, enlightening and empowering. It aims to give you the facts you need to make informed choices, and to enable you to work in partnership with the health professionals to achieve the best outcome for you and your baby.

- *BEING PREGNANT, GIVING BIRTH* won't tell you the right answers – but it will help you to decide what is best for you.

Work and Home
FINDING THE BALANCE

A NATIONAL CHILDBIRTH TRUST GUIDE

Can I cope with the demands of work and home?
How do I deal with changed priorities?
Should we use a childminder, nanny or nursery?
How do we avoid employing the 'nanny from hell'?
Can I work and breastfeed?

- Mixing parenting with other work can be stressful and demanding but it also has its rewards and pleasures. In *WORK AND HOME* parents talk about how they have tried to achieve the right balance between work and home throughout the changing stages of family life.

- Mothers in all types of work situations – women who work full time, part time, freelance, job share or role reverse – describe how they juggle their working lives with caring for their families.

- Parents who use childminders, nannies, au pairs, nurseries, friends and relatives, nanny share or child swop, talk about the pros and cons of each form of childcare. Their experiences will help you to consider the different options that are open to you.

- *WORK AND HOME* won't tell you the right answers – but it will help you to decide what is best for you and your family.

Breastfeeding Your Baby
A NATIONAL CHILDBIRTH TRUST GUIDE

How does breastfeeding work?
How do mothers breastfeed premature babies?
What's special about breast milk?
Can you breastfeed twins?
Will I enjoy breastfeeding?

- More and more evidence is confirming that 'breast is best' for both baby and mother and increasing numbers of women are choosing to breastfeed, yet sometimes 'the natural thing to do' can be fraught with difficulties.

- This book written by three breastfeeding counsellors draws on the experience of the National Childbirth Trust – which deals with over 114,000 enquiries a year – to answer the questions parents have about breastfeeding.

- Women talk about their experience of breastfeeding, from the first few days when they are learning with their baby, through to becoming confident together, returning to work, and weaning.

- Other women describe feeding twins, premature babies and older babies. They talk about how they coped with problems such as soreness, growth spurts, babies with colic, and feeding a baby with special needs.

- Mothers describe what helped and what hindered. *BREASTFEEDING YOUR BABY* supplies the facts and the figures, along with detailed information boxes to get you off to a good start.

- *BREASTFEEDING YOUR BABY* won't tell you the right answers – but it will help you to decide what's best for you and your child.

Breastfeeding Your Baby

Jane Moody, Jane Britten and Karen Hogg

A NATIONAL CHILDBIRTH TRUST GUIDE